Biblical Institute:

A SYNOPSIS OF

LECTURES ON THE PRINCIPAL DOCTRINES

—OF—

SEVENTH-DAY ADVENTISTS.

OAKLAND, CAL.:

STEAM PRESS OF THE PACIFIC S. D. A. PUBLISHING HOUSE.

1878.

2005 06 07 08 09 10 11 12 · 5 4 3 2 1

Copyright © 2000, 2005 TEACH Services, Inc.
ISBN-13: 978-1-57258-175-1
ISBN-10: 1-57258-175-1
Library of Congress Control Number: 00-105027

The cover picture was taken from Uriah Smith's
The Marvel of Nations, Battle Creek, Michigan, 1887.

Published by
TEACH Services, Inc.
www.TEACHServices.com

PREFACE.

In the following pages is given a synopsis of the lectures delivered at the Biblical Institute, held by Elders James White and U. Smith, in Oakland, California, April 1–17, 1877. The design in these pages has been to give the principal facts, dates and references, connected with the important subjects presented, in as brief a manner as possible, and these, it is believed, will serve in connection with the review questions to give a general idea of the teachings of the Scriptures on these great themes, and furnish a good basis for further study.

We would call especial attention to the questions as a feature upon which rests in large measure the value of the book. Those who use the book for class exercises will of course use the questions. And we would recommend their use even by the general reader.

It will be hardly necessary to say to those who may use this work in class exercises, that the Lessons as here divided are not intended to measure the length of the recitations. A Lesson embraces an entire subject; but it will be found profitable to devote quite a number of recitations in many instances to a single lesson. We commend a thorough study of these all-important themes to those everywhere who desire to acquaint themselves with the prophetic word.

The Biblical Institute.

LESSON ONE.

THE MILLENNIUM.

THE word, millennium, signifies a thousand years. The popular view of what is called the temporal millennium is that the gospel of Jesus Christ will yet so far control the minds and hearts of men that the whole world will be converted, and become holy by its influence, and that this happy state will continue one thousand years; and that during this time Christ will reign with his people spiritually, and that at the close of the millennium he will come the second time when the judgment will take place.

But a careful examination is sufficient to fully convince the intelligent student that the sacred Scriptures do not teach that at any period of time all men will be converted to God. There were but few righteous men from Adam to Moses. And the numbers of the just in the Jewish age, compared with the multitudes of the unbelieving, were very small. Neither does God's plan in the Christian age embrace the conversion of all men. The gospel is preached to all nations, and thus God visits "the Gentiles, to *take out of them* a people for his name."

REVIEW QUESTIONS ON LESSON ONE.

1. What does the word millennium signify? 2. What is the popular view of the millennium? 3. What facts stand in the way of this view? 4. For what purpose is the gospel

Acts 15 : 14. Among the finally saved will not be found all of any one generation; or all of any one nation; but some out of every age and every tongue will join in the song to the Lamb: "Thou wast slain and hast redeemed us to God by thy blood *out of* every kindred, and tongue, and people, and nation." Rev. 5 : 9.

From the very nature of the case the conversion of the world is an impossibility. God is the same during all time. He deals with men and nations impartially. The devil is the same, excepting that the experience of six thousand years has made him more artful in seducing men and women into sin. The fallen race is the same, only that each succeeding generation degenerates physically, mentally and morally, till the world becomes fully ripe for her final doom. This is seen in the metalic image of Dan. 2. Here five universal kingdoms are the subject of prophecy. Four of these pertain to the mortal state, one to the immortal. The four earthly monarchies, Babylon, Persia, Grecia and Rome, are severally represented by gold, silver, brass and iron. We not only see in the symbol the depreciation of value from gold to silver, to brass and to iron, but the last divided condition of earthly governments, just before the opening glories of the immortal kingdom, is represented by iron mixed with miry clay.

God's plan to convert sinners, and to save all who would obey him and believe in Jesus, has been in operation about six thousand years. A crucified and risen Jesus has been preached with the Holy Spirit sent down from heaven for more than eigh-

preached? 5. Of whom will the company of the redeemed be composed? 6. Why is the conversion of the world an impossibility? 7. What is seen in the metallic image of Dan. 2? 8. How long has the plan of salvation been in operation? 9. How long has a risen Jesus been preached to

teen centuries; yet the world has not been converted. And the prospect of its conversion to Bible
holiness never looked darker than at the present
time. In the forcible words of another we would
inquire:—

"And what are the present prospects of a church
that has set out in all confidence to convert the
world? How may those now putting on the har-
ness boast of greater expected success than is
warranted by the experience of those who have
put it off after having fought the good fight? The
prophets could not convert the world; are *we*
mightier than they? The apostles could not convert the world; are we stronger than they? The
martyrs could not convert the world; can we do
more than *they?* The church for eighteen hundred
years could not convert the world; can *we* do it?
They have preached the gospel of Christ; so can
we. They have gone to earth's remotest bounds;
so can we. They have saved 'some;' so can we.
They have wept as so few believed their report; so
can we.

"Has God a mightier Saviour—a more powerful
Spirit? Has he another gospel which will save
the world? Where is it? Is there any way to
the kingdom other than that which leads through
much tribulation? Is there another way to the
crown besides the way of crosses? Can we reign
with him unless we first suffer in his cause?" *

The doctrine of the world's conversion, and a
temporal millennium, being based upon false inter-
pretations, and incorrect quotations of certain portions of the sacred Scriptures, it is proper that we
should here notice those texts usually quoted to

the world? 10. What is the result so far? 11. What is
the outlook for the future? 12. Upon what is the doctrine

---

* Preface to Voice of the Church.

4   THE BIBLICAL INSTITUTE.

pove this doctrine, and show that they do not mean
what they are said to prove :—

1. "Ask of me, and I shall give thee the heathen
for thine inheritance, and the uttermost parts of
the earth for thy possession." Ps. 2 : 8. As sufficient evidence that this text does not prove the
conversion of the world, we quote the verse following it : "Thou shalt break them with a rod of iron;
thou shalt dash them in pieces like a potter's
vessel."

2. The stone cut out of the mountain without
hands, shall roll until it becomes a great mountain
and fills the whole earth. All the proof for the
world's conversion found in the above, is in quoting
the text wrong. Here is the text as it reads :
"Thou sawest till that a stone was cut out without
hands, which smote the image upon his feet that
were of iron and clay, and brake them to pieces.
Then was the iron, the clay, the brass, the silver
and the gold, broken to pieces together, and became
like the chaff of the summer threshing floors ; and
the wind carried them away, that no place was
found for them; and the stone that smote the
image became a great moutain, and filled the whole
earth." Dan. 2 : 34, 35.

In this remarkable passage, the following points
are worthy of notice : (1.) The stone smote the
image upon his feet, and brake the iron, clay, brass,
silver and gold to pieces together. Here is destruction, not conversion. (2.) They became like the
chaff of the summer threshing floors, and the wind
carried them away, that no place was found for

of the world's conversion based ? 13. What is Ps. 2 : 8
sometimes quoted to prove ? 14. What shows that it does
not refer to the world's conversion ? 15. How is Dan. 2 :
34, 35, sometimes quoted ? 16. How does this differ from a
true version of the text ? 17. What is the first point worthy
of notice in this text ? 18. The second ? 19. The third ?

them. Here is illustrated the removal of all earthly governments. (3.) Then the stone became a great mountain, and filled the whole earth. In this prophecy, the stone has nothing in common with the image. The image, a symbol of earthly governments, all wicked men, is first removed, and then the stone fills the whole earth. But if it be urged that the dashing of the heathen, (Ps. 2 : 9) and the breaking of the image, (Dan. 2 : 34) mean the conversion of the world, then Paul's words : " The God of peace shall bruise Satan under our feet shortly," means the conversion of Satan.

3. A nation shall be born in a day. Here is another incorrect quotation. Isa. 66 : 8 reads : " Who hath heard such a thing ? who hath seen such things ? shall the earth be made to bring forth in one day ? or shall a nation be born at once ? for as soon as Zion travailed, she brought forth her children." This text has no allusion to the conversion of sinners ; but evidently refers to the resurrection of the just.

4. " The kingdoms of this world are become the kingdoms of our Lord and of his Christ." But let it be borne in mind that this is under the third woe, when it is also said : " And the nations were angry, and Thy wrath is come, and the time of the dead, that they should be judged, and that thou shouldst give reward unto thy servants the prophets, and to the saints, and them that fear thy name, small and great ; and shouldst destroy them which destroy the earth." Rev. 11 : 15, 18.

5. "And this gospel of the kingdom shall be preached in all the world, for a witness unto all nations ; and then shall the end come." Matt. 24 :

20. How is Isa. 66 : 8 sometimes misquoted ? 21. To what does it evidently refer ? 22. What is to be said of Rev. 11 : 15, 18 ? 23. How do believers in the world's conversion

14. Those who teach the world's conversion would have the gospel preached to all nations, every individual hear it, believe it, obey it, and all become holy by it. What then? The end? No, not until the world has enjoyed a sinless period of one thousand years. But the text does not say that every individual will even hear this gospel of the kingdom. It does not state that any one will be converted and made holy by it. And we find it far from intimated that the world would be converted and remain so a thousand years.

6. "They shall beat their swords into plowshares and their spears into pruninghooks; nation shall not lift up a sword against nation, neither shall they learn war any more." Micah 4:3. See also Isa. 2:4. The reader will please notice that Micah 4:1, speaks of the exalted state of the professed church of Christ in the last days. Mountains mean earthly governments. The church, here represented by "the mountain of the Lord's house," was to be exalted above the hills. It was to be established in the tops of the mountains.

In verses 2-5 is a statement, not of what the Lord declares would take place in the last days, but what the multitudes of popular professors, who are looking for the conversion of the world, would say. The statement commences thus: "And many nations shall come, and say." Verse 2. But the Lord speaks in verses 6 and 7, as follows: "In that day, saith the Lord, will I assemble her that halteth, and I will gather her that is driven out, and her that I have afflicted." "In that day" when "many nations"

have Matt. 24:14 fulfilled? 24. What then takes place? 25. What points are falsely inferred from the text? 26. What texts are quoted from Micah and Isaiah on this subject? 27. Who makes the statement of Micah 4:2-5? 28. Where are the Lord's words recorded and what are they?

are prophesying of peace and safety, the Lord's remnant people are driven out and afflicted. But we have more and very decisive testimony in regard to the state of the nations in the last days by the prophet Joel. This subject may appear still more clear and forcible by arranging what many nations say, and what the Lord says, side by side in the following manner :—

MANY NATIONS SAY.	THE LORD SAYS.
And many nations shall come, and say, Come, and let us go up to the mountain of the Lord, and to the house of the God of Jacob ; and he will teach us of his ways, and we will walk in his paths ; for the law shall go forth of Zion, and the word of the Lord from Jerusalem. And he shall judge among many people, and rebuke strong nations afar off ; and they shall beat their swords into plowshares, and their spears into pruninghooks ; nation shall not lift up a sword against nation, neither shall they learn war any more." Micah 4 : 2, 3.	Proclaim ye this among the Gentiles : Prepare war, wake up the mighty men, let all the men of war draw near ; let them come up. Beat your plowshares into swords, and your pruninghooks into spears ; let the weak say, I am strong. Assemble yourselves and come, all ye heathen, and gather yourselves together round about ; thither cause thy mighty ones to come down, O Lord. Let the heathen be wakened, and come up to the valley of Jehoshaphat ; for there will I sit to judge all the heathen round about. Joel 3 : 9–12.

7. " They shall all know me, from the least of them unto the greatest of them." Jer. 31 : 34. This is in the promise of the new covenant, and relates, first, to the condition of each individual with whom the new covenant is made ; and secondly, to the fullness of the blessings of the gospel, when all are brought into harmony with God in the everlasting state. Both ideas are embraced in the promise. But that every individual will be converted, or that all of any generation this side of the immortal state will be

29. What does the Lord say according to Joel ? 30. What does Jer. 31 : 34 teach ? 31. What is wrongly inferred from

converted and come to the knowledge of God, the Scriptures do not teach.

8. The glory of the Lord shall fill the earth, as the waters cover the sea. "But as truly as I live, all the earth shall be filled with the glory of the Lord." Num. 14:21. "They shall not hurt nor destroy in all my holy mountain; for the earth shall be full of the knowledge of the Lord, as the waters cover the sea." Isa. 11:9. "For the earth shall be filled with the knowledge of the glory of the Lord as the waters cover the sea." Hab. 2:14. "Blessed are the meek; for they shall inherit the earth." Matt. 5:5. This glorious state, however, is not brought about by the conversion of all men. It is introduced by the destruction of sinful men, the restitution of the earth to its condition as it came from the hand of the Creator, and the gift of immortality to the meek of all ages. "For evil doers shall be cut off; but those that wait upon the Lord, they shall inherit the earth. For yet a little while, and the wicked shall not be; yea, thou shalt diligently consider his place, and it shall not be. But the meek shall inherit the earth; and shall delight themselves in the abundance of peace." Ps. 37:9-11.

9. "For behold, I create new heavens and a new earth; and the former shall not be remembered, nor come into mind. But be ye glad and rejoice forever in that which I create; for behold, I create Jerusalem, a rejoicing, and her people a joy. And I will rejoice in Jerusalem, and joy in my people, and the voice of weeping shall be no more heard in her, nor the voice of crying." "The wolf and the lamb shall feed together, and the lion shall eat straw like the

---

it? 32. Quote Num. 14:21; Isa. 11:9; Hab. 2:14, and Matt. 5:5. 33. What connection has this glorious state with the conversion of all men? 34. How is it introduced? 35. Quote Ps. 37:9-11. 36. How is Isa. 65:17-25 applied?

bullock; and dust shall be the serpent's meat. They shall not hurt nor destroy in all my holy mountain, saith the Lord." See Isa. 65 : 17-25 ; also chapter 11 : 6-9.

This prophecy is said to be a figurative description of the condition of things during the temporal millennium. We, however, regard it as a prophetic description of the state of things after the restitution of the earth and man to their primeval glory. Before the fall, man was upright, and the earth and all the living creatures that God had created upon it, as viewed by the Creator, were seen to be "very good." Gen. 1 : 31. The Scriptures do not teach the annihilation of all things by the fires of the great day, and the creation of all new things for the future state. But they do distinctly teach the restitution of all things. Thus saith the great Restorer : " Behold, I make all things new." Rev. 21 : 5. Isaiah and the Revelator both speak of the new heavens and the new earth. The prophet Isaiah is either giving a figurative description of a very happy condition of things in this mortal state, or he is portraying the literal glories of the restitution after the second advent and the resurrection of the just. To the figurative view we find serious objections :—

(1) Our temporal millennium friends, in order that all parts of their figurative theory may harmonize, must have in their figurative new heavens and earth, figurative houses, figurative vineyards, and they must eat the figurative fruit thereof, and behold around them figurative wolves, and figurative lions,

---

37. What is the more evident application ? 38. What was man's condition before the fall ? 39. Do the Scriptures teach the annihilation of all things by the fires of the great day ? 40. What do they teach in this respect ? 41. What is the testimony of Rev. 21 : 5 ? 42. What two views are the only ones that can be taken of Isaiah's language ? 43. What is the first serious objection to the figurative view ?

feeding with figurative lambs and figurative bullocks, to say nothing of figurative serpents. If it be said that the gospel is to convert all these wolves, and lions, and serpents, we reply that if they are converted, they are no longer wolves and lions and serpents, and during the entire period of the millennium there will be none but figurative lambs and doves.

(2.) The apostle has so clearly identified the three worlds, namely, the one before the flood, the one that now is, and the new earth which is to come, as to entirely preclude the figurative view. He says: " For this they willingly are ignorant of, that by the word of God the heavens were of old, and the earth standing out of the water and in the water; whereby the world that then was being overflowed with water perished. But the heavens and the earth, which are now, by the same word are kept in store, reserved unto fire against the day of judgment and perdition of ungodly men." " Nevertheless, we, according to his promise, look for new heavens and a new earth, wherein dwelleth righteousness." 2 Pet. 3 : 5–7, 13.

No fact can be more plainly stated than that the world that perished by the flood is the same as that which now is, and is reserved unto fire. This is to be changed by fire, and then will appear the new heavens and the new earth, according to the promise of God. And it is a remarkable fact that the promise referred to by the apostle is found only in Isa. chapter 65. Thus, the apostle links the three worlds together. Are the first two worlds literal? So is the third. Is the new earth, mentioned by

---

44. What is the second objection ?   45. Quote 2 Peter 3 : 5–7, 13.   46. What fact is plainly stated in this testimony ? 47. How does that compare with the earth that now is ? 48. What is to succeed this present earth ?   49. In what single place is the promise found which is referred to by

Isaiah, figurative? So are all three worlds figurative. But if they are all literal, then we see a harmony in Scripture respecting them. If they be regarded as figurative, then we are left to the following conclusion :—

That in the days of figurative Noah, the figurative heavens and earth, being overflowed by figurative water, perished figuratively. But the figurative heavens and earth, which are now, are reserved unto figurative fire, against the figurative day of judgment and perdition of ungodly figurative men. Nevertheless, we, according to his figurative promise, look for figurative new heavens and new earth, wherein dwelleth figurative righteousness.

True, the sacred writers use figures and parables. But we should believe that God in his word means just what he says, unless the connection shows good reasons why a figure or parable is introduced. If God does not mean what he says, in his word, who will tell us what he does mean? In case that God does not mean what he says, the Bible ceases to be a revelation, and he should give us another book to teach what this one means. But the Bible is the very book in which God has plainly spoken to the children of men.

With this view of the sacred Scriptures, we see spread out before us the living realities of the new earth, in all their grandeur and glory, as when Adam was lord of Eden. Before the transgression, all was purity and peace, even among the beasts which God had created. And who can say that these, with

---

Peter? 50. If the heavens and earth referred to, be figurative, what does it prove respecting this present earth, and the earth before the flood? 51. What rule should be followed in interpreting figures and parables? 52. If God does not mean what he says, what would be necessary? 53. With the literal view of the Scriptures, what do we have described before us in these passages? 54. What text is

natures such as the Creator first gave them, will not
be in place in the earth restored from the fall, as
well as in the earth before the fall?

Having examined the principal texts quoted to
prove the conversion of the world, and having shown
that they do not mean what they are said to mean,
we will call attention to some of the many direct
proofs that no such state of things can exist prior to
the second advent.

1. The prevalence of the little horn. "I beheld,
and the same horn made war with the saints and
prevailed against them; until the Ancient of Days
came, and judgment was given to the saints of the
Most High; and the time came that the saints possessed the kingdom." Dan. 7:21, 22. "But the
saints of the Most High shall take the kingdom, and
possess the kingdom forever, even forever and ever."
Verse 18. Here it will be seen that the little horn
makes war with the saints until they take the kingdom, and when they once obtain the kingdom, they
hold it forever and ever. Where, then, is there room
for that period of peace and triumph of the church
called the temporal millennium?

2. The apostasy. In 2 Thess. 2:1-7, Paul states
what would take place before the second coming of
Christ. Is it the triumph of the world's conversion?
No, it is the sad apostasy, the falling away, and the
manifestation of the papacy, the man of sin who will
continue to the end. The apostle speaks of the manifestation and destruction of this blasphemous power
in these words: "And then shall that wicked be
revealed, whom the Lord shall consume with the

referred to as direct proof that there can be no such thing as
a temporal millennium? 55. What power is referred to by
the little horn of Dan. 7? 56. How long does this horn
make war upon the saints? 57. How is this little horn to
be destroyed? 58. What room is there then for that period

spirit of his mouth, and shall destroy with the brightness of his coming." Verse 8.

3. The wicked continue with the righteous as illustrated by the parable of the wheat and tares, until the end of the Christian age. See Matt. 13: 24–30. The friends of the doctrine of the world's conversion find this parable directly in their way, and they have wearied themselves in laboring to explain it away. But, as our divine Lord, by special request, gave an explanation of it, modesty suggests that we accept his explanation. See verse 36–43. We simply repeat, "The field is the world." "The good seed are the children of the kingdom." "The tares are the children of the wicked one." "Let both grow together until the harvest." "The harvest is the end of the world."

4. Persecution and tribulation were to be the portion of the church of God in all ages. The apostle speaks of the faithful who had lived and suffered before, who "had trial of cruel mockings and scourgings, yea, moreover of bonds and imprisonments; they were stoned, they were sawn asunder, were tempted, were slain with the sword; they wandered about in sheepskins and goatskins; being destitute, afflicted, tormented (of whom the world was not worthy); they wandered in deserts, and in mountains, and in dens and caves of the earth. And these all, having obtained a good report through faith, received not the promise; God having provided some better thing for us, that they without us should not be made perfect." Heb. 11 : 36–40. He also points

of triumph to the church known as the temporal millennium? 59. What is the next text quoted to disprove this doctrine? 60. How does it answer this purpose? 61. What is the third argument against the temporal millennium? 62. Whose explanation of this parable should we take? 63. According to this explanation what is shown? 64. What was to be the portion of God's church in all ages? 65.

to the future, and says: "Yea, and all that will live godly in Christ Jesus shall suffer persecution." 2 Tim. 3 : 12.

5. The last days of human probation have been regarded as the favored period for the completion of the great work of converting the world. But the prophets of the Old Testament nowhere represent God as saying that the last days would be glorious. Jesus and the apostles of the New Testament never speak of the last days as a period of triumph to the church; but rather as the days of her peril, which demand especial watching; the days of her mourning and tears and importunate prayers for deliverance. Paul describes the last days thus: "This know also, that in the last days perilous times shall come; for men shall be lovers of their own selves, covetous, boasters, proud, blasphemers, disobedient to parents, unthankful, unholy, without natural affection, truce-breakers, false accusers, incontinent, fierce, despisers of those that are good, traitors, heady, high-minded, lovers of pleasures more than lovers of God; having a form of godliness, but denying the power thereof. From such turn away." 2 Tim. 3 : 1–5.

6. Peter says: "There shall come in the last days scoffers, walking after their own lusts and saying, Where is the promise of his coming?" 2 Pet. 3 : 3, 4. How could these scoffers arise and deny his coming, and persecutions and perils exist in the last days, if all were converted long before his coming?

7. The last days embrace the very last day, reaching down to the coming of the Son of man. The

How does this affect the doctrine of the temporal millennium? 66. When is the millennium according to the views of its advocates, to be fulfilled? 67. How do the prophets of the Old Testament, and the writers of the New, represent the last days? 68. Quote 2 Tim. 3 : 1–5. 69. What is Peter's testimony? 70. To what are the days of the coming of

days of the coming of the Son of man were to be like the days of Noah and Lot. " And as it was in the days of Noah, so shall it be also in the days of the Son of man. They did eat, they drank, they married wives, they were given in marriage, until the day that Noah entered into the ark, and the flood came and destroyed them all. Likewise also as it was in the days of Lot; they did eat, they drank, they bought, they sold, they planted, they builded; but the same day that Lot went out of Sodom it rained fire and brimstone from heaven, and destroyed them all. Even thus shall it be in the day when the Son of man is revealed." Luke 17 : 26–30.

8. Destruction, not conversion, awaits the world at the very time when many popular professors cherish the delusive hope of a good time coming. They see no danger, and brand as fanatical alarmists those who obey the prophetic injunction, " Blow ye the trumpet in Zion, and sound an alarm in my holy mountain; let all the inhabitants of the land tremble; for the day of the Lord cometh, for it is nigh at hand." Joel 2:1. But, says the apostle : " When they shall say, Peace and safety, then sudden destruction cometh upon them." 1 Thess 5 : 3.

9. The way to destruction is broad, and many go in it; and the way to life is narrow, and but few find it. When one asked Jesus : " Are there few that be saved?" he answered: "Strive to enter in at the strait gate; for many, I say unto you, will seek to enter in, and shall not be able." Luke 13 : 23, 24. Again it is recorded : " Enter ye in at the strait gate, for wide is the gate, and broad is the way, that leadeth to destruction, and many there be which go in thereat; because strait is the gate, and narrow is

the Son of man likened ? 71. When many are indulging the hope of good, what awaits the world? References. 72. What does Christ say in reference to the broad and narrow way? 73.

the way, which leadeth unto life, and few there be
that find it." Matt. 7 : 13, 14. The doctrine of the
world's conversion, and that of universal salvation,
are both directly opposed to this passage. The one
has the way to life narrow at first, but growing
wider, until all walk in it; while the other has the
way to life always wide enough for all the world.
But our Lord states a great fact in this passage,
which existed when spoken, ever had existed, and
which would exist until the close of probation;
namely, that the way to destruction was broad, and
many would go in it; and that the way to life was
narrow, and few would find it.

But when the few of each successive generations,
from righteous Abel to the close of probation, who
have bent their lonely footsteps in the narrow path
to Mount Zion, shall reach their everlasting rest,
they will constitute that " great multitude, which
no man could number, of all nations, and kindreds,
and peoples, and tongues," arrayed in Heaven's purity. Not one of these had come out of that imaginary period of a converted world. No; not one.
What an imposing scene! " And one of the elders
answered, saying unto me, What are these that are
arrayed in white robes ? and whence came they ?
And I said unto him, Sir, thou knowest. And he
said to me, These are they which came out of great
tribulation, and have washed their robes and made
them white in the blood of the Lamb." Rev. 7.

How does this statement affect the doctrine of the world's
conversion? 74. If this doctrine is true, how should Christ
have described it? 75. Of what are the great multitude
composed who will finally reach Mount Zion? 76. What is
the experience of them all in this world?

LESSON TWO.

THE SECOND ADVENT.

TEXT: Let not your heart be troubled ; ye believe in God, believe also in me. In my Father's house are many mansions ; if it were not so, I would have told you. I go to prepare a place for you. And if I go and prepare a place for you, I will come again, and receive you unto myself ; that where I am, there ye may be also. John 14 : 1-3.

Our Lord was tenderly introducing to his disciples the subject of his ascent to heaven. "Little children, yet a little while I am with you." John 13 : 33. "Simon Peter said unto him, Lord, whither goest thou ? Jesus answered him, Whither I go, thou canst not follow me now ; but thou shalt follow me afterwards." Verse 36. This statement caused distress and consternation in the minds of the disciples, and led Peter to say to his Lord : "Why cannot I follow thee now ? I will lay down my life for thy sake." Verse 37. Then follow the comforting words of the text, assuring the sorrowing disciples that their Lord would come again, and receive them to himself.

The certainty of the second advent of Christ, the manner and object of his coming, and the nearness of the event, are points of thrilling interest to all who love our Lord Jesus Christ.

He will *appear* the second time. Paul speaks directly upon this point : "So Christ was once offered

---

REVIEW QUESTIONS ON LESSON TWO.

1. What was our Lord's subject in John 14 : 1-3 ? 2. What was the conversation between Christ and Peter ? 3. What was the effect upon the disciples ? 4. What question did Peter then ask ? 5. What followed ? 6. What points of thrilling interest are involved in the doctrine of the second coming of Christ ? 7. What is Paul's testimony in Heb. 9 :

to bear the sins of many.   And unto them that look for him, shall he *appear* the second time without sin unto salvation."   Heb. 9 : 28.   Again he says : " Looking for that blessed hope, and the glorious *appearing* of the great God, and our Saviour Jesus Christ."   Titus 2 : 13.   Another apostle testifies to this point thus : " Beloved, now are we the sons of God, and it doth not yet appear what we shall be ; but we know that, when he shall *appear*, we shall be like him ; for we shall see him as he is." 1 John 3 : 2.

The second advent of Christ will be personal and visible.   This proposition is sustained by a large amount of testimony from the highest authority.

1. The Son of God himself, when addressing his disciples upon the subject of his second advent, pointed forward to the generation that should witness the signs of that event in the sun, moon and stars, and said : " They shall see the Son of man coming in the clouds of heaven with power and great glory."   Matt. 24 : 30.   See also Mark 13 : 26 ; 14 : 62 ; Luke 21 : 27 ; John 14 : 3.

2. Holy angels at his ascension made a most definite and decisive declaration relative to his personal and visible second advent.   As a cloud was receiving him from their sight, " behold, two men [angels] stood by them in white apparel, which also said, Ye men of Galilee, why stand ye gazing up into heaven? This same Jesus which is taken up from you into heaven shall so come in like manner as ye have seen him go into heaven."   Acts 1 : 10, 11.   " Behold, he cometh with clouds, and every eye shall see him."   Rev. 1 : 7.

---

28 ?   8. How does he speak of the subject to Titus ?   9. What is John's testimony ?   10. What then will be the nature of the second advent ?   11. What are the words of Christ himself upon this point ? References.   12. What was the testimony of angels to the disciples at the ascension?

3. Paul testifies to the personal and visible second advent of Christ in language not to be misunderstood : " The Lord himself shall descend from heaven with a shout, with the voice of the Archangel, and with the trump of God ; and the dead in Christ shall rise first; then we which are alive and remain shall be caught up together with them in the clouds, to meet the Lord in the air ; and so shall we ever be with the Lord." 1 Thess. 4 : 16, 17. See also Titus 2 : 3 ; 1 John 3 : 4.

At the second coming of Christ, the voice of the Archangel will be heard, the righteous dead will be raised, and the living righteous will be changed to immortality. It is then that victory over death and the grave is triumphantly shouted by all who receive the gift of eternal life at the last trump. " Behold, I show you a mystery : We shall not all sleep, but we shall all be changed, in a moment, in the twinkling of an eye, at the last trump ; for the trumpet shall sound, and the dead shall be raised incorruptible, and we shall be changed. For this corruptible must put on incorruption, and this mortal must put on immortality. So when this corruptible shall have put on incorruption, and this mortal shall have put on immortality, then shall be brought to pass the saying that is written, Death is swallowed up in victory. O death, where is thy sting ? O grave, where is thy victory ? " 1 Cor 15 : 51–55.

Again the apostle sets forth the hope and joy of the true church of Jesus Christ in all ages, while passing through persecutions and great tribulation, and while her members have been falling under the

13. Who will see him at his coming ? 14. What is Paul's testimony in 1 Thess. 4 : 16 ? 15. Whose voice is heard at the second coming of Christ ? 16. What change then passes upon the righteous, dead and living ? 17. When is the shout of victory over death to be given ? 18. What is set

power of death and the grave, in the consoling words found in 1 Thess. 4 : 13–18.

When the Lord shall appear the second time, sinners then living will be destroyed by fire, and the earth will be desolated.   2 Thess. 1 : 7–10 ; 2 : 8.

The man of sin, the papacy, is to be destroyed with the brightness of Christ's coming.   And, at the same time, those that know not God, the heathen, and those that obey not the gospel of our Lord Jesus Christ, will perish under the vengeance of flaming fire that attends the revelation of the Son of God from heaven.   When the heathen, the papists, and all others who do not obey the gospel of Christ, shall be destroyed, there cannot be one wicked person living.

Christ's explanation of the parable of the tares of the field proves the destruction of all wicked men who shall be living at the time of his second coming. "The field is the world ; the good seed are the children of the kingdom ; but the tares are the children of the wicked one ; the enemy that sowed them is the devil ; the harvest is the end of the world ; and the reapers are the angels.   As therefore the tares are gathered and burned in the fire ; so shall it be in the end of this world.   The Son of man shall send forth his angels, and they shall gather out of his kingdom all things that offend, and them which do iniquity, and shall cast them into a furnace of fire."   Matt. 13 :38–42.   That will be a clean work.   When all things that offend, and they which do iniquity, shall be gathered out of the earth, there cannot be one sinner left in it.

The prophet describes the day of the destruction

forth in 1 Thess. 4 : 13–18 ?   19.   What becomes of the living wicked when Christ comes ?   20.   In what condition is the earth for a time left by that event ?   21.   When and how is the papacy to be destroyed ?   22.   What is proved by the parable of the tares ?   Reference.   23.   What are the de-

of the wicked, and the desolation of the earth, in these fearful words : " Behold, the day of the Lord cometh, cruel both with wrath and fierce anger, to lay the land desolate; and he shall destroy the sinners thereof out of it." Isaiah 13 : 9. " Behold, the Lord maketh the earth empty, and maketh it waste, and turneth it upside down, and scattereth abroad the inhabitants thereof." Chap. 24 : 1. " The land shall be utterly emptied, and utterly spoiled; for the Lord hath spoken this word." Verse 3.

The voice of the Lord proclaimed to the prophet the blindness and deafness of apostate Israel, which led him, in anxiety and anguish of spirit, to cry : " Lord, how long?" And the Lord answered : " Until the cities be wasted without inhabitant, and the houses without man, and the land be utterly desolate." Isa. 6 : 11.

God speaks by the weeping prophet. The terrors of the day of the coming of the Son of man are portrayed in most fearful words. In the general slaughter there will be no escape for wicked men, though their profession be as high as heaven. " Thus saith the Lord of hosts, Behold, evil shall go forth from nation to nation, and a great whirlwind shall be raised up from the coasts of the earth. And the slain of the Lord shall be at that day from one end of the earth even unto the other end of the earth; they shall not be lamented, neither gathered, nor buried ; they shall be dung upon the ground. Howl, ye shepherds, and cry ; and wallow yourselves in the ashes, ye principal of the flock ; for the days of your slaughter and of your dispersions are accomplished; and ye shall fall like a pleasant vessel. And the shepherds shall have no way to flee, nor the principal of the flock to escape." Jer. 25 : 32–35.

scriptions given by Isaiah of this day? References. 24. What does Jeremiah say of it? 25. What will be the con-

Isaiah is carried forward in prophetic vision to the point of time just prior to the general desolation, and describes the state of things when false professors shall be aroused to their lost condition. "Now will I rise, saith the Lord; now will I be exalted; now will I lift up myself. Ye shall conceive chaff, ye shall bring forth stubble; your breath, as fire, shall devour you. And the people shall be as the burnings of lime; as thorns cut up shall they be burned in the fire. Hear, ye that are far off, what I have done; and ye that are near, acknowledge my might. The sinners in Zion are afraid; fearfulness hath surprised the hypocrites. Who among us shall dwell with the devouring fire? who among us shall dwell with everlasting burnings?" Isa. 33 : 10–14.

Again the Lord hath spoken by another prophet: "I will utterly consume all things from off the land, saith the Lord. I will consume man and beast; I will consume the fowls of the heaven, and the fishes of the sea, and the stumbling-blocks with the wicked; and I will cut off man from off the land, saith the Lord." Zeph. 1 : 2, 3. Read also carefully, chap. 3 : 8.

The second coming of Christ is a subject of great importance to the church. This is evident from the amount of testimony relative to it, in connection with the resurrection of the just and the Judgment, found both in the Old and New Testaments. The inspired writers, in their threatenings against the ungodly, in their words of hope and encouragement for the saints, and in their exhortations to repentance and holy living, hold up the great fact of the second coming of the Son of man, as that which

---

dition of false professors at this time? Reference. 26. What testimony is given from Zephaniah? 27. What shows the second coming of Christ to be a subject of great importance to the church? 28. How do the inspired writers use this question? 29. How early in the world's history was it

should alarm and arouse, and also comfort the people of God.

Before Adam passed from the stage of life, Enoch, the seventh in the line of his descendants, proclaimed this doctrine in the ears of the impenitent, " Behold," said he, " the Lord cometh with ten thousand of his saints, to execute judgment upon all." Jude 14. And as we pass from book to book through the Bible, we find that the prophets, Jesus, and the apostles, have made the same use of the doctrine ; and in the very last book, John describes a coming day, when all classes and ranks of men, because they have not prepared for the coming of Christ, will call for rocks and mountains to fall on them, and hide them from the overwhelming glory of his presence, as he appears in the clouds of heaven. Rev. 6 : 14-17.

Christ's coming is also held prominently forth in the sacred writings, as the time when the righteous will be rewarded. " When the chief Shepherd shall appear," says Peter, " ye shall receive a crown of glory that fadeth not away." 1 Pet. 5 : 4. And Paul looks forward to the day of Christ's appearing as the time when not only he, but all who love the appearing of their Lord, shall receive the crown of righteousness which is laid up for such. 2 Tim. 4:8.

Most frequently, however, is this great doctrine used as an incentive to repentance, watchfulness, prayer, and holy living. " Watch," is the emphatic injunction of the Son of God in connection with the numerous declarations of his second coming in the gospels.

Paul exhorts to deny ungodliness and worldly lusts, and to " live soberly, righteously, and godly, in this present world ; looking for that blessed hope,

announced, of which we have an explicit record ? Reference. 30. When will the righteous be rewarded ? References.

and the glorious appearing of the great God and our
Saviour Jesus Christ." Titus 2 : 12, 13.

James says : " Be ye also patient ; stablish your
hearts ; for the coming of the Lord draweth nigh.
Grudge not one against another, brethren, lest ye be
condemned. Behold, the Judge standeth before the
door." James 5 : 8, 9.

Peter says : " But the end of all things is at hand ;
be ye therefore sober, and watch unto prayer." 1
Pet. 4 : 7. And again : " What manner of persons
ought ye to be in all holy conversation and godliness, looking for and hasting unto the coming of the
day of God." 2 Pet. 3 : 11, 12.

Such is the use which holy men, who spoke as
they were moved by the Holy Ghost, have made of
the doctrine of the second coming of Christ. Have
not they, therefore, lost the spirit of the gospel, who
openly contend against so prominent and weighty
and precious a doctrine, or who even pass it by in
silence ?

The second personal appearing of Jesus Christ is
most absurdly applied to several different things.
Some teach that death is the second coming of Christ.
There can be but a single second advent of Christ ;
while this misty sentiment has as many appearings
of Jesus as there are deaths. The early disciples
did not receive the idea that death was the second
coming of Christ. See John 21 : 21–23. When they
understood their Lord to intimate that John might
remain until his return, they at once concluded that
he would not die. Death is the life-taker, and man's
last enemy. 1 Cor. 15 : 26. Christ is coming to give
life to the just, and to " destroy him that hath the
power of death, that is, the devil." Heb. 2 : 14.

---

31. What exhortations do the apostles base upon the doctrine ? 32. Absurd applications of this subject : state and
answer the first one named. 33. The second. 34. The

Again, conversion is said to be the second coming of Christ. Then there are as many second comings of Christ as there are conversions. There can be but one second appearing of Christ. And again the manifestations of the Holy Spirit are said to be the second advent of Christ. Hence, men talk of the spiritual coming of Christ, and of his spiritual reign for one thousand years. But here, also, they are involved in the difficulty of a plurality of second comings of Christ; for in this case they would have Christ appear at each gracious manifestation of the Holy Spirit. There can be but a single second advent of Christ.

The distinction between the manifestations of the Holy Spirit and the personal presence of Christ at his second appearing is made very plain in the Script-ures. John 14 : 16 ; 16 : 5, 7, 8.

And again Shakers see the second appearing of Christ in the person of Ann Lee. And the Mormons see the fulfillment of the prophecies relative to the coming and kingdom of Christ in the gathering of "the Latter-day Saints." And the Spiritualists gen-erally agree in saying, Lo, here is the second advent of Christ in the manifestations of Spiritualism.

In the prophetic discourse of Matt. 24 and 25, cov-ering the entire Christian age, our Lord, after speak-ing of the tribulation of the church under papal per-secution, says of our time : " Then if any man shall say unto you, Lo, here is Christ, or there ; believe it not. For there shall arise false christs, and false prophets, and shall show great signs and wonders ; insomuch, that if it were possible, they shall deceive the very elect." Matt. 24 : 23, 24. The word *then* in this passage points to a specific period of time when, " Lo, here is Christ, and Lo, he is there," would be heard. Our Lord here describes the spiritual deceptions of the present age. False christs arose not far from the first advent, to deceive the Jews in regard to that event (Matt. 24 : 5); likewise false christs and false prophets have arisen at this day to deceive the people on the subject of the second advent.

Dr. Henshaw, the late bishop of Rhode Island, speaking of the doctrine of the temporal millennium, in his Treaties on the Second Advent (page 115), says :—

"So far as we have been able to investigate its history, it was at first advanced by the Rev. Dr. Whitby,* the commentator, and afterwards advocated by Hammond, Hopkins, Scott, Dwight, Bogue, and others, and has been received without careful examination by the majority of evangelical divines in the present day. But we may safely challenge its advocates to produce one distinguished writer in its favor who lived before the commencement of the eighteenth century. If antiquity is to be considered as any test of truth, the advocates of the pre-millennial advent and personal reign of Christ with his saints upon the earth, need have no fears of the results of a comparison of authorities with the supporters of the opposite theory."

And from the modern and popular error of the temporal millennium and the spiritual reign of Christ have grown those mystical applications by which the plainest declarations of Scripture relative to the second appearing of the Life-giver, are applied to

---

Have we reached the time of the false christs and false prophets therein described ? 37. What is Dr. Henshaw's testimony in reference to the time when the doctrine of the temporal millennium was introduced ? 38. From what have sprung the mystical applications here referred to ? 39. Why

---

* Daniel Whitby, D. D., was born A. D. 1638, in England, and died A. D. 1727.

death, to conversions, to the manifestations of the Holy Spirit, to Shakerism, to Mormonism, and to Spiritualism.

And why not receive such mystical teachings? The reason is given in the next verse : " For as the lightning cometh out of the east, and shineth even unto the west; so shall also the coming of the Son of man be."

The time of Christ's coming is near. The signs of his second advent, in the sun, moon, and stars, have been fulfilled.* He is near even at the doors. " Verily, I say unto you, This generation shall not pass away till all these things be fulfilled." Those who suppose that our Lord here speaks of the generation living, who listened to his teachings, should consider the following facts:—

1. It is certainly true that what is embraced in the phrase, " all these things," was not fulfilled in that generation. The darkening of the sun and moon, and the falling of the stars, mentioned by our Lord, did not occur in that generation.

2. It could not be the generation living in the days of his flesh, for he said to them (Luke 11 : 29), " There shall no sign be given it, but the sign of Jonas the prophet." It is evident that our Lord refers to the generation who were to see the signs fulfilled, and who were to be instructed by the parable of the fig tree. 1 Cor. 15 : 51, 52 ; 1 Thess. 4 : 17 ; Ps. 95 : 10.

The proclamation of the coming and kingdom of

not receive these mystical views? 40. What can be said touching the time of Christ's appearing? 41. How does Christ speak of the generation? 42. To what generation does he refer? 43. Give references showing this use of lan-

*The historical facts relative to the supernatural darkening of the sun and moon May 19, 1780, and the falling stars of November 13, 1833, will be given in a discourse devoted to the subject of the signs.

Christ is given to the last generation. God did not
send Noah to preach to the next to the last generation before the flood, but to the last. The
very generation which was destroyed by the
waters of the flood, saw Noah build the ark, and
heard his warning voice. So God has raised up
men to give the solemn warning to the world at
the right time to give force to the warning. And
the very generation of men that live after the three
great signs are fulfilled, and who hear and reject
the warning message from heaven, will drink the
cup of the unmingled wrath of God.

In comparing Noah's days and ours, the Lord
continues: "For as in the days that were before
the flood, they were eating, and drinking, marrying and giving in marriage, until the day that Noe
entered into the ark, and knew not until the flood
came and took them all away; so shall also the
coming of the Son of man be." A picture of the
present condition of the mass of mankind is here
drawn. How dark the features! The people of
the last generation will be like those before the
flood while the ark was preparing. Noah preached,
and warned them of the coming flood, and they
mocked. He built the ark, and they scoffed and
jeered. He was a preacher of righteousness. His
works were calculated to give edge to, and set home
to the heart, what he preached. Every righteous
sermon, and every blow struck in building the ark,
condemned a careless scoffing world. As the time
drew nearer, the people were more careless, more
hardened, more bold and impudent, and their con-

guage. 44. To what generation is the proclamation of the
coming kingdom given? 45. How is this illustrated by the
case of Noah? 46. What great fact does Christ set forth by
his reference to the days of Noah? 47. Do our own times
correspond to this picture? 48. How will the preaching of

demnation surer. Noah and his family were alone. And could one family know more than all the world?

By most people, the evidences of the soon coming of Christ are considered insufficient to base faith upon. But the testimony and acts of one man condemned the people destroyed by the flood. The evidences then were sufficient, otherwise the world would not have been condemned. But a hundred times more convincing evidences come pouring in upon us that the day of the Lord is near and hasteth greatly. We follow down the numerous prophetic chains of Daniel, and of the Revelation, and we find ourselves in every instance standing just before the day of wrath. We see the signs spoken of by prophets, by Christ, and in the epistles, fulfilling or fulfilled. And at the right time, and in the right manner, to fulfill certain prophecies, a solemn message arises in different parts of the world: "Blow ye the trumpet in Zion, and sound an alarm in my holy mountain; let all the inhabitants of the land tremble; for the day of the Lord cometh, for it is nigh at hand." Joel 2:1. Wherever we look, we see prophecy fulfilling. While the knowledge of God and the Spirit of holiness are departing, spiritual wickedness, like a flood, covers the land.

If the signs are of such a nature, and are fulfilled in such a manner as to compel all to believe in the coming of Christ, how can it be as it was in the days of Noah? Men were not then compelled to believe. But eight believing souls were saved,

Christ's coming be received by the masses? 49. How will they look upon the evidences of this doctrine? 50. Is it necessary that all believe a doctrine to establish its truthfulness? 51. How do the evidences concerning the Lord's coming compare with the evidences that were given of a coming flood? 52. What are some of these evidences? 53.

while all the world besides sank in their unbelief beneath the waters of the flood. God has never revealed his truth to man in a manner to compel him to believe.

Just before the end, the world will be hardened in sin, and indifferent to the claims of God. Men will be careless about hearing warning of danger, and blinded by cares, pleasures and riches. An unbelieving and infidel generation will be eating, drinking, marrying, building, planting, and sowing. This world is their god, and all their energies of body and mind are devoted to its service. And the evil day is put far away.

The faithful watchman who sounds the alarm as he sees destruction coming, is held up before the people from the pulpits of our land, and by the religious press, as a "fanatic," a "teacher of dangerous heresies;" while in contrast is set forth a long period of peace and prosperity to the church. So the churches are quieted to sleep.

Now we hear the peace-and-safety cry from the pulpit, and all the way along down to the grog-shop. "Where is the promise of his coming?" is murmured from the impious lips of a thousand last-day scoffers. But the scene will speedily change. "For when they shall say, Peace and safety, then sudden destruction cometh upon them." The scoffing of the haughty scoffer will be turned to wailing. "The lofty looks of man shall be humble, and the haughtiness of men shall be bowed down, and the Lord alone shall be exalted in that day." Isa. 2:11.

The last plagues, in which is filled up the wrath

of God, now bottled up in heaven, waiting for mercy to finish her last pleadings, will be poured out Unmingled wrath of Jehovah! And not one drop of mercy? Not one! Jesus will lay off his priestly attire, leave the mercy seat, and put on the garments of vengeance, never more to offer his blood to wash the sinner from his sins. The angels will wipe away the last tear shed over sinners, while the mandate resounds through all heaven, Let them alone. The groaning, weeping, praying church on earth, who in the last message employs every power to sound everywhere the last note of warning, lest the blood of souls be found in her garments, is now hushed in solemn silence. The Holy Spirit has written within them these prophetic words of their soon expected Lord: "He that is unjust, let him be unjust still; and he which is filthy, let him be filthy still; and he that is righteous, let him be righteous still; and he that is holy, let him be holy still. And, behold, I come quickly." Rev. 22:11, 12.

The doctrine of the second appearing of Christ has been held by the church ever since her Lord ascended to the Father to prepare mansions for her reception. It is the event that consummates her hopes, terminates the period of her toils and sorrows, and introduces her eternal repose. What sublime scenes will then open before the waiting children of God! The blazing heavens will reveal the Son of God in his glory, surrounded by all the holy angels. The trumpet will sound and the just will come forth from the grave immortal. And all —Redeemer and redeemed, attended by the heavenly host—will move upward to the mansions prepared for them in the Father's house.

To those who really love their absent Lord, the

theme of his soon return to bestow immortality
upon the dead and living righteous is fraught with
unspeakable blessedness. This event with all its
grand results, has always been the hope of the
church. Paul could look over eighteen long centuries, and speak of it as " that blessed hope, and the
glorious appearing of the great God and our Saviour
Jesus Christ." Titus 2 : 13. And Peter exhorts :
" Looking for and hasting unto the coming of the
day of God." 2 Pet. 3 : 12. And Paul again, after
speaking of the descent of the Lord from heaven,
the resurrection of the dead in Christ, and their
ascent with the living righteous to meet the Lord
in the air, says, " Wherefore comfort one another
with these words."

The present is the waiting, watching time. It is
the period designated by the emphatic words, "Here
is the patience of the saints ; here are they that
keep the commandments of God and the faith of
Jesus." Rev. 14 : 12. In definite time we would
find relief from the suspense to which our present
position subjects us. The Lord appeals to us thus :
" Watch ye therefore ; for ye know not when the
Master of the house cometh, at even, or at midnight
or at the cock-crowing, or in the morning ; lest
coming suddenly he find you sleeping. And what
I say unto you I say unto all, " Watch." Mark 13 :
35–37.

---

those who love their Lord regard it ?   61. What is the present position of the church ?

LESSON THREE.

THE GREAT IMAGE OF DANIEL CHAPTER II.

An image of gigantic form was shown to Nebuchadnezzar in a dream. Its head was of gold, breast and arms of silver, sides of brass, legs of iron, feet and toes part of iron and part of clay. Beginning with the most precious metals, there is a uniform descent till it ends with the basest. Finally a stone cut out of the mountain without hands smote the image upon the feet, dashed it to atoms, the wind carried away the fragments like chaff, and the stone became a great mountain and filled the whole earth.

This indicates that the image denotes something which occupies the territory of the earth, inasmuch as the stone which succeeds it, expanding into a mountain, occupies its place and fills the earth. With this the dream ends, and the state of things thus introduced is to be eternal. First there is change and degeneracy, indicated by the different metals of the image; lastly a permanent, eternal, glorious condition of things, shown by the mountain filling the earth.

In his interpretation of the image, Daniel told Nebuchadnezzar, Thou art this head of gold. Verse 38. He did not mean Nebuchadnezzar as an individual; for he was speaking of kingdoms. Verses

---

REVIEW QUESTIONS ON LESSON THREE.

1. What was shown to Nebuchadnezzar? 2. Of what was this image composed? 3. What became of the image? 4. As the stone in taking the place of the image, occupies the earth, what place had the image occupied? 5. What is indicated by the transition from gold to less valuable metals, ending in iron and clay? 6. What did Daniel in his interpretation say to Nebuchadnezzar? 7. Did he mean Neb-

39, 40. One part of the image could not represent a kingdom, and another part an individual. This would be inconsistent. The head of gold therefore symbolizes that kingdom over which Nebuchadnezzar was ruler.

Who, then, was Nebuchadnezzar ? King of the old Chaldean or Babylonian monarchy. This was the head of gold. It is sometimes objected to Adventism that it has no starting point ; that the first steps have to be assumed or taken for granted, whereas its great feature is, as in this instance, that the starting point is given and the stakes set for us in unmistakable language in the Scriptures themselves.

An old Assyrian empire, founded by Nimrod the great grand-son of Noah, Gen. 10 : 6–10, had ruled in Asia for 1300 years. On the ruins of this was founded the Chaldean or Babylonian empire of the Scriptures, by Belcsis, the Baladan of Isa. 39 : 1, B. C. 747. In prophecy it dates from B. C. 677, because then it became connected with the people of God, by the capture of Manasseh, king of Judah. 2 Chron. 33 : 11. It reached the hight of its glory under Nebuchadnezzar to whom this dream was given.

From this point the road was steep and short to its decline and overthrow. The kings and their reigns were as follows : Nebuchadnezzar 43 years. Evilmerodach, his son, 2 years. Neriglissar, his

---

uchadnezzar as an individual ? 8. How do you prove that kingdoms are here represented ? 9. Who was Nebuchadnezzar ? 10. By whom was the old Assyrian empire founded ? Reference. 11. How long did it rule in Asia ? 12. What was erected upon its ruins ? 13. Where, and under what name is the founder of the new empire mentioned in the Scriptures ? 14. From what year does it date in prophecy ? 15. Why ? Reference. 16. When did it reach the hight of its greatness ? 17. How many kings reigned after Nebuchad-

son-in-law, 4 years. A son of Neriglissar, nine months, not counted in Ptolemy's canon, and lastly Nabonadius, son of Evilmerodach, grand-son of Nebuchadnezzar, the Belshazzar of the book of Daniel, who reigned 17 years, and with whom that kingdom came to an end.

The kingdom that succeeded Babylon, represented by the breast and arms of silver, was Medo-Persia. Dan. 5 : 30, 31. Cyrus overthrew Babylon B. C. 538, it having continued from 677, B. C. 139 years. 538 marks the beginning of the Medo-Persian kingdom and 331, B. C. its close, when Darius was overthrown by Alexander the Great, at the battle of Arbela. The Persian kingdom continued 207 years.

The third kingdom, the one which succeeded Persia, was Grecia. Dan. 8 : 5–7, 21.

We are to look for one more universal kingdom and only one, for there were to be but four in all. Therefore, whatever universal kingdom we find anywhere this side of Grecia, that must be the kingdom represented by the legs of iron. Such a kingdom is brought to view in Luke 1. Cæsar Augustus sent out a decree that all the world should be taxed. Then he had jurisdiction over all the world. His kingdom was universal. But Cæsar Augustus was a Roman Emperor. Here we find the fourth and last universal empire, Rome, the legs of iron. The clay of the feet and toes

nezzar, and how long ? 18. What kingdom succeeded Babylon ? Reference. 19. By what is this represented ? 20. When did Cyrus overthrow Babylon ? 21. How long had Babylon continued from its introduction into prophecy ? 22. What marked the end of the Persian kingdom ? 23. How long did Persia continue ? 24. What kingdom succeeded Persia ? Reference. 25. How many universal earthly kingdoms do we look for after Grecia ? 26. Where is such a kingdom brought to view ? 27. Who was Cæsar Augustus ? 28.

denotes the degeneracy which came into the kingdom, and the ten toes the ten kingdoms into which
the Roman empire was finally divided by the
incursions of the northern barbarians. Rome in
prophecy dates from its league with the Jews, B. C.
161, seven years after its conquest of Macedonia.
Its division into ten parts was accomplished
between the years 356 and 483 A. D. Grecia ruled
from B. C. 331, to B. C. 161, a period of 170 years,
and Rome from B. C. 161, to its division in 483, a
period of 644 years.

The two legs do not denote the division of Rome
into the Eastern and Western empires. If they do,
Rome should have been thus divided from the
beginning of its history, or the legs should have
been united down to the ankles, as it was not till
A. D. 330 that the seat of empire was moved from
Rome to Constantinople. But history forbids the
former, and consistency forbids the latter.

" In the days of these kings " the kingdom of God
is to be set up. Not in the days of any one of the
previous kingdoms which had passed away, nor of
Rome in its undivided state, when it was but one
kingdom. It is not till after we find a plurality of
kingdoms existing cotemporaneously, that we can
look for the setting up of the kingdom of God, and
we do not find these cotemporaneous kingdoms till
we find Rome breaking up into its final divisions

What is denoted by the clay of the feet and toes ?   29. What
is represented by the ten toes ?   30. From what point does
it date in prophecy ?   31. When was it divided into ten parts !
32. How long did Grecia rule ?   33. How long did Rome
reign to its division into ten kingdoms ?   34. Are Eastern
and Western Rome symbolized by the two legs of the image ?
35. If so, when should Rome have been divided ? 36. When,
by whom, and where, was the seat of empire moved from
Rome ?   37. In the days of these kings ; what kings ? 38.
Why may not some one of the first three kingdoms be meant,

356 to 483 A. D. Not till then was the image complete ready to be smitten by the stone upon the feet. The kingdom represented by the stone could not therefore have been set up in the days of Christ and his apostles 483 years before this division was completed. The fact is therefore forever settled that the kingdom represented by the stone is not a spiritual kingdom, but is literal like the four preceding it; and that it is yet future; for nothing to answer to the setting up of this kingdom has taken place since 483 A. D.

It will be asked if those kings or kingdoms are still in existence, in the days of which the God of Heaven was to set up his kingdom. If they were established so long ago as 483, have they not all passed away? We answer, No. They are the kingdoms which, as Dr. Scott remarks, have generally been known since that time as the ten kingdoms of western Europe. Many of them can easily be traced to the present time. Originally they were the Huns, Ostrogoths, Visigoths, Franks, Vandals, Suevi, Heruli, Burgundians, Anglo-Saxons and Lombards. And we have now the French from the Franks, the English from the Anglo-Saxons, the Portuguese from the Suevi, the Spanish from the Visigoths, the modern Italians from the Ostrogoths, and the Huns, and Lombards from the original stock of that name.

The image is all complete. We are still in the

---

or Rome before its division? 39. When was the image complete so that it could be smitten upon the feet? 40. Was the kingdom represented by the stone set up in the days of Christ or his apostles? 41. Why not? 42. Is this kingdom a literal kingdom and why? 43. Is it yet future, and why? 44. Are those kingdoms still in existence? 45. What is Dr. Scott's remark? 46. What were the names of the ten kingdoms originally? 47. What modern nations do we now find descended from them? 48. Is the image now complete?

days of these kings, and wait for the setting up of
the kingdom of God, which is the next and only
remaining event in this line of prophecy.

CLASS QUESTIONS ON LESSON III. WITH ANSWERS.

1. Dan. 2. It has been stated by some speakers
that the reason the Lord chose gold, silver, brass,
and iron to represent the four kingdoms in the great
image, was because those kingdoms would represent
themselves by these metals. Is there any historical
proof of this assertion?

ANS. An iron crown was used in the later years
of Rome as their symbol of power; and this iron
crown appeared as a historical object down to within
a few hundred years of the present time. But we
know of nothing to sustain the statement in reference to the other kingdoms. That some regard was
had to the relative strength of the kingdoms, in the
metals by which they were represented, is evident
from the language of the prophecy itself: "And
the fourth kingdom shall be *strong* as iron." Verse
40. But inasmuch as the image closes with a mixture of miry clay, the idea of degeneracy from beginning to end, from gold to mud, is still more strongly
presented.

2. Dan. 2 : 45. What is the mountain out of
which the stone was cut that smote the image on
its feet?

ANS. The great mountain of grace, that system
of favor to men which led God and his Son to
devise the way of salvation, and which led Christ to
enter upon the work of redemption which will

----

49. Are we still in the days of these kings? 50. What is
the next event in this line of prophecy?

result in his finally having a kingdom filling the whole earth, after all the evil kingdoms of this world like the shattered fragments of broken potters' vessels shall have been cleared away.

3. At what date was Rome divided into its eastern and western divisions?

ANS. As the prophecy takes no note of this division it is a point of no importance so far as concerns an interpretation of the prophecy. It is however a matter of historical interest as one of the steps which prepared the way for the overthrow of the Western empire. Swinton's Outlines of the World's History, p. 193, speaks on this point as follows:—

"Constantine made a change which had a great effect upon the later history of the Roman world. He removed the capital of the empire to the old Greek city of Byzantium, on the Bosphorus, which he greatly enlarged and called New Rome, but which has been better known ever since as Constantinople (Greek *polis*, a city—the city of Constantine). Even before this, Rome had, as we have seen, ceased to be the usual dwelling-place of the emperors, who commonly lived at Milan, Nicomedia (Bithynia), and elsewhere; but the transfer of the capital to a Greek city is a proof of how completely the empire had come to overshadow Rome and Italy. Theodosius was the last emperor who reigned over the whole Roman empire. On his death in A. D. 395, the vast dominion was divided between his two sons,—Honorius ruling in the West, and Arcadius in the East. From that date the history of Rome divides itself into two distinct histories, that of the Western or Latin empire, and that of the Eastern, Greek or Byzantine empire."

LESSON FOUR.

THE VISION OF DANIEL CHAPTER VII.

THE symbolic language of the Scriptures is to be explained by the literal. All the figures of the Bible are defined by the literal language of the Bible. We have here the sea, winds, and four great beasts, none of which, of course, are to be regarded as literal. The sea, rivers, or waters, used as figures, denote "peoples, multitudes, nations and tongues." Rev. 17:15; Isa. 8:7. Winds denote political strife and war. Jer. 25:32, 33. The beasts denote four kingdoms that arose on the earth, one after the other. Dan. 7:17, 23. The fourth beast is the fourth *kingdom;* therefore the other beasts denote kingdoms though they are like this one sometimes called kings.

The consistency of the figures as illustrating the events of human history is at once seen. In the most populous civilized portions of the earth, which from earliest history have been western Asia, and Europe, political strife has moved among the people. As a consequence, revolution has succeeded revolution, and four great kingdoms have one after another arisen and fallen.

We have seen from the great image of Dan. 2, that there were to be but four universal kingdoms from

REVIEW QUESTIONS ON LESSON FOUR.

1. How is the symbolic language of Scripture to be explained? 2. Are the figures of the Bible explained by the Bible? 3. What figures are here introduced? 4. What is symbolized by the sea? References. 5. What by the wind? Reference. 6. What do beasts, when used as symbols, represent? 7. What is said of the fourth beast? 8. To what portion of the earth must we therefore look for the fulfillment of this representation? 9. How many universal kingdoms have existed on the earth, beginning in the time of

Daniel's day to the end of time. The fourth beast of this vision of Dan. 7, denotes the last one of these earthly governments; for he is given to the burning flame, and the kingdom passes into the possession of the saints with a perpetual title.

The four beasts of Dan. 7 therefore denote the same four kingdoms that are represented by the great image: the first beast, the lion, symbolizing Babylon, B. C. 677 to B. C. 538; the second, the bear, Medo-Persia, B. C. 538 to 331; the third, the leopard, Grecia, B. C. 331 to 161; the fourth, the great and terrible nondescript, Rome, B. C. 161 to A. D. 483.

The lion had at first two wings as of an eagle, representing the rapid conquests and ruling power of Babylon under Nebuchadnezzar, who raised it to the hight of its power. The wings were plucked and a man's heart given to it—as it was under the last king, the weak and pusillanimous Belshazzar.

The bear raised itself up on one side, showing the ascendency of the Persian element in the Medo-Persian empire, as more fully brought out in the symbol of the ram of chapter 8. The three ribs denote, probably, the three provinces especially devoured by this kingdom, Babylon, Lydia, and Egypt, which greatly stimulated the Persian lust for power, or said to it, Arise and devour much flesh.

The leopard had four wings, denoting the rapidity of Grecian conquests under Alexander; and four

Daniel? 10. By what is the last one of these governments here symbolized? 11. What kingdoms, therefore, are brought to view by these beasts? 12. Give the dates of Babylon. 13. The dates of Persia; of Grecia; of Rome. 14. What was signified by the two wings of the lion? 15. What period of the empire was fitly represented by the lion with a man's heart and no wings? 16. What is shown by the bear raising himself up on one side? 17. What by the three ribs? 18. How did they say to it, Arise and devour much flesh? 19. What is shown by the four wings of the leopard?

heads, signifying the division of the kingdom into four parts after Alexander's death, more particularly noticed under the symbol of the goat of chapter 8.

The fourth great and terrible beast had ten horns. These are declared to be ten kingdoms which should arise out of this empire. Dan. 7 : 24. These correspond to the ten toes of the image. Rome was divided into ten kingdoms between the years A. D. 356 and 483, as follows: Huns, A. D. 356, Ostrogoths, 377, Visigoths, 378, Franks, 407, Vandals, 407, Suevi, 407, Burgundians, 407, Heruli, 476, Anglo-Saxons, 476, Lombards, 483. This enumeration of the ten kingdoms is given by Machiavel in his History of Florence, lib. 1. The dates are furnished by Bishop Lloyd, and the whole is approved by Bishop Newton, Faber and Dr. Hales.

Among these ten horns another little horn diverse from the others thrust itself up, plucking up three in its course. This was the papacy, established in 538. The decree of Justinian, emperor of the East, declaring the pope the head of all the churches, was issued in 533; but before it could be carried out, three Arian powers who stood opposed to papal doctrines and assumptions had to be removed out of the way, namely, the Heruli, Vandals and Ostrogoths. The Ostrogoths were forced into a final retreat from

20. What by the four heads? 21. What do the ten horns of the fourth beast represent? 22. To what do these correspond in the image of chapter 2? 23. Between what years was Rome divided? 24. Name the ten kingdoms and the dates when they arose. 25. Who gives this enumeration of the kingdoms? 26. Who furnishes the dates? 27. What celebrated scholars endorse this work of Machiavel and Bishop Lloyd? 28. What was seen coming up among the ten horns? 29. What does this little horn represent? 30. When was the papacy established? 31. When was Justinian's decree issued? 32. Why does not papal supremacy date from the year of this decree instead of 538? 33. What were the three horns plucked up by the papacy, and why?

Rome in March 538, and Justinian's decree was carried into effect.

This horn spoke great words. Witness the titles the pope has assumed, and received from his flatterers. He has worn out the saints of the Most High. Between fifty and one hundred millions of martyrs testify on this point. He has thought to change times and laws; *the* law, say the Septuagint, the German and Danish translations; pointing out the law of the Most High. This the papacy has thought to do, by endeavoring to change the fourth commandment, substituting the first day of the week for the Sabbath, in place of the seventh, which the commandment enjoins. See Hist. of the Sabbath and Catholic Catechisms. They have been given into his hands a time, times, and dividing of time, or half a time: three times and a half. A time in Scripture signifies a year. Dan. 4:16, compared with Josephus who says that the "seven times" were seven years. Three times and a half are therefore three years and a half. As the Bible year consists of 360 days (12 months of 30 days each) three and a half of such years give us 1260 days; and these days being symbolic, a day for a year, Eze. 4:6; Num. 14:34, we have 1260 years for the continuance of papal supremacy. This is the same as the 1260

---

34. When were the Ostrogoths forced to abandon Rome? 35. In what way has the pope spoken great words against the Most High? 36. How has he worn out the saints? 37. What has he thought to change? 38. What reading is given by the Septuagint, German and Danish versions? 39. How has the papacy endeavored to change the law of God? 40. Where is proof of this found? 41. For how long a time were the saints, times and laws given into the hands of this little horn? 42. How long a period is meant by "a time"? 43. How many days in "a time times and a half"? 44. Are these days literal or symbolic? 45. How much time is represented by a symbolic day? References. 46. How much literal time have we, therefore, for the continuance of papal

days and 42 months of Rev. 12 and 13 applied to the same power. Reckoned from 538, they bring us to 1798. Feb. 10, of that year, Berthier acting under the French Directory, took Rome, and carried the pope into exile where the next year he died. Here sat the judgment of verse 26, and his dominion was taken away (temporarily overthrown but not consumed), and has been waning away both temporarily and spiritually from that time to the present.

In verses 9 and 10 judgment of another kind is brought to view: the investigative Judgment of the Heavenly Sanctuary, commencing in 1844. In connection with that a special utterance of great words is heard by the prophet. The great Ecumenical Council held in Rome in 1870, furnishes a marked fulfillment. There by a deliberate vote of the highest dignitaries of all the Catholic world, 538 against 2, July 21, 1870, the pope was decreed to be infallible. In two months from that time, Sept. 20, 1870, Rome surrendered to the troops of Victor Emanuel, and the last vestige of the pope's temporal power departed. His destruction in the burning flame must be at hand.

The fifth kingdom of this vision which the saints take and possess forever, is the one under the whole heaven, including the territory of these beast kingdoms. It is therefore the same as the kingdom of

---

supremacy? 47. Where and in what terms is this same period of time elsewhere mentioned? 48. Reckoned from 538, to what year do they bring us? 49. What took place in that year? 50. What judgment is brought to view in verse 26? 51. What, in verses 9 and 10? 52. When were the greatest and most presumptuous words of the papacy heard? 53. On what day was the vote on infallibility taken? 54. How did the vote stand? 55. What took place two months later? 56. Into whose hand does the kingdom finally pass? 57. Where is it located and what is its extent? 58. What relation does this show between this kingdom and

Dan. 2, which fills the whole earth. What folly then to talk of the kingdom of Dan. 2 being set up at the first advent of Christ, since it is not set up till after the papacy has run its allotted career, and is destroyed, an event that takes place only at the second coming of Christ in power and glory. 2 Thess. 2: 8.

CLASS QUESTIONS ON LESSON IV. WITH ANSWERS.

1. Dan. 7 : 8. Of what are the *eyes* and *mouth* symbolical ?

ANS. This little horn being a symbol of the papacy, the eyes in the horn would appropriately indicate the far-seeing policy, shrewdness and cunning of that power. In some of the great papal processions in Rome, there is borne before the pope a banner or shield covered on both sides with eyes, to denote that that church is all eyes, everywhere present, watching the actions of all men. Well was it said of that horn that it had eyes like the eyes of man. The mouth would indicate clearly the other great feature of this church, its utterance of presumptuous words, and assumption of blasphemous titles.

2. Dan. 7 : 13. What is meant by the Son of man coming with the *clouds of* heaven, when he comes to the Ancient of Days ?

ANS. This scene certainly does not take place on this earth, or within the region of our atmosphere. The Ancient of Days is not here. The Son of man goes before him to receive a kingdom, which

---

the kingdom of God of chapter 2? 59. What then shall be said of the idea that the kingdom of Dan. 2 was set up at the first advent of Christ ?

he does not receive before his work as priest is ended; hence it does not refer to his ascension at the time of his first advent; for then he went to his Father to act as priest before him. But he receives his kingdom before he returns. Luke 19:12. Hence this scene transpires in Heaven. The clouds therefore are not the clouds of our atmosphere which may be referred to in expressions respecting his return to this earth. We know of no clouds in Heaven but the clouds of angels that ever surround their Lord; and we think these are the ones intended here.

3. Dan. 7:23. What marked the establishment of Rome as a universal empire?

ANS. Rome reached the hight of its greatness under Octavian, known as Augustus Cæsar. The date from which it may most probably be considered a universal empire, was the time when it had made itself master of all the divisions of the preceding or goat kingdom. And when it made Egypt a province, it had then absorbed into itself all the kingdom of Alexander. This was B. C. 30. But it was introduced into prophecy earlier than this, that is, when the league was made between it and the Jews in B. C. 161. After that the prophet saw it extending itself toward the east, the south, and the pleasant land. This was fulfilled when it made Syria and Palestine Roman provinces in B. C. 65 and 63, and Egypt, as already stated, B. C. 30.

4. Dan. 7:25. Is the word "times" in this verse in the Greek or Hebrew of such form as to denote just two times; that is, is it in the dual number, so that the expression might be read, "a time, two times, and half a time, making three times and a half?

ANS. No argument, we think, can be drawn

from the dual number on this verse. The Hebrew does not make that distinction in numbers, and in the Greek the form is frequently identical with the regular plural. But the expression is none the less definite; for no number being expressed, the law of language would require us to understand the least number that could be expressed by the plural, which is two. As many as two it must be, or it could not be put in the plural; but to say that it is more than two, would be pure assumption for there is nothing to indicate it. And this conclusion is made certain by comparing this language with other prophecies in reference to the same period of time, in which it is cálled 42 months and 1260 days. Rev. 12 : 6, 14 ; 13 : 5. This would be a time (1 year 360 days) two times (or years 720 days) and half a time (180 days) making in all 1260 days.

5. Dan. 7 : 25. Some claim that the 1260 years of papal supremacy began somewhere in the 8th century when Pepin ascended the throne. How can this be answered ?

ANS. The point marked in the prophecy as the beginning of papal supremacy is not when the pope became a temporal prince, but when he had power to persecute the church of God. This was not by virtue of any grant from Pepin, nor from Phocas, but from Justinian. Croly, on the Apocalypse, says that the highest authorities among the civilians and annalists of Rome spurn the idea that Phocas was the founder of the supremacy of Rome ; they ascend to Justinian as the only legitimate source. Baronius, the great Catholic historian, formally gives the whole detail of Justinian's grants of supremacy to the pope. Gavazzi, Lectures, p. 66, says : " The celebrated letter of Justinian to the pope in the year

533, not only recognizing all previous privileges, but enlarging them, and entitling the pope and his church to many immunities and rights, afterward gave origin to the pretensions displayed in the canon law." See also De Cormenin, vol. 1, p. 114. This decree made in 533 was not carried into effect till 538, and we must date the period from the time when the saints, times and laws were actually given into his hands. It was this spiritual control, not temporal, that is marked by the prophecy.

6.   Dan. 7 : 25. If the Bible year is only 360 days, how were the seasons regulated, as there are in reality in every year 365 days, 5 hours, 48 minutes and 49 seconds ?

Ans.   The regular year of the Jews was 12 months of 30 days each, which would give just 360 days for the year.   But this falling so much short of a real year, the seasons would have been entirely thrown out of place in a short time, unless some method had been adopted to remedy the difficulty. The simple method adopted by the Jews was this : Every third year an extra month was intercalated. Their 12th month was called Adar, and this extra month was called ve-Adar, or the second Adar, and was made of sufficient length just to make up the time they had lost, and bring the year up with the sun again.   But this third year, lengthened out indefinitely by this thirteenth month, was exceptional.   The regular year was 360 days in length ; and hence in the reckoning of all prophetic periods the year of 360 days must be taken.   But the years which they symbolize are of course the actual years, $365\frac{1}{4}$ days in length.

7.   What judgment is spoken of in Dan. 7 : 26 ?

Ans.   Political judgment on the papacy at the end of its specified period of 1260 years.   National calamity and overthrow are sometimes spoken of in the Scriptures as judgments. In Acts 7 : 7, Stephen speaks of the overthrow of the Egyptians at the exode as follows: "And the nation to whom they shall be in bondage will I judge, said God; and after that shall they come forth and serve me in this place." It could therefore be properly said that the (threatened) judgment upon the Egyptian nation sat at that time. So the period of papal supremacy was limited to 1260 years, and at the end of that time judgment was rendered and his dominion taken away. That this judgment refers exclusively to the papacy is evident from the remainder of the verse. It was at the time when his dominion was taken away which we know was in 1798; and a consuming process was to follow, which has since been fulfilled till now the last vestige of his temporal power is gone, and the end must be near. This judgment is not the same as that of verses 9 and 10, which has been explained in remarks on the sanctuary, nor the same as that of verse 22, which seems to refer to the time when the saints will have their part to act in apportioning judgments upon the wicked, 1 Cor. 6 : 2, which will be during their reign of a thousand years with Christ. Rev. 20 : 4.

LESSON FIVE.

THE VISION OF DANIEL CHAPTER VIII.

THE symbols of this chapter are mostly explained in the chapter itself. The ram with two horns, the higher of which came up last, represented the kings, or the kingdom, of Media and Persia, the two horns symbolizing the two elements in the nation, the Medes and Persians. The Persian came up last and attained the controlling influence. Hostilities first broke out between the Babylonians and the Medes, whereupon Cyaxeres, king of the Medes, summoned to his aid his nephew Cyrus, the son of his sister who had been married to Cambyses the king of Persia. Cyrus, responding with an army of 30,000 Persians, was at once placed by Cyaxeres in command of the joint forces of the Medes and Persians. On the taking of Babylon, B. C. 538, Cyaxeres (who is called Darius in Dan. 5 : 31), as civil ruler, took the throne. On his death, two years later, B. C. 536, he made Cyrus his successor, and the same year, Cambyses, the father of Cyrus dying, Cyrus was brought also to the Persian throne. The two were then united in one ; and thus was founded the Medo-Persian empire, the ruling house being in the Persian line. This power pushed its conquests

---

REVIEW QUESTIONS ON LESSON FIVE.

1. What symbols are introduced in chapter 8 ? 2. Where are these symbols mostly explained ? 3. What does the ram with two horns represent ? 4. What do the two horns symbolize ? 5. Which was the higher ? 6. How did this come up last ? 7. Who was Cambyses ? 8. Whom did Cambyses marry ? 9. Who was Cyrus ? 10. When was Babylon taken by Cyrus ? 11. Who was then placed on the throne of the kingdom ? 12. What name is given to Cyaxeres in Dan. 5 : 31 ? 13. When did Darius die ? 14. What change then took place in the position of Cyrus ? 15. How extensive was the

especially in the directions named, northward, westward and southward, till in the days of Ahasuerus, Esther 1 : 1, it reigned over one hundred and twenty-seven provinces, from India to Ethiopia.

The rough goat is explained to be the king of Grecia. Verse 21. The great horn between his eyes was the first king. Id. This shows that the word king as first used has the sense of kingdom ; as it would be absurd to speak of the first king of a king. This first king was Alexander the Great, who having defeated the last Persian king, Darius Codomannus, at the battle of Arbela, Oct. 1, B. C. 331, found himself master of the world. This horn was broken and four came up in its place, denoting the four parts into which his empire would be divided. Eight years after the battle of Arbela, Alexander gave himself up to beastly drunkenness to that degree that he died Nov. 12, B. C. 323, aged only 33. Prideaux gives a just estimate of the man, when he calls him " the great cut-throat of the age in which he lived." In the name of Aridæus, then called Philip, bastard brother of Alexander's and also an idiot, and by Alexander's two infant sons, Alexander Ægus and Hercules, all being under the guardianship of Perdiccas, the unity of the empire was for a time maintained. But it did not take long to put these all out of the way, and within fifteen years after Alexander's

---

Persian empire in the days of Ahasuerus ?   Reference.   16. What is symbolized by the rough goat ?   17. What, by the great horn between his eyes ?   18. What does this show in relation to the use of the word king in these prophecies ? 19. Who was the first king ?   20. When and how did he become master of the world ?   21. How was this horn broken ?   22. Give the date of his death, and his age at the time.   23. What estimate of Alexander is given by Prideaux ? 24. How was the unity of the empire for awhile maintained ? 25. How long before these were all put out of the way ?   26.

death the kingdom was divided into four parts, between his four leading generals: Cassander had Macedon and Greece; Lysimachus had Thrace and those parts of Asia that lay upon the Hellespont and Bosphorus; Ptolemy had Egypt, Libya, Arabia, Palestine and Cœle-Syria, and Seleucus had Syria and all the East. These kingdoms are called, in brief, Macedonia, Thrace, Syria and Egypt. They date from about B. C. 308.

The little horn denotes a succeeding kingdom to arise in the latter part of the reign of the four horns, a kingdom of fierce countenance, strange language, a wonderful destroyer, to stand up against the Prince of princes, and at last to be broken without hand. This horn was not Antiochus Epiphanes as claimed by some, for he was not "exceeding great" in comparison with Medo-Persia and Grecia that went before. He did not increase his dominions, was not another horn, but only one (the 8th in order) of the 26 kings that constituted the Syrian horn of the goat. He did not stand up against the Prince of princes (Christ), but died 164 years before our Lord was born.

This horn must symbolize Rome, as in the parallel visions of Dan. 2 and 7. Rome came out of one of the horns of the goat, as it conquered Macedonia B. C. 168, and in 161 became connected with the people of God by its league with the Jews; 1 Mac. 8; Josephus' Antiq., b. xii., c. x., sec. 6; Prideaux, vol. ii., p. 166; thus becoming a subject of prophecy, and appearing to the prophet

What then took place? 27. Name the four kingdoms. 28. Name their respective rulers. 29. What is the date of their rise? 30. What is denoted by the little horn? 31. To whom is this symbol sometimes applied? 32. Why can it not apply to Antiochus Epiphanes (pronounced An-*ti*-o-kus E-*pif*-a-neez)? 33. What kingdom does answer to the little

to come out of the Macedonian horn. It extended its conquests toward the east, south, and pleasant land (Palestine), making provinces of the following countries : Syria, B. C. 65 ; Palestine, B. C. 63 ; Egypt, B. C. 30. It stood up against the Prince of princes, nailing Christ to the cross. By Rome the daily was taken away and the transgression of desolation set up ; that is, there was a change in the religion of the empire, Paganism (the daily desolation) was taken away, and the papacy (the transgression of desolation, or the abomination that maketh desolate) was set up. Dan. 12 : 11. An host was given him : the hordes of barbarians that overran the empire, but were converted to the papal faith.

This horn of Daniel 8 must not be confounded with the little horn on the fourth beast of Dan. 7. That symbolized the papacy exclusively. This embraces Rome through its whole career both pagan and papal. In other words, this horn of Dan. 8, is the same as the great and terrible beast of Dan. 7, in both its phases.

In verse 14 is introduced the period of 2300 days, the sanctuary and its cleansing. All the vision was sufficiently explained to the prophet with the exception of the time. But Daniel says, verse 27, "I was astonished at the vision, but none under-

horn of this prophecy ? 34. How can Rome be said to come out of one of the horns of the goat ? 35. In what directions did Rome extend its conquests ? 36. When were Syria, Palestine and Egypt made Roman provinces ? 37. How did Rome stand up against the Prince of princes ? 38. What is meant by the daily ? 39. How was the daily taken away by Rome ? 40. What was put in its place ? 41. To whom was the host of verse 12 given ? 42. Who constituted this host ? 43 Is this horn of the vision of Dan. 8, the same as the horn of the fourth beast of Dan. 7, and why ? 44. What is introduced in verse 14 ? 45. How much of the vision had been explained to Daniel ? 46. Yet what does Daniel say in verse

stood it." Although Gabriel had been commanded to make him understand it, Daniel fainted before an explanation of the time was reached, and the angel was obliged to postpone further instruction.

CLASS QUESTIONS ON LESSON V. WITH ANSWERS.

1. Dan. 8 : 13. What is to be understood by the phrase, " How long the vision ? "

ANS. We think it has reference to the time embraced in the vision. How long a period is covered by the vision during which the sanctuary and the host shall be trodden under foot? The answer, Unto two thousand three hundred days, does not point out definitely the close of the time, but only brings to view the last event which will close up the matter so far as the sanctuary and the host are concerned, bringing eternal deliverance to the people of God. These days therefore must cover most of the time of the vision, embracing the duration of the great kingdoms noticed in the prophecy. To call the days literal, not quite six years and a half, would be simply ridiculous. They must be prophetic days, signifying so many years.

2. Dan. 8 : 17. " At the time of the end shall be the vision." End of what ?

ANS. We think the expression " the time of the end " here means the same as when found in other passages ; namely, a period of time commencing in 1798, and extending to the end, in which the main prophetic periods should terminate, and those events

---

27 ? 47. To what must this have reference ? 48. Why did not Gabriel go on till he had explained to Daniel every part of the vision ? 49. Had he been commanded to explain it ? 50. What may we therefore still look for ?

and movements transpire which were to warn the world and prepare a people for the end. Then "shall be the vision;" that is, be opened, begin to be understood. It was closed up and sealed to that time. Then it would be unsealed. Since that time the great light has arisen on prophetic subjects which has shown the end to be near, and given rise to the extensive Advent movement of the present generation.

3. Dan. 8:19: "Behold I will make thee to know what shall be in the last end of the indignation." What is meant by the last end of the indignation?

ANS. The manner of expression here used shows that the indignation covers a period of time. We think that it is the indignation which God permits to come upon his people from opposing powers, the same as mentioned in verse 13, How long shall be the vision . . . *to give* both the sanctuary and the host to be trodden under foot? In Eze. 21:27, God speaks concerning the throne of Israel, when subjected to the King of Babylon, " I will overturn, overturn, overturn it; and it shall be no more till he come whose right it is, and I will give it him." Three overturns from Babylon awaited it, that is, to Persia, to Grecia and to Rome. Then it should be no more; national existence ceased, but the spiritual Israel have lived among the nations, but still in subjection to earthly powers. And so it will be till He come whose right it is, Christ, who shall take the throne of his Father David, and rule over his people forever. Again, it was said to Daniel (12:7), " When he shall have accomplished to scatter the power of the holy people " (that is, shall have finished the scattering of their power, or their oppression among the nations) " all these things shall be fulfilled." This all shows that God's people were to be overturned, scattered, and subject to indignation, till the times, or rule, of the Gentiles should be fulfilled. And in the verse under notice, the Lord says to Daniel, I will make thee to know what shall be in the last end of this time of indignation. Then he goes on to predict the final downfall of earthly kingdoms, and lastly points Daniel forward to the cleansing of the sanctuary, which puts away the sins of God's people, and is the first step toward their deliverance, which will be the full end of the indignation, followed by their glorification and eternal inheritance.

4. What followed the league formed between the Jews and the Romans in B. C. 161 ?

ANS. The cruel oppression of the Syrians roused such a spirit of resistance among the Jews that under the leadership of the Maccabees, aided by the friendship of the Romans, they achieved their complete liberation from Syrian tyranny. Smith's History of the World, vol. iii., p. 170, speaks of " the long list of nations in Europe and Asia, to which the Roman Senate sent letters requiring them to protect the Jews residing among them." Thus matters continued till internal dissensions invited the Romans to interfere in a manner more positive than by the existing league of amity and friendship. In the days of Pompey there were two aspirants for the office of high-priest, the high-priest holding also the position of prince or ruler of the people. Powerful factions followed their respective leaders, Aristobulus and Hyrcanus; and to put an end to the strife, appeal was made to Pompey who was then in the East settling the affairs of Syria, to decide the question. Aristobulus, perceiving that Pompey would give the decision in favor of

Hyrcanus, retired to Jerusalem and made immediate preparation to defend his claims by force of arms. This brought Pompey with all his army against the city. Aristobulus finally relenting came out to surrender to him the keys of the city; but his party by a sudden outburst of fanaticism refused him entrance. The party of Hyrcanus threw open the gates. The others retreated to the temple and its fortified precincts where they were besieged by Pompey. After three months the place was taken and the defenders massacred, the blood of the priests themselves being mingled with that of the sacrifices they were offering at the altar. Aristobulus graced the triumph of Pompey at Rome. Hyrcanus was restored to the priesthood, but *stripped of the royal title*. Judea became a Roman province, till the dismemberment of the Roman Empire.

In this act of the abolition of the royal title, or the office of king, may perhaps be seen a fulfillment of Dan. 8:10, and Rev. 12:4. These texts speak of the casting down of some of the stars by this Roman power. Stars must here be used in a symbolical sense, signifying persons in places of eminence or power. Rev. 12:4, says a third of them were cast down. Of these three offices, kings, priests and counselors, or members of the Sanhedrim, a third, or the office of king was abolished.

LESSON SIX.

THE 70 WEEKS AND 2300 DAYS.

IN the ninth chapter of Daniel we find a further explanation of Daniel 8. Mark the connection between the two chapters. 1. Gabriel appears again to Daniel, verse 21, the very one who in the vision of chapter 8 had been commanded to make him understand that vision, but who had not yet completed that mission. 2. Daniel refers to the vision at the beginning in which he had seen this angel. This must be the vision of chapter 8, as no other had intervened between that and this. 3. Gabriel said, " I am now come forth to give thee skill and understanding," the very work he was intrusted with in chapter 8, but had been obliged on Daniel's account, to postpone. 4. The angel then himself refers back to the vision of chapter 8, saying, " understand the matter " and consider " the vision." 5. He then commenced with the very matter omitted in chapter 8, namely, the explanation of the time : " Seventy weeks are determined upon thy people." The word here rendered determined signifies " cut off." Seventy weeks are cut off. From what ? From the 2300 days. Wherever the 70 weeks commence, there the 2300 days begin.

REVIEW QUESTIONS ON LESSON SIX.

1. Where do we find a further explanation of Dan. 8 ? 2. Who on this occasion appeared to Daniel ? 3. To what does Daniel refer ? 4. What vision must this be ? 5. What did Gabriel say ? 6. How do these words suggest a connection with chapter 8 ? 7. To what does the angel himself then refer ? 8. With what point does the angel here commence his explanation ? 9. What are his words ? 10. What does the word rendered " determined " signify ? 11. From what are the seventy weeks cut off ? 12. Does the commencement

Gabriel then proceeds to give the starting point. When a commandment should go forth to restore and build Jerusalem, the seventy weeks would begin. The first decree that was issued after this time, in any wise affecting Jerusalem, was the decree of Cyrus B. C. 536 for the return of the Jews and the rebuilding of the temple. Ez. 1. But this only provided for the temple, and fell far short of granting the " restoration " to which the prophecy points. This work was hindered by the enemies of the Jews in the reign of Artaxerxes the Magian, B. C. 522. Ez. 4. The decree of Cyrus was reaffirmed by Darius Hystaspes, B. C. 519, and the work on the temple again went forward. But this decree like that of Cyrus was too limited in its provisions. At length Ezra obtained a decree from Artaxerxes Longimanus, in the seventh year of his reign, B. C. 457, Ez. 7 : 7, containing provisions for the complete restoration of the Jewish State. This decree, written in the original in Chaldaic or Eastern Aramaic, the language of the Persian court, is found in full in Ez. 7 : 12–23. When this went forth the prophecy was met, all three of the decrees constituting " the commandment," as expressed in Ez. 6 : 14, and the date of its going forth being that point when the last one with its full provision, was

---

of the seventy weeks determine the commencement of the 2300 days? 13. What event does Gabriel name as the starting point of the seventy weeks? 14. What was the first decree issued after the giving of this vision? 15. For what did this decree provide? 16. How and when was this work hindered? 17. Who re-affirmed the decree of Cyrus and when? 18. What must be said of the provisions of this decree? 19. What was the next decree? 20. Under what king and in what year did this decree go forth? Reference. 21. What provisions were contained in this decree? 22. In what language was this originally written? 23. Where is it found in full? 24. Was the prophecy met in this decree? 25. How much did it take to constitute the "commandment"?

carried into effect by Ezra. Ez. 7:9. The commission to Nehemiah 13 years later, was no decree and is not to be taken into the account.

Seven weeks or 49 years were allotted to the literal work of building the city, and arranging the affairs of the State. This was completed in the last act of reformation by Nehemiah, in the fifteenth year of Darius Nothus, B. C. 408, exactly 49 years from the commencement of the work by Ezra, B. C. 457. Sixty-two weeks, 434 years more, were to extend to Messiah the Prince. Christ was set forth as the Messiah, or the Anointed, at his baptism when he was anointed with the Holy Ghost. Acts 10:37, 38; 4:27; Luke 4:18, etc. This period therefore reaches to his ministry, which commenced in A. D. 27. For John began his ministry in the fifteenth year of Tiberius Cæsar, Luke 3:1, which was in A. D. 27, and Christ entered upon his work six months later, which would bring us to the autumn of that year. And to this point exactly, the 69 weeks or 483 years bring us, reckoned from

---

Reference. 26. What can be said of the commission granted to Nehemiah? 27. How much time was allotted to the building of the city? 28. How and when was this completed? 29. What is the next division of time, and to what does it reach? 30. What is the meaning of the word Messiah? 31. When was Christ set forth as the Messiah? References. 32. Does this period then reach to his birth or to the commencement of his ministry? 33. When did Christ's ministry begin? 34. When did John commence his ministry? Reference. 35. What year was the 15th of Tiberius Cæsar? 36. How long after the commencement of John's ministry did Christ enter upon his? (A priest could not enter upon his office before the age of 30. See Num. 4:3, 23, 35, 39, 43, 47. It is supposed that John and Christ followed the same rule; and as Christ was six months younger than John, he would begin his work six months later. Of him it is said that he was about 30 years old at his baptism, and so was doubtless fully 30, when he began his public ministry.) 37. To what point do the 69 weeks or 483 years bring us reckoned

B. C. 457, in the autumn when Ezra commenced his work at Jerusalem. Here Christ went forth proclaiming, "The time is fulfilled," Mark 1 : 15, which can have reference to nothing else but the fulfillment of this period which was to bring us to the Messiah the Prince.

After the 7 weeks and the 62 weeks he was to be cut off, or in the middle of the 70th week, cause the sacrifice and oblation to cease. These expressions point unmistakably to the crucifixion of Christ. The ministry of Christ continued just three years and a half; for he attended but four passovers, at the last of which he was crucified. John 2 : 13 ; 5 : 1 ; 6 : 4 ; 13 : 1. If the sixty-ninth week ended in the autumn of A. D. 27, the middle of the 70th week, three and a half years further on, would be in the spring of A. D. 31, and right there the crucifixion took place. See Hales' Chronology. We go forward three years and a half more to the termination of that week, and find ourselves at the end of the 70 weeks in the autumn of A. D. 34. How much yet remains of the 2300 years? 2300−490=1810; and 34+1810=1844, where the whole period of 2300 years expired. So definitely and easily is the application of this period of 2300 years ascertained. The seventh year of Artaxerxes when Ezra received his

from the autumn of B. C. 457 ?   38. Why do we reckon from the autumn ?   39. What announcement did Christ make at the commencement of his preaching ?   40. To what must this have had reference ?   41. What was to take place after the 7 weeks and the 62 weeks ?   42. When were the sacrifice and oblation to cease ?   43. To what must these expressions refer ?   44. How long was Christ's ministry ?   References. 45. To what point do $3\frac{1}{2}$ years from the autumn of A. D. 27 bring us ?   46. On what authority is the crucifixion placed in the spring of 31 ?   47. Where did the 70 weeks terminate ? 48. How many days remain of the 2300 after the expiration of the 70 weeks?   49. Where then did the 2300 days end ? 50. What celebrated work fixes the 7th of Artaxerxes to the

commission is placed in B. C. 457 by Ptolemy's canon, and the accuracy of that canon is demonstrated by the concurrent agreement of more than 20 eclipses. The starting point for the 2300 days cannot therefore be moved from B. C. 457, without showing the inaccuracy of Ptolemy's record of these eclipses. But Prideaux says that they have been repeatedly calculated and have been found invariably to fall where Ptolemy has placed them.   Connection, vol. i., p. 242.

CLASS QUESTION ON LESSON VI. WITH ANSWER.

1. How and why is Christ's birth dated B. C. 4; and how old was he at his crucifixion?

Ans. The computation of time known as the Christian era was not introduced till A. D. 532. The birth of Christ was then placed on what was supposed to be good evidence in the year of Rome 753.   Six centuries afterward it was discovered that Christ was actually born something over three years before this date, so that the date of his birth stands B. C. 4.   But as the system had been adopted by nearly all Europe, and had been in use six hundred years, it was seen that any attempt to correct it would result in inextricable confusion. It was therefore thought best to let it remain.   See Hales' Chronology, Bliss' Chronology, Smith's History of the World, etc.   This does not affect historical dates, nor the reckoning of prophetic periods in the least, as all the years called B. C. are reckoned down to the point which has been adopted as the dividing line between B. C. and A. D.;

---

and all years this side are reckoned from that point. Christ probably entered upon his ministry at thirty years of age, and continuing three years and a half before his crucifixion, he would consequently be at that time, in the spring of A. D. 31, thirty-three years and six months of age.

LESSON SEVEN.

THE SANCTUARY.

THE prophecy of Dan. 8:14 simply declares that at the end of the 2300 days the sanctuary shall be cleansed. The subject of the sanctuary thus becomes the central and controlling question in this prophecy. If we regard it as something which is to be cleansed only at the coming of Christ, then the 2300 days must extend to Christ's coming. Many hold it in this light, and hence their continual efforts to re-adjust the prophetic periods, and set new times for the Lord to come.

The word sanctuary occurs in the Bible 146 times, and both the definition of the word and its use, show it to mean a holy or a sacred place, and a dwelling place for God. This fact should guard any one against applying it to any object which will not bear this definition, or to which it is not applied in the Scriptures.

The earth is not the sanctuary; for it is not a

REVIEW QUESTIONS ON LESSON SEVEN.

1. What is stated in Dan. 8:14? 2. How does the subject of the sanctuary affect our views of the coming of Christ? 3. How many times does the word sanctuary occur in the Bible? 4. What is the definition of the word? 5. Why may not the earth be the sanctuary? 6. Why not the land

holy or sacred place; and the Scriptures never call it the sanctuary.

The land of Canaan is not the sanctuary, for the same reasons. Neither can the term be applied to any limited portion of the land, as to Jerusalem, or Mt. Zion; for though these were spoken of while the Hebrew people maintained the favor of God, as holy, and a place where God would dwell, it is evidently because his temple was there, which he had caused to be erected for his habitation. For this reason Moses once speaks of the mountain of inheritance as the sanctuary, Ex. 15 : 17, just as David calls Judah in one instance, the sanctuary, Ps. 104 : 2, and in another instance, Mt. Zion; Ps. 78 : 68; but the tribe was not the mountain, any more than the mountain was the sanctuary; but the tribe possessed the mountain, and upon the mountain was the sanctuary "built," says David, "like high palaces." Ps. 78 : 69. However, Paul settles the question so far as pertains to the whole Mosaic dispensation, covered by the first covenant, and tells us emphatically that another object was the sanctuary during that time. Heb. 9 : 1, 2.

The church is not the sanctuary; for it is nowhere called such. One text, mentioned above, Ps. 104 : 2, is sometimes quoted to prove the church the sanctuary; but that has been already explained; and even if it was to be taken in its most rigidly literal sense, it would only prove that a particular tribe, and not the whole church was the sanctuary.

of Canaan? 7. Can the term be applied to any limited portion of the land, as to Mt. Zion or Jerusalem, and why not? 8. What does David say of the tribe of Judah, and how is his language explained? 9. What does David say of the sanctuary in Ps. 78 : 69? 10. How does Ps. 78 : 54, 69, explain Ex. 15 : 17? 11. What bearing does Paul's language in Heb. 9 : 1, 2, have upon this part of the subject? 12. Is the church the sanctuary? 13. What can be said of Ps.

But the statement quoted from Paul, Heb. 9:1, 2, applies to this very time when Judah constituted a portion of God's people, and he tells us that something else was then the sanctuary. And further, if the church ever constituted the sanctuary, even then it could not be the sanctuary of Dan. 8:14; for there the church is brought to view by the term "host" as an object entirely distinct from the sanctuary.

But to return to Paul's statement in Heb. 9:1, 2. What is that which he says was the sanctuary during the continuance of the first covenant? Answer, The tabernacle built by Moses in the wilderness of Sinai, which was afterward embodied in the temples of Solomon, Zerubbabel and Herod. This is described in full in Ex. 25, and onward. This settles the subject of the sanctuary down to the time of Christ. The only question now to be decided is, Has there been a sanctuary since that time? and if so, what?

These questions are definitely answered in the writings of Paul. He says that the second covenant has a sanctuary, the same as the first. The new covenant was introduced and ratified by Christ. He is its minister. His ministry is performed in Heaven. He is there a minister of the sanctuary, the true tabernacle which the Lord pitched and not man. Heb. 8:1, 2. The sanctuary of this covenant is, therefore, where the minister is, in

104:2? 14. If at any time the church was the sanctuary, could it be the sanctuary of Dan. 8:14, and why? 15. What does Paul say was the sanctuary of the first covenant? Reference. 16. Where is this described? 17. How much is settled by Paul's language? 18. What question remains? 19. Has the new covenant a sanctuary? 20. When and by whom was the new covenant introduced and ratified? 21. Where does Christ perform his ministry? 22. While in Heaven of what is he a minister? 23. Where then is the

Heaven. The sanctuary of the first covenant was a type of the Heavenly sanctuary of the new. Moses, when he made the tabernacle, made it after a pattern. Ex. 25 : 9, 40 ; 26 : 30 ; Acts 7 : 44 ; Heb. 8 : 5. That was made with hands (by men) ; Heb. 9 : 24 ; the one in Heaven, not by men, but by the Lord, Heb. 8 : 2 ; 9 : 11. The earthly sanctuary is twice called a figure, and once a pattern of the sanctuary in Heaven. Heb. 9 : 9, 23, 24. The Heavenly sanctuary is called the greater and more perfect tabernacle, and the true, in comparison with the earthly. Heb. 9 : 11, 24.

But more than this, John in his vision of things in Heaven saw there the antitype of the golden candlestick, the altar of incense, the golden censer and the ark of God's testament, all instruments of the sanctuary, the presence of which unmistakably proves the existence of the sanctuary where they were seen. And John also had a view of the sanctuary itself, which he brings to view under the name of "the temple of God in Heaven." Rev. 4 : 1, 5 ; 8 : 3 ; 11 : 19. Thus it is called also by David and Habakkuk. Ps. 11 : 4 ; Hab. 2 : 20. It is called God's "holy habitation" by Jeremiah and Zechariah. Jer. 25 : 30 ; Zech. 2 : 13.

Having found the sanctuary, we now inquire, What is its cleansing ? With the sanctuary there were connected instruments of service and a priest-

---

new covenant sanctuary ? 24. What relation did the sanctuary of the first covenant bear to that of the new ? 25. What was Moses commanded when about to make the tabernacle ? References. 26. How is the earthly sanctuary spoken of in Heb. 9 : 9, 23, 24 ? 27. What is the Heavenly sanctuary called in comparison with the earthly ? 28. What was shown to John in vision ? References. 29. What is the Heavenly sanctuary called by David and Habakkuk ? References. 30. What by Jeremiah and Zechariah ? References. 31. What was connected with the sanctuary ? 32.

hood. The sanctuary contained two apartments, separated by a vail. The first was called the holy place, the second the most holy. In the holy place, were the candlestick with seven branches, the table of show-bread, and the altar of incense. In the most holy was the ark, containing the tables of the ten commandments. The cover of the ark, beaten out of a solid piece of gold with the figure of a cherub on either end, was the mercy-seat. In this sanctuary the priests ministered. This ministry is described in Lev. 1 and onward. When a person had sinned, he brought his offering to the door of the tabernacle to the priest, laid his hands upon the head of his offering, and confessed upon him his sin, took his life, and the blood was taken by the priest into the sanctuary and sprinkled before the vail. His sin was thus transferred to the sanctuary. This went on through the year continually, sin all the while accumulating in the sanctuary, till the tenth day of the seventh month, when the priest performed a special service in the most holy place, to close the yearly round of ministration, called the cleansing of the sanctuary. On this day two goats were brought and set apart by lot to the Lord and to Azazel. See Lev. 16 : 8, margin. The blood of

How many apartments had the sanctuary? 33. What was the first called? 34. The second? 35. What was in the first apartment? 36. What in the second? 37. How was the cover of the ark made, and what was it called? 38. Who ministered in this sanctuary? 39. Where is this ministry described? 40. What was done by a person who had sinned? 41. What was done with the blood of the victim? 42. What effect did this have on the person's sin? 43. How long did services like this go on? 44. What was meanwhile accumulating in the sanctuary? 45. When was the service changed? 46. Where was this special service performed? 47. What was it called? 48. To perform this service what did the priest first take? Lev. 16 : 5, 7. 49. How and to whom were these goats set apart? 50. What was done with the

the goat for the Lord was taken and sprinkled by the priest upon the mercy-seat in the most holy place, to make atonement for the sanctuary, and for the sins of the people. Coming out he confessed over the scape-goat all the sins of the people and thus placed them upon his head. Lev. 16 : 21. This goat was then sent away by the hand of a fit man into the wilderness. Thus the sanctuary was cleansed, and sin was put away from the people.

But all this was a figure. That sanctuary, those offerings, the work of the priests, all were figures. Paul says of the priests that they " served unto the example and shadow of heavenly things." Heb. 8 : 4, 5. All looked forward to the greater and more perfect priesthood after the order of Melchisedec, performed, Paul says, by Christ in Heaven. Christ is at once the antitype of the offering and the priesthood. He first shed his blood and provided the offering. Then he entered upon his work as priest. What the earthly priests did in figure he does in fact. They transferred the sins of the penitent to the earthly sanctuary in figure. He transfers them to the Heavenly sanctuary in fact. We come to Christ for pardon, and this is the way we receive it. To deny this is to deny all that Paul has taught us in the book of Hebrews respecting the relation of the work of those ancient

blood of the goat set apart for the Lord ? 51. For what purpose was this blood sprinkled upon the mercy-seat ? 52. On coming out from the sanctuary what did the priest do ? 53. Where did this place the sins of the people ? 54. What was then done with this goat ? 55. In what condition did this leave the sanctuary and the people ? 56. What was the nature of all this service ? 57. Unto what did Paul say that these priests served ? 58. To what did all their service look forward ? 59. Of what is Christ the antitype ? 60. What did he first provide ? 61. Upon what work did he then enter ? 62. What is the nature of his work compared with that of the earthly priests ? 63. When we receive pardon

priests to the work of Christ as our High Priest in Heaven.

The Heavenly sanctuary must be cleansed for the same reason that the earthly was cleansed. This Paul expressly states. Heb. 9 : 22, 23. Any who object to things being cleansed in Heaven, must settle that with the apostle. The cleansing, however, was not from physical uncleanness but from sin. When was this to be cleansed ? At the end of the 2300 days in 1844. There was no other sanctuary then in existence but the Heavenly sanctuary of the new covenant; hence that is the one to which that prophecy applies. How is the cleansing in this case to be performed ? Just as in the type, by a closing service in the most holy place. The high priest passes into the most holy which he enters only for this purpose, makes the atonement by the offering of blood upon the mercy-seat, and closes the round of sanctuary service. In the type this round was completed every year. In the antitype it is performed once for all. The type and the prophecy of the 2300 days hold us to the conclusion that in 1844 Christ entered upon his final work as priest in the second apartment of the sanctuary in Heaven. In the type, one day of the year was set apart to this work, and a portion of the day was actually employed in the service. In the antitype the time is indefinite, but it must be comparatively brief.

As this concludes Christ's work as priest, with it

---

from Christ what disposition is made of our sins ? 64. Must the Heavenly sanctuary be cleansed, and why ? 65. Where is this stated ? 66. From what is it to be cleansed? 67. When was it to be cleansed ? 68. What proof that the Heavenly sanctuary must be the one referred to ? 69. How is its cleansing to be performed ? 70. How often is a round of service performed in the antitype ? 71. What must we conclude, therefore, took place in 1844? 72. In the type how much time was employed in this service ? 73. In the

probation ends, as there is no more mercy to be offered. And when that point is reached, all cases are decided for eternity. But this work of decision is a work of Judgment. It must be the first part of that three-fold work of Judgment solemnly declared in God's word to await all mankind : first, to decide all cases; secondly, to determine the rewards or punishments ; thirdly, to execute the sentence written. But Christ does not make his second advent till his work as priest is done. Therefore before the coming of Christ a portion of the work of Judgment transpires and probation ends. This accords with Rev. 22 : 11, 12 : "He that is unjust let him be unjust still, . . . and he that is holy let him be holy still. And, behold, I come quickly." It accords also with the necessities of the case ; for when Christ appears there is no time allotted for a work of Judgment, yet all the righteous dead are then raised, leaving the wicked to sleep on for a thousand years, and all the righteous living are changed in a moment, in the twinkling of an eye. This conclusively shows that decision must have been rendered in their cases before the coming of the Lord.

In the cleansing of the sanctuary we have just the time and place for this preliminary or investigative work of Judgment. This is the very nature of the work of Christ at this time to put away sin and so decide who are righteous. This involves an examination of the books of record containing the

antitype, how much ? 74. What ends with Christ's work as priest? 75. What is this work of decision ? 76. What part of the Judgment must it be ? 77. What part of his work does Christ finish before his second advent ? 78. What must therefore take place before Christ comes ? 79. What scripture sustains this view ? 80. How does it meet the necessities of the case ? 81. What subject provides for this necessary preliminary work of Judgment? 82. What is the work of Christ during this time ? 83. What does this involve ? 84.

deeds of every man's life; for all Judgment is rendered according to every man's works written in the books. Rev. 20:12. Hence in the account of the opening of this scene in the most holy of the Heavenly sanctuary, as given in Dan. 7:9, 10, we read that "the Judgment was set and the books were opened." This is before the coming of Christ; for it is before the destruction of the papal beast on account of the great words of the little horn. Verse 11. Here is where the Son of man is brought to the Ancient of Days, and receives his kingdom, which kingdom he receives before his return to this earth. Dan. 7:13, 14; Luke 19:12.

Here sins, repented of and pardoned, are blotted out; Acts 3:19, 20; which work being ended, Christ is sent the second time to this earth. But if at this time a person's sins are not in a condition to be blotted out, his name is blotted out of the book of life. Rev. 3:5. Here Christ confesses the names of his people before his Father, receiving of the Father acceptance of them through him.

This is the finishing of the mystery of God, brought to view in Rev. 10:7. The mystery of God is the gospel to all nations. Eph. 3:3 compared with Gal. 1:12; Eph. 1:9; 3:9; Rom. 16:25, 26; Col. 1:25, 27. The finishing of this mystery, must be the close of the gospel work which will cease when Christ's work as priest is done. Therefore the cleansing of the sanctuary, the investiga-

From what is all Judgment rendered? Reference. 85. What scene does Dan. 7:9, 10 describe? 86. What is said of the books at this time? 87. What shows that this is before the coming of Christ? 88. Where does the Son of man receive from the Ancient of Days his kingdom? 89. Does he receive his kingdom before his return to earth? Reference. 90. To what does Acts 3:19, 20, apply? 91. When will Rev. 3:5 be fulfilled? 92. What is the mystery of God? References. 93. What is the finishing of this

tive Judgment, and the finishing of the mystery of God, are all one and the same work.

The commencement of this work is marked by the end of the great period of 2300 days, and the commencement of the sounding of the 7th angel, the last of the series of the 7 trumpets. The angel of Rev. 10 announces the close of prophetic time. Verse 6. This must be prophetic time ; for literal time, duration, continues in the days of the 7th angel subsequently mentioned ; and probationary time continues in the announcement of another message of mercy. Verse 11. Prophetic time ends with the 2300 days, which is the longest prophetic period and reaches down to the latest point. Hence Rev. 10 : 6 brings us to the conclusion of the 2300 days. Then, said the angel to Daniel, shall the sanctuary be cleansed. Then, said the angel to John, shall the mystery of God be finished; which is the same thing. This he said would be in the days when the 7th angel should begin to sound ; that it would occupy the first years of his sounding. And again John says, when the 7th angel began to sound, the temple of God was opened in Heaven, and there was seen in his temple the ark of his testament. Rev. 11 : 19. This introduces us into the second apartment of the Heavenly sanctuary ; but the work in that apartment is the cleansing of the sanctuary, the investigative Judgment, the finishing of the mystery of God, which consequently commenced when the 7th angel began to sound.

mystery ? 94. To what does Rev. 10 : 7 apply ? 95. How is it shown that Rev. 10 : 6 applies to prophetic time ? 96. With what does prophetic time end ? 97. To what point does Rev. 10 : 6 bring us ? 98. What did the angel say to Daniel and John would then take place ? 99. Are these the same ? 100. What trumpet marked the commencement of this work ? 101. What event is given in Rev. 11 : 19 to mark the sounding of the 7th angel ? 102. To what work does this

The sins being borne from the sanctuary in the type, were laid upon the head of the scape-goat, which was then sent away to perish. This was the shadow of some service in connection with the Heavenly sanctuary by which our sins are to be put away in fact forever. Upon whom could they more appropriately fall at last than upon the devil, the author and instigator of sin? Satan is the antitypical scape-goat. Azazel, Lev. 16: 8, margin, is held on good authority to mean the devil. True, Christ is said to have borne our sins; but that was upon the cross before he commenced his priestly work. He never after bears them except as priest; and the last he does with them is to lay them upon the head of their author, the devil, who is sent away with them to a land not inhabited. The account of this binding of Satan is found in Rev. 20 : 1–3. At the end of the thousand years, being loosed out of his prison by the resurrection of the wicked whom he then again has power to deceive, even to bring them up against the camp of the saints, Rev. 20 : 8, 9, he is, with them, forever destroyed by fire from God out of Heaven. Then comes the day of the execution of the Judgment, and perdition of ungodly men. 2 Pet. 3 : 7. Sins are then put away forever. Evil is destroyed root and branch. A new heavens and earth succeed the old. Verse 13. The saints enter upon their everlasting inheritance, and the universal song of jubilee goes up from a holy and happy universe to God and the Lamb. Rev. 5 : 13.

---

introduce us? 103. What was done with sins borne from the sanctuary? 104. Who is the antitypical scape-goat? 105. What does the word Azazel mean? 106. When did Christ bear our sins? and in what sense? 107. When does the scape-goat, or Satan, bear them? 108. Where is the account of the binding of Satan found? 109. What takes place at the end of the thousand years? 110. What day is this? Reference. 111. What follows?

CLASS QUESTIONS ON LESSON VII. WITH ANSWERS.

1. How could Christ be said to be within the vail in Paul's day, as in the Old Testament that phrase applies to the most holy?

ANS. This question assumes too much. Neither in the Old Testament nor the New, is the term "the vail," confined to that vail which divided between the holy and the most holy place. The term is applied equally to the vail which constituted the door of the sanctuary and hung at the entrance to the holy place. The same term, both in Hebrew and Greek, is used to describe this vail, that is used in describing the other. Ex. 26:31, 36. Paul is careful to make a distinction between the two. In Heb. 9:3, he speaks of the *second* vail, showing that there must be a *first* vail. And inasmuch as he has used the term second in speaking of that vail in this instance, the clearest principle of logic would compel us to understand him as referring to the other vail whenever in his writings this term is not used. In Heb. 10:19, 20, he shows that we go within the vail when we go into the holy place. For the word "holiest" is, in the Greek, in the plural number, and should be rendered the holies, or holy places: "Having therefore, brethren, boldness to enter into the holy places by the blood of Jesus, by a new and living way which he hath consecrated for us through the vail." Here the singular number is used in speaking of the vail, but the plural in speaking of the holy places, showing us, that, as he uses the term, we pass through "the vail" in entering the holy place, just as much as in entering into the most holy. Hence, when he says that Christ is entered within the vail in Heb. 6:19, 20, he does not necessarily mean into the most holy place.

2. Please explain Heb. 10 : 20. How is Christ's flesh the vail?

ANS. It isn't. The difficulty arises from this misunderstanding of the text. Verses 19 and 20 read as follows: "Having therefore, brethren, boldness to enter into the holiest [holies] by the blood of Jesus, by a new and living way which he hath consecrated for us, through the vail, that is to say, his flesh." What is his flesh? Not the vail, but the way. A little transposition of terms will show more plainly this idea; thus, "By a new and living way, that is to say, his flesh, which he hath consecrated for us through the vail." How is his flesh a way through the vail? Because it is by his offering of himself that we gain access there. Paul says, Heb. 9 : 12, that "by his own blood he entered in once [Gr. once for all] into the holy place" [Gr. plural, holy places]. And it is by his sacrifice, his blood, that we also find entrance there. With this understanding of the text it is consistent with other scriptures, and the figure is a beautiful one; but with the other view it is involved in unexplainable inconsistencies and difficulties; for we might well inquire, in the language of the question, how his flesh could be the vail; and, in that case, what is the new and living way?

3. Does Christ actually use his blood in the work of cleansing the sanctuary? If so, how is it provided? If not, how could the earthly service be said to be a *shadow* of that service?

ANS. We do not see how the work in the most holy would require the actual presence of Christ's blood, any more than his work in the holy place, in order to be the substance of which the work of the earthly sanctuary was a shadow. The question then would be simply whether he has, during his eighteen hundred years of ministry, actually presented his blood in the sanctuary or ministered by virtue of its merits. In the case of Christ there would appear to be no necessity for the actual presence of his blood, as in the case of the earthly sacrifices; for in the latter there was no blood provided which had any merit independent of its actual presence. But as the blood of Abel and the martyrs is represented as crying unto God, so the great fact that Christ had died upon the cross and shed his blood for men, would be a sufficient response to every petition for pardon and forgiveness of sin. But Christ was himself the offering. He doubtless bears the marks of his crucifixion. Would not his presence therefore under these circumstances be the equivalent of the actual presentation of blood and even more? John represents Christ as presenting all the features of his offering before his Father in Heaven. "I beheld," he says, "and lo, in the midst of the throne, and of the four beasts, and in the midst of the elders, stood a Lamb as it had been slain." Rev. 5:6.

4. How can the sins of the people be conveyed into the most holy place, as the high priest went in there only once a year?

Ans. The high priest stood as a representative of all the sins for which he had performed a ministration through the year. And this is doubtless the reason why a complete round of service was limited, in the type, to the short period of a year, so that the same person might minister in the most holy on the day of atonement, who had ministered through all the year in the holy place. Thus on the day of atonement all the sins for which offering had been made during the year, would be represented in him, and his offering in the most holy place, would have reference to them all. This would be emphatically true of Christ, who was himself the offering. When Christ appears before the ark, he appears both as our sacrifice and our priest, a representative in a double sense of all the sins which have been brought to him for pardon.

5. If the sanctuary services were a type of the true, and the cleansing of the sanctuary is now going on, how can our sins be forgiven, as our high priest must now be within the vail?

ANS. The service in the most holy availed for the sins of the people the same as the service on other days. We cannot suppose that there was one day in every year, under the type, during which there was no forgiveness of sin, such as was provided for that time. Nothing passed over to the next year's account. And the efficacy of the work of atonement availed in individual cases according to their own action. They were to afflict their souls, or repent of their sins, even up to the moment when the atonement was made and the year's work was done. Doing this their sins were borne away, otherwise they were left upon them. And in the greater and more perfect ministry of our Lord, it is still more apparent that there is pardon for sin while the service in the most holy, or the cleansing of the sanctuary, is going forward. Christ's blood, when once shed, avails not only for sins committed in the past, but makes provision as well for the future. His blood, or which would be the same thing the merits of his sacrifice, are ministered in both apartments. And Paul says that we have boldness to enter into the holies, or both the holy and most holy places, by the blood of Jesus. Heb. 10:19. We enter into the most holy as well as the holy through that blood. But entering in there through

the blood of Christ must mean simply obtaining
the forgiveness of our sins through him. And that
we do while he is in the most holy as well as while
he is in the holy place.

6. Was the sanctuary of the second covenant,
as was seen by John, Rev. 4:5; 8:3, 4; 11:19, in
existence at the time when God gave Moses a pattern of the tabernacle for the first covenant?

Ans. We see nothing in the way of supposing
that the Heavenly sanctuary was then in existence;
but there was no priestly service performed in it till
Christ commenced his ministry there. Paul says
that the way into the holiest of all (holies, plural)
was not yet made manifest while as the first tabernacle was yet standing. Heb. 9:8. That is to say,
the way into the true holy places, the Heavenly
sanctuary, was not laid open before the world, the
attention of men was not called to it, and there was
no ministration there, while the first tabernacle
stood and its services were effectual. These services
then took the place of everything else. And when
the time came for the shadow to give place to the
substance, the work began in the temple in Heaven.

7. Who was mediator between God and man
while Christ was upon earth, and especially from
the time of his death till the commencement of his
ministry in Heaven?

Ans. We understand that Christ has been the
mediator between God and man ever since the plan
of salvation was devised. Down to the cross the
fact of a Redeemer to come was the great fact in
reference to which men acted in approaching to God.
They signified their faith from Adam to Calvary by
the offering of the blood of beasts. Since Calvary
the great fact has been a Redeemer already come, in
whom we show our faith through the ordinances of

the gospel. The time for decision to be made up in any case, with a few exceptions, does not come till the work of atonement in the closing up of the service of the Heavenly sanctuary. And the decision will be rendered in every case according to the faith manifested in that Redeemer, whether before or after Christ, as the evidence shall appear in the record of the books above. And whether or not Christ was in the presence of his Father, at the time such faith was manifested, would be immaterial. Man's acts of faith would go on record as well while Christ was on earth as while he was in Heaven; as well while he was in the grave, as when among the living; as well at any time before he commenced his work of ministry in Heaven, as after.

8. Was the daily round of service in the tabernacle performed on the day of atonement?

Ans. The daily round of general sacrifices was performed on the day of atonement as upon other days, besides some special general offerings upon that day, as upon other feasts, and besides the specific offering of the atonement. Num. 29:7–11. But while the work of atonement was going forward, the ordinary individual offerings at the door of the sanctuary could not be offered. There was no occasion for these, since all the people were represented in the offering which the priest was presenting in the most holy place. For a person at the same time to be offering at the door of the tabernacle would be to present two different offerings at once, which would be uncalled for, and manifestly improper; and what would be more objectionable still, it would divert to another service the attention which the Lord required all to fix upon the work of atonement.

9. In the first tabernacle God's glory was manifested between the cherubim over the ark in the most holy place. Can it be inferred from the type that that is also God's position in the Heavenly sanctuary? But Rev. 4:5 shows us the throne of God in the holy place. How can this be reconciled?

Ans. By not supposing that God or his throne is always confined to the same place or position. We do not understand the Scriptures to teach that the Lord was always in one place. Sometimes he met with Moses at the door of the tabernacle. Ex. 29:43. His throne is represented as a movable, living throne. Eze. chapters 1 and 10. When the scene of the cleansing of the sanctuary opened, the Ancient of Days, Jehovah, took a position which he had not before occupied. Dan. 7:9. On the change of ministration from the holy into the most holy place, God's throne was evidently moved from the one to the other.

10. How can Christ be a sanctuary, and at the same time be administering as high priest in the same. Eze. 11:16; Isa. 8:14?

Ans. These texts can have no reference to the sanctuary in Heaven. They do not say that Christ should be the sanctuary, but "*as* a sanctuary," and "*for* a sanctuary." The word sanctuary is sometimes used to signify a place of refuge and defense. And Christ would be such to his people, while dispersed through the land of their captivity. But the word rendered sanctuary in the texts referred to is not *hagion*, the word used to describe the sanctuary of worship, both as type and antitype, but *hagiasma*, a sacred or consecrated place.

11. Please give an explanation of the original of Rom. 3:25. How can Christ be said to be the mercy-seat?

Ans. He cannot. Those who make this assertion from Rom. 3:25, as some of our opponents do, are simply misled by their ignorance of the language they try to handle. There is a neuter Greek noun, *hilasterion*, which means mercy-seat. There is another in the masculine gender, *hilasterios*, which means "one who makes expiation, a propitiator, or propitiatory sacrifice." In the accusative singular this latter word takes the same form as the other, *hilasterion*. The construction of Rom. 3:25 demands the use of the accusative case; and hence, this masculine noun being of the same form as the neuter noun, our friends have mistaken it for the neuter noun, and declare that Christ is the mercy-seat. They think thereby to break down the idea of the antitypical sanctuary, held by S. D. Adventists. But their attempt is wholly abortive; for the word is the masculine noun *hilasterios*, and means, a propitiator, or one who makes expiation.

12. Rom. 5:11. What does Paul mean by saying, "We have now received the atonement," when the atonement did not begin until 1844? This is urged as an objection against our views of the Heavenly sanctuary.

ANS. The whole difficulty lies in giving a wrong meaning to the word there rendered atonement. The word is *katallagee*, and simply means "reconciliation, restoration to favor," never atonement. The words used in the Old Testament for atonement are *exilasis, exilasma*, and the verbs, *exilaskomai*, and *exileoo*. Reconciliation the church has all along received through Christ; but we receive the atonement only when it is made as the closing service of our Lord in the sanctuary above.

13. Is the antitypical table of show-bread in the Heavenly sanctuary? What was it designed to typify?

Bib. Ins. 6

ANS. Inasmuch as the candlestick and altar of incense were seen in the Heavenly sanctuary, it would seem fair to infer that the table was not lacking though it seems nowhere to be brought directly to view. Its significance as a type may be perhaps inferred in a measure from its use in the earthly sanctuary. Bread was kept upon it before the Lord, a loaf for each tribe. New fresh loaves were placed upon the table every Sabbath, and the old were to be eaten by the priests in the holy place. The other instruments symbolized channels through which the blessings of the Lord come to us; as the candlestick, the Spirit of God; the altar of incense, the acceptance of our prayers with God; the mercy-seat, the way of pardon and peace; and when it is said in the Scriptures that man shall not live by bread alone but by every word that proceedeth out of the mouth of the Lord, does it not bring to view that which may fitly be illustrated by the show-bread which the priests were to eat? Does it not represent these words of the Lord by which we live, his grace and favor which continually sustain us? In the absence of positive testimony it becomes no one to do more than suggest; and these remarks are offered only as suggestions.

LESSON EIGHT.

THE MESSAGES OF REVELATION CHAPTER XIV.

HAVING seen that the cleansing of the sanctuary is a work of Judgment, a key is placed in our hands for an explanation of the messages of Rev. 14. The first message, verses 6, 7, is symbolized by an angel flying in the midst of heaven, having the everlasting gospel to preach to them that dwell on the earth, saying with a loud voice, "Fear God, and give glory to him; for the hour of his Judgment is come; and worship him that made heaven and earth, and the sea and the fountains of waters."

Let us see what we are warranted to expect from the terms of the message, that we may know what to inquire for as a fulfillment. The scope of the message is the gospel either as a whole or in some of its special phases; and the burden of its announcement is that the hour of God's Judgment is come. Some Judgment work connected with the gospel we are therefore to look for. But the gospel brings to view no work of this kind except that connected with the close of the probation of the human race, near the end of time. Still it cannot be any phase of the Judgment after probation has ended; for two other proclamations to men follow it before the Lord appears as symbolized by one

---

REVIEW QUESTIONS ON LESSON EIGHT.

1. How does the subject of the sanctuary help us to understand the three messages of Rev. 14? 2. By what is the first message symbolized? 3. What does he have to preach? 4. What are his words? 5. What is the scope of this message? 6. What is the burden of its announcement? 7. What are we therefore to look for? 8. What Judgment is brought to view by the gospel? 9. Can this be any Judgment that takes place after probation ends? 10. Why?

like the Son of man on the white cloud. Verse 14. It can therefore be no other than the work of investigative Judgment which we have seen takes place above, as the sanctuary is cleansed, immediately preceding the coming of Christ. And further, it is a time message, based on the prophetic periods; for it announces the hour of God's Judgment come, and must consequently bring us to the commencement of that work.

With these data before us, where shall we look for that message? We need not stop even to inquire if it was given by the apostles, or the reformers, or any class of religious teachers previous to our own day; for if given at any time before the last generation it would not be true. The apostle reasoned of a Judgment *to* come, Acts 17 : 31 ; 24 : 25 ; and it is recorded of Luther that he thought the day of Judgment was about 300 years distant from his day. But our own generation has witnessed such a proclamation as the message announces. In the great Advent movement of 1840 to 1844 and onward, the fulfillment is seen.

This movement was one of the right nature : it was based on the prophetic periods and proclaimed time. It was of sufficient extent : it went to every missionary station on the globe. See Exposition of Matt. 24. This angel of Rev. 14 : 6, is the same as

---

11. What therefore is the nature of this Judgment, and when and where does it take place? 12. What is the nature of this message, and on what is it based? 13. To what must it bring us? 14. Was this message given by the apostles or reformers? 15. Can such a message be given till we reach the last generation? 16. What did the apostles say about the Judgment? References. 17. How far off did Luther think it was from his day? 18. What has our own generation witnessed? 19. What was this movement? 20. On what was this Advent movement based? 21. What was its extent? 22. What relation has this angel to the angel of

the angel of Rev. 10. Evidence of this is found in the chronology of this latter movement, the nature of the message, and the terms in which the proclamation of this angel is uttered. Rev. 10:6. But this angel utters his oath on the authority of a little book which he has in his hand open. This is unquestionably the book which Daniel had been told to close up and seal to the time of the end, and the fact that the angel now had it in his hand open, shows that his message is given this side of the time of the end. He proclaims the end of prophetic time, and following that the finishing of the mystery of God. In Rev. 14:6, 7, it is the finishing of the prophetic periods, and then the hour of God's Judgment. The finishing of the mystery of God, and the hour of God's Judgment, therefore, occupy the same time and bring to view the same work—a work to be fulfilled in the cleansing of the sanctuary, commencing in 1844 and now going forward.

Having located the first message, the others must follow in order. The second has received as marked a fulfillment as the first. Babylon is brought to view under the symbol of a woman in Rev. 17: 5. This does not mean the wicked world, or

---

Rev. 10? 23. Where is the evidence of this found? 24. From what does this angel utter his oath? 25. In what condition is the little book? 26. What book is probably intended by this? 27. What directions had been given in regard to this book? 28. How long was it to be closed up and sealed? 29. What is shown by the fact that the angel now has the book open? 30. What does this angel proclaim? 31. What is the proclamation of Rev. 14:6, 7? 32. This being the same angel, what relation does the hour of God's Judgment have to the finishing of the mystery of God? 33. In what is this work to be fulfilled? 34. When did it commence? 35. How does locating the first message affect the others? 36. Has the second message received a marked fulfillment? 37. What is the symbol taken to represent

worldly powers; for the woman is seated upon a beast which represents the civil power. Verse 3. A woman is the symbol of a church; a lewd woman representing a corrupt or apostate church, Eze. 16; and a virtuous woman, a pure church. Rev. 12:1. But Babylon is not confined to any one church; for this woman of Rev. 17:5 has daughters of the same character with herself. Parity of reasoning would lead us to include under this term all heathen systems of religion, as well as portions of the so-called Christian world. Babylon means mixture and confusion. The name is derived from Babel, where God rebuked men's impious attempt to build a tower to Heaven, by confounding their language. The great fault here charged upon Babylon is that she made all nations drink of the wine of the wrath of her fornication, or corrupted them with her false doctrines.

The fall of Babylon is not the loss of temporal power by the papacy, nor the destruction of the city of Rome. For the papacy does not lose her temporal power because she made the nations drink of her false doctrines; but that is the very means by which she obtained and so long held it. And it cannot mean the destruction of Rome; for Babylon is where the people of God are largely represented. Rev. 18:4. But this has never been true of Rome,

---

Babylon? 38. Why does not this woman, or Babylon, represent the wicked world? 39. Of what is a woman the symbol? 40. Is Babylon confined to any one church, and why? 41. What must be included under this term? 42. What does the term Babylon mean? 43. From what is it derived? 44. What is the great fault charged upon Babylon? 45. What is meant by the wine of the wrath of her fornication? (The word rendered "wrath" has also the definition of "violent passion," which rendering would make the prophet's figure more consistent.) 46. Why is not the fall of Babylon the loss of temporal power by the papacy? 47. Why can it not mean the destruction of the city of

and especially it was not when the second message
of Rev. 14 was given. And, secondly, it is after
Babylon's fall that the people of God are called out,
which would be an absurdity if applied to the fall
and burning of Rome. And, thirdly, after the fall,
Babylon fills up with hateful birds and foul spirits,
which makes the application to the destruction of
Rome still more ridiculous.

The fall of Babylon is a moral fall, as is shown
by Rev. 18 : 1–3. But, the proclamation of this fall
being connected with the great Advent movement
of our own days, it must apply to some portion of
Babylon which was at that time in a condition to
experience a moral change for the worse. But this
announcement, Babylon is fallen, could not then be
said of the heathen world, which has for ages been
lost in darkness and corruption; nor of the Romish
church, for that has for generations been as low as
it is possible for any organization, religious or secular, to descend. It must therefore have reference
to those classes who have partially come out from
Romish errors, but stopped short of receiving all
the light that was offered them. This is true of
the great mass of Protestant sects. They ran well
for a season, and had a large measure of the graces
of the Holy Spirit and the blessing of God to witness to what truth they were willing to receive.
But their theology is still hideously deformed by
enormous errors drawn from Rome, which they refuse
to abandon. A reception of the first message would
have healed their divisions and made a beginning

Rome ? 48. When are God's people called out? 49. What
happens to Babylon after her fall? 50. What therefore
must be the nature of her fall? 51. To what portion of
Babylon must this proclamation apply ? 52. What must be
said of the great mass of the Protestant sects? 53. What
condition is their theology still in ? 54. What would the

of the work of correcting their errors. We know this from the effect it did have on those who received it, who came from all these denominations. But they rejected the message, and shut it out of their houses. The cry was then raised, Babylon is fallen; and although the distinctive call of Rev. 18:4, "Come out of her my people," which we apply to the future, was not given, yet some 50,000 persons did come out from the theological bondage to which they were subjected, an earnest of a still greater separation to take place, as we believe, in the near future, when Rev. 18:2 is more completely fulfilled in them, and the cry of verse 4 shall be given.

This state of religious declension among the popular churches has been a marked condition with them since 1844. The most devoted among them saw and deeply deplored it then. See testimonies in work entitled, The Three Messages. Their condition in this respect has not improved since; and the spasmodic and emotional efforts of a Knapp, Hammond, Moody, and other modern revivalists, are not affording any permanent improvement. There is an advance truth for this age, and no permanent work of religious reform can be accomplished except in connection therewith.

The third angel followed them; and now the message deepens into a most close and pointed warning, and a denunciation of wrath more terrific

first message have done for them? 55. How do we know this? 56. How did they treat the message? 57. What cry was then raised? 58. What was the result? 59. What do we look for in the future? 60. What has marked the condition of these churches since 1844? 61. Have they themselves admitted and deplored it? 62. Has their condition improved since? 63. What can be said of the efforts of modern revivalists? 64. Where only can we look for permanent religious reformation? 65. What is the burden of

than anything elsewhere to be found in the Bible, against uniting with anti-Christian powers in the last work of opposition against God, upon which they will embark before the end. It is announced with a loud voice that if any man worship the beast or his image, or receive his mark in his forehead or hand, he shall drink of the wine of the wrath of God poured out without mixture into the cup of his indignation. The terms here employed are without dispute highly figurative; and hence many conclude at once that they cannot be understood. But surely God would never denounce judgments so terrible as these and then clothe the warning in such terms that it could not be understood, and so men not know whether they were exposing themselves to the punishment or not. This is certainly the last message to go forth before the coming of Christ; for the next scene is one like the Son of man coming on a white cloud to reap the harvest of the earth. None but Christ does this. This message consequently reaches to the close of probation; and whoever is giving the true Advent message, will be urging upon the people a warning of this nature. If we have reached the last days and the coming of Christ is at the doors, the time has come for this message. It is due. Yet there are those who will presume to call themselves Adventists, and proclaim the coming of Christ very near, who entirely ignore this message, leave it out of their preaching, and profess to know nothing about it. Are such standing in the light and giving the true message? Assuredly not.

---

the third message which follows? 66. Against what does it utter its warning? 67. Can this message be understood? 68. What relation has this message to the coming of Christ? 69. To what point must it reach? 70. Is this message now due? 71. What will that people be doing who are giving

Seventh-day Adventists claim to be giving this message. People have a right therefore to demand of us an explanation of the terms and figures employed in the message; and we stand ready to give it. This is the burden of our work, to warn against the worship of the beast, and urge in contrast obedience to God. An exposition of the symbols introduced, involves an examination of Rev. 12 and 13.

CLASS QUESTIONS ON LESSON VIII. WITH ANSWERS.

1. In what manner did Wm. Miller fulfill the oath of the angel of Rev. 10, that time should be no more?

ANS. We do not understand that the angel of that chapter symbolizes any individual, but only a movement. The movement was the great Advent movement of 1844. That met the prophecy in every particular. It was based on the records of a little book which had been closed up and sealed till the time of the end, but was now open, namely, the prophecies of Daniel. The whole burden of the movement was a proclamation of time; that the 2300 days would terminate in 1844, and that no prophetic period would extend beyond that year. This we understand is what is meant by the oath that time should be no more, as that must refer to prophetic time. In the proclamation of time, therefore, under the first message, the oath of the angel respecting time was fulfilled. But there was a disappointment, in consequence of a mistake, connected with that movement; how then could it be a ful-

the true Advent message? 72. What do S. D. Adventists claim? 73. What have people a right to demand of us? 74. What is the burden of our work? 75. Where do we look for an explanation of the symbols of the message?

fillment of prophecy? Such a question is no embarrassment to us; for we do not regard the mistake as pertaining to anything brought to view in the work of that angel. He swore to time; and the time proclamation was all right. The mistake was not there, but in the event to occur at the end of the prophetic period which reached to that point, which has since been fully explained in the subject of the sanctuary. But this question is an embarrassing one to those who believe the mistake was in the time. That chapter so clearly represents the past Advent movement, that such an application cannot well be questioned. But how then shall it be explained, since, according to their view, the whole burden of the angel's message that time should be no more proved to be a mistake, as prophetic time did not then expire? They endeavor to get out of the dilemma at the expense of the angel, by saying that as he was clothed with a cloud, see verse 1, there were some things hidden from his view. So he swore to time, but when the cloud cleared away he saw that he had made a mistake. That is to say, this angel got lost in the fog, and in his bewildered state roared out his message over sea and land that time should be no more; but when the fog cleared away, he saw that that was all wrong, and told John that he must go to work and prophesy again! That somebody is in the fog is clear enough; no doubt about that; but it isn't the angel.

2. If Babylon does not signify the ungodly world, how is it that a third part of Babylon, Rev. 16:19, is interpreted to be paganism?

Ans. Because paganism is a system of religion; and it is all these multiplied forms of false and apostate systems of religion that we understand to be included in mystic Babylon.

3. Are we to understand that there will be two Judgments ?

ANS. Considered as a whole, the Judgment is one; but viewed in reference to its different phases, it may be considered as three-fold. 1. We have the investigative Judgment in the sanctuary, in which the Father sits as Judge, accepting those who come to him through Christ, as Christ confesses their names before him. Rev. 3 : 5. This is the hour of God's Judgment brought to view in the first message, and decides all cases, drawing the dividing line between all the righteous and the wicked. Then Christ comes; and his coming is called a coming to Judgment, as it is the carrying out of the decisions of the sanctuary, in giving reward to a certain extent to his people. 2. Then comes the second phase of the Judgment, the work of a thousand years, during which time the saints, having themselves been judged and accepted, act with Christ, apportioning to the wicked of each generation the punishment due to their crimes. Rev. 20 : 4; 1 Cor. 6 : 2, 3. This work completed, we come 3. To the third and last division of the Judgment, at the end of the thousand years, when the sentence written is executed. Rev. 20 : 9. This is called in 2 Pet. 3 : 7, the day of Judgment; but Peter immediately specifies what part of the Judgment by adding, "and perdition of ungodly men." At the same time that this final sentence is executed upon the wicked the saints receive the completion of their reward. Matt. 25 : 34.

4. Does not Matt. 25 : 31–34 seem to teach that the Judgment is after Christ comes ?

ANS. This brings to view simply the carrying out of the decisions of the investigative Judgment in the sanctuary by separating the righteous from the wicked. This takes place when Christ comes. If we confine it to those living on the earth when Christ appears, this separation is shown by the change to immortality which instantly passes upon all the righteous. And if we extend the application so as to include all the dead, the separation is equally apparent; for all the righteous dead are at once raised from their graves, leaving all the wicked dead behind. The rest of the chapter passes on to the execution of the wicked, and the full reward of the righteous, at the end of the thousand years, as noticed in the preceding question.

5. Can persons now in the churches who have heard the third angel's message, and do not obey it, nor separate themselves from the churches, be saved?

ANS. A person's present position does not decide his eternal destiny, unless the day of his probation is past. That persons live in some instances for long periods disregarding known duties and refusing to acknowledge and obey clearly perceived light, is beyond question, the Lord bearing with them, and giving them opportunity to repent. That there are multitudes of such at the present time in the churches and the world, is doubtless true. How long the Lord will bear with them, ere he will say, "Ephraim is joined to his idols, let him alone," we know not. It is at best a most dangerous position. One thing is certain that a person must, ere mercy ceases to plead with him, obey all the light of which he has any perception, or he will be lost. Jesus said, "Walk while ye have the light, lest darkness come upon you; for he that walketh in darkness, knoweth not whither he goeth." Such are sure to stumble and fall.

6. Is not the call now going forth, "Come out of her my people"? Rev. 18:4.

ANS. As a specific call we do not think it is now going forth. Circumstances and influences conspire more or less to separate those who receive the truth from previous organizations. Frequently churches will not retain a person in their communion if he conscientiously endeavors to obey the law of God by keeping the seventh day. Perhaps more who have come among S. D. Adventists from other churches have left those churches because they have for this reason been thrust out, than from any other cause. Others, failing to receive spiritual benefit, and having no freedom to speak of their new-found faith and hope, voluntarily leave their former connection of bondage for a new one of freedom. But we look for proud and popular churches to grow more and more conformed to the world, to go into greater spiritual darkness, and alienation from God, and for a mighty cry to go forth in consequence, "Come out of her my people," which will reach all that can be saved in her communion.

7. Will there be a second cry, "Babylon is fallen"?

ANS. We think there will be. In consequence of rejecting the truth, Babylon fills up with foul spirits, and unclean and hateful birds, even becoming the habitation of devils. The nations are corrupted with her false doctrines; she has formed unlawful connection with the world, and through her pride and extravagance the merchants of the earth wax rich. These things become so apparent, at length, that a strong announcement is made of this fact, and in connection therewith goes forth the cry, "Come out of her my people." We look for this to be fulfilled near the close of probation, for then her plagues are about to fall.

8. What is the meaning of 2 Cor. 6:17: "Wherefore come out from among them, and be ye separate, saith the Lord, and touch not the unclean thing; and I will receive you"?

Ans. We think this has more reference to marriage relations with unbelievers than to anything else, as it is said in verse 14, "Be not unequally yoked together with unbelievers." Why the translators should supply the word "thing" to the adjective unclean, is a mystery; since it is an adjective of the masculine or feminine gender, and refers to persons. The word "touch" means to have relation together as man and wife. We take the passage and its connections to be a general prohibition resting upon believers not to marry unbelievers. Yet it may not have the force in the present condition of society in Christian lands that it did in the days of the apostle; for the word unclean means vicious or lewd; and the pagan world bore, and still bears, notoriously that character. It would scarcely have been possible for a Christian in Paul's day to unite with a pagan, without yoking himself or herself to a person of that character.

LESSON NINE.

REVELATION XII. AND XIII.

THE last part of Rev. 13 brings to view the very agents against which warning is uttered in the third angel's message. A beast with two horns like a lamb makes an image to a preceding beast, and enforces the worship and mark of that beast. This antecedent beast is described in Rev. 13 : 1–10. But this beast receives his seat and power and great authority from a symbol still preceding him—a great red dragon, described in Rev. 12 : 3, 4. With this chapter the vision opens. John beholds a woman (the gospel church), clothed with the sun (entering the light of the gospel dispensation), the moon (the typical dispensation) under her feet (just past), and upon her head a crown of 12 stars (the 12 apostles). To the expectant church appears a man child who was to rule all nations with a rod of iron, and who was caught up to God and to his throne. This can be none other than Christ. The dragon endeavored to devour this child as soon as he was born. This Rome tried to do when Christ was born. The dragon therefore is here a symbol of Pagan Rome.

REVIEW QUESTIONS ON LESSON NINE.

1. What is brought to view in the last part of Rev. 13? 2. What does the beast with two horns do? 3. Where is this antecedent beast described? 4. From what does this beast receive his seat and great power? 5. Where is this dragon described? 6. With what does this line of prophecy begin? 7. What does the woman represent? 8. What is meant by her being clothed with the sun? 9. By having the moon under her feet? 10. By having upon her head a crown of twelve stars? 11. Who was the man child which then appeared? 12. What did the dragon endeavor to do to this man child? 13. What government endeavored to do this? 14. Of what then is the dragon here a symbol? 15. What

The dragon gave his seat, power and great authority to some other power represented by the following beast like a leopard. Rev. 13 : 1–10. To what power was the dragon's seat, ancient Rome, given up? Answer. To the papacy. The seat of empire was moved to Constantinople, and the bishop of Rome soon ascended in the city of Rome, a higher throne than her pagan emperors had ever occupied. Great power was given to him; or, in other words, supremacy was conferred upon him, by the decree of Justinian, emperor of the East, carried out in 538. The parallel between this beast, Rev. 13 : 5–10, and the little horn of the fourth beast of Dan. 7 : 21, 25, 27, conclusively shows that it represents the papacy. This being so the time of his captivity, verse 10, was at the end of the 1260 years in 1798.

1. At this time another power is introduced upon the scene. "I beheld *another* beast." This was therefore no part of the papal beast. It was no kingdom or nation in Western Europe; for had it been, it would have been one, or some part of one, of the ten horns of the first beast. It was no kingdom of Eastern Europe, Western Asia, or Northern Africa; for these had all been appropriated to the symbols introduced in the 2d, 7th and 8th of Daniel. And John does not say, I saw the lion, bear, leopard, the fourth beast, or any of his ten horns,

---

did the dragon do with the place he had occupied as his seat? 16. To what power was Rome, the dragon's seat, given? 17. What took place in Rome, shortly after the seat of empire was moved to Constantinople? 18. How, when, and by whom, was great power given to the Roman bishop? 19. What is shown by the parallel between this beast and the little horn of the 4th beast of Dan. 7? 20. When was the time of his captivity? 21. What is introduced at this point of time? 22. Why was not this any part of the papal beast? 23. Why not some kingdom in Western Europe? 24. Why not some kingdom in Eastern Europe, Western Asia, or

coming up, but "another" beast. We are obliged to look to the western hemisphere for the territory of this power. And we must look to the leading power which has arisen here, which is our own government.

2. The chronology is equally decisive in fixing the application to our own country. This power was seen coming up when the previous one went into captivity; which was in 1798. If we look the earth all over what new power do we find coming up in a manner to attract the attention of the world, at that time? None but our own government.

3. It comes up out of the earth, in contrast with the sea out of which the preceding beast arose; that is, it arose in territory previously unknown and unoccupied by the peoples, nations and tongues of civilization. This is true of our own government, but of no other one equally prominent.

4. John saw this two-horned beast coming up in 1798. Our own nation was just then "coming up," and has continued to come up since that time, in a manner that finds no parallel in the history of any nation on the earth. Look at a few items of its progress in a hundred years. The population in 1775, was 2,803,000; now, over 40,000,000. Territory in 1783, at the time our independence was acknowledged, 815,615 square miles; now, 3,578,392 square miles. Agricultural interests 100 years ago

Northern Africa? 25. To what part of the world are we therefore obliged to look for this power? 26. To what government? 27. What can be said of the chronology of this symbol? 28. When was this power seen coming up? 29. What new nation was then arising to the notice of the world? 30. With what is its coming up out of the earth contrasted, and what does this signify? 31. Of what government is this true? 32. Have the United States "come up" in a manner to meet the prophecy? 33. What was its population in 1775, and what is it now? 34. What was its territory in 1783, and

were small and in the hands of uneducated men. First patent for cast iron plow in 1797. About 400 patents on this implement alone have since been granted. Then the seed was sown and crops harvested by hand. Drills, seed-sowers, cultivators, ← reapers, mowers and threshing machines, are inventions all within the memory of living men. Present product (1876), corn, 900,000,000 bushels; wheat, 270,000,000; rye, 22,000,000; oats, 300,000,000; potatoes, 165,000,000; hay, 28,000,000 tons; barley, 28,000,000 bushels; cotton, 2,000,000,000 lbs.; sugar, 120,000,000 lbs. Cotton crop in 1792, value, $30,-000; now, $180,000,000. Fruit, then unknown; now valued at $40,000,000. Horned cattle, number, 30,000,000; horses, 10,000,000; sheep, 30,000,000; swine, 26,000,000. In 1848 gold was discovered in California. The product to this time is over $800,- ← 000,000, with a present capacity of $70,000,000 a year. Railroads 65,000 miles, enough to reach twice and a half around the globe. More than 1,000 cotton factories, 580 daily newspapers, 4,300 weeklies, and 625 monthly publications. Between the years 1817 and 1867 the growth of the territorial domain of this country was 1,968,008 square miles. This is over 1,400,000 square miles of territory more than was added by any other one nation during this time, and more than 800,000 square miles more than were added by all the other nations of the earth put together. Mitchel speaks of it as "the most striking

---

what is it now? 35. What is its present gold-producing capacity? 36. How many miles of railroad has it? 37. How many cotton factories? 38. How many daily newspapers? 39. How many weeklies? 40. How many monthlies? 41. In the 50 years between 1817 and 1867 what was the territorial growth of this country? 42. How much more was this than that of any other nation during this time? 43. How much more than that of all other nations put together during the same time? 44. How does Mitchel speak of this?

instance of national growth to be found in the history of mankind." Emile de Girardin calls it "unparalleled progress." The *Dublin Nation* speaks of it as a most "wonderful American empire emerging." Can any one doubt what nation has been "coming up" during this time ? And the one that has been coming up must be the one symbolized by the two-horned beast of Rev. 13.

5. And all this has been accomplished in a quiet and peaceful manner. The symbol arose out of the earth. This nation has not been established by the conquest and overthrow of other nations, as the nations of Europe have been, but simply by standing up in defense of its right against the mother country. The word translated "coming up" in Rev. 13 : 11, means to grow like a plant out of the earth. And respecting the rise of these United States, the *Dublin Nation* says : "No standing army was raised, no national debt sunk, no great exertion was made, but there they are." G. A. Townsend, New World Compared with the Old, p. 462, speaks of "the mystery of our coming forth from vacancy." Again he says, p. 635 : "The history of the United States was separated by a beneficent providence far from this wild and cruel history of the rest of the continent, and *like a silent seed we grew into empire*." Edward Everett spoke of the "peaceful conquest" through which the banners of the cross have here been borne over mighty regions. Mark how wonderfully this harmonizes with the language of the prophecy, which

45. Emile de Girardin ? 46. The *Dublin Nation?* 47. By what must the nation that has thus been coming up be symbolized ? 48. In what manner has this been accomplished ? 49. What does the word translated "coming up" mean ? 50. What is the testimony of the *Dublin Nation* on this point ? 51. How does Mr. G. A. Townsend speak of it ? 52. What terms does Edward Everett use ? 53. How do these expressions compare with the prophecy ? 54. What do

says this power was to come up like a plant out of the earth.

6. This power had two horns like a lamb. This at once suggests two things: the youthfulness of the power, and an innocent or lamb-like profession embodied in two great principles. Just these features our own government exhibits, in the great principles of civil and religious liberty, which it guarantees to all its citizens. America is recognized as the youngest among the nations. The motto of the Egyptian exhibit at the Centennial was, "The oldest nation of the earth to the youngest sends greeting." These two features, youth and a lamb-like exterior, are found in our own government but in no other.

7. This beast has no crowns upon its horns, showing that it does not represent a kingly or monarchical form of government. Ours is the only notable government answering to this specification.

8. It represents some government where the power is in the hands of the people; for when any acts are to be performed, it says to them that dwell on the earth that *they* should do it. Rev. 13 : 14. It is in other words, a republic; and this points unmistakably to our own government.

9. It is also a Protestant government, or at least a non-Catholic power; for it causes them which occupy its territory to worship the first beast, which denotes Catholicism. But if it was a Catholic country it would be the beast itself, and worshiping the

the two horns of this symbol suggest? 55. What two great principles in this government answer to these? 56. What is shown by the fact that this beast has no crowns upon his horns? 57. Is our own government such a one? 58. What proves that the law-making power is in the hands of the people? 59. What form of government must it therefore be? 60. Does this fix it to our own government? 61. What kind of a government is it shown to be in regard to its religion,

beast would be worshiping itself. But the two-
horned beast enforces the worship of a power distinct from itself; and that power being Catholicism,
the beast itself symbolizes not a Catholic, but a
Protestant country.

10. He doeth great wonders, real miracles, makes
fire come down from heaven and deceives them that
dwell on the earth. In Rev. 19 : 20, the same works,
wrought for the same purpose, are ascribed to the
false prophet. The two-horned beast and the false
prophet are therefore the same power. But Rev.
16 : 13, 14, shows that the agency by which the false
prophet works his miracles is the spirits of devils
that go forth for this purpose. A wonderful work,
wrought by spirits of devils, is therefore another
feature of this power. And behold it has made its
appearance in modern Spiritualism which has arisen
in this country; and from this point has spread to
all the nations of the earth.

Considering these facts, that the power represented by the two-horned beast must be located in
this hemisphere, and be just coming into notoriety
about the year 1798, and be a lamb-like power, re-
publican in form of government and Protestant in
religion, and the place where the wonder workings
of Spiritualism should first spring forth, and one
that should make such progress as has no parallel
in the history of nations—can any one for a moment doubt that our government is the one represented? No reason can be given why any nation

and why? 62. What remarkable acts does it perform? 63.
To whom are the same works ascribed in Rev. 19 : 20? 64.
What relation do the two-horned beast and false prophet
therefore have to each other? 65. By what agency does the
false prophet work the miracles? Reference. 66. What is
therefore revealed to us as another feature of this two-horned
beast? 67. In what has this made its appearance? 68.

should be noticed in prophecy, which will not apply in a pre-eminent degree to our own nation.

What remains to be fulfilled, is embodied principally in two propositions : This power is to cause an image to be made to the beast, and to enforce the reception of the mark of the beast. An image to the beast must be something resembling the beast. The beast, Catholicism, was a church clothed with civil power. An ecclesiastical organization clothed with civil power would bear some resemblance to it, or be an image of it. A State church in this land of multiplied sects, is probably an impossibility. How, then, can we have here such an image ? There can be a union formed on such points as the different religious denominations hold in common. The principal of these are three : 1. The first day of the week as the Sabbath, adored from various standpoints and under different titles as the Lord's Day, the Christian Sabbath, the American Sabbath, etc. ; 2. The Immortality of the Soul. 3. Water Baptism. The question of such a union among the churches, under the seductive title of a "Union in Christ" is now extensively agitated. Papers are published in the interest of the movement and earnest advocates are devoting to it their best powers. It finds a strong under current of favor in all the churches.

The movement in reference to the mark is equally advanced, and bears more openly upon its face its evident design. This will be apparent from a brief consideration of what the mark is, and the movement now on foot in reference to it.

What remains to be fulfilled ? 69. What must an image of the beast be ? 70. What was the beast ? 71. Can we look for a State church here ? 72. In what way then can we have such an image ? 73. Is the question of the union of the churches on common points of faith already agitated and urged ? 74. What can be said of the movement in reference

What is the mark of the beast? It is not of course a literal mark. Prophecy would not couple together a symbolic beast, and a literal mark of that beast. Marks were sometimes used by generals and masters in ancient times to distinguish their followers and servants. The mark of the beast must be some institution of the beast which will distinguish its followers. But we show ourselves followers or servants of any power only by obeying its authority; and authority is always manifested through law.

From what other company are the followers of the beast distinguished? From the followers of God; inasmuch as the warning which goes forth against the worship of the beast and the reception of his mark is designed to keep men loyal to the requirements of Heaven. "Here are they," says the third message, "which keep the commandments of God." But we can show ourselves followers of God only by keeping his law. Therefore the issue in reference to which the third message warns us is a conflict between the law of God and the law of this beast power, by our action toward which we are to show ourselves either the worshipers of the beast or the followers of God.

This accords with the prophecies which reveal the leading characteristic of this Catholic power, in connection with which we must of course look for the mark of that power. Daniel, describing it under the symbol of the little horn of the fourth beast of his seventh chapter, says: " He shall think to change

to the mark? 75. Is the mark of the beast a literal mark? 76. How were marks sometimes used anciently? 77. What then must be the mark of the beast? 78. How is authority always manifested? 79. How is it shown that the mark distinguishes beast worshipers from the worshipers of God? 80. With what prophecies does this harmonize? 81. What does Daniel say of this power? 82. What is the reading of

times and laws." Dan. 7:25. The Septuagint, German and Danish translations read, "*the* law." Here is meant unquestionably the law of God. Among the works of this power we shall therefore find this attempt to change the law of God. Paul states of him the same thing. He speaks of him in 2 Thess. 2, as the man of sin, son of perdition, etc., and says that he would endeavor to exalt himself above all that is called God, or that is worshiped. How could he do this? He could do it in no other way but by promulgating a law which conflicts with the law of God. To do this independently of the law of God, would be to show himself professedly opposed to God, which this power is not to do; for Paul says that he would sit in the temple of God, and show himself that he is God, or set himself forth as God. He must therefore take hold of the law of God and change it, and demand obedience to the change, as if God was its author. And this is just what Daniel said he would think to do; that is, to change the law of God.

The mark of the beast is therefore simply this change which he has attempted to make in the law of God. And what is this? We take testimony from its own mouth. See Catholic Catechisms. It is its change of the fourth commandment, wherein it has put the first day of the week in place of the seventh, which God has not ceased to enjoin. And this Catholic power has not contented itself with simply making this change, but it admits that God has never enjoined it and that the Scriptures do not

<hr>

the Septuagint, German and Danish translations? 83. What law is intended? 84. How does Paul speak of the same power? 85. What is the only way in which this power could exalt itself above God? 86. How does this answer to the words of Daniel? 87. What is therefore the mark of the beast? 88. What change has this power attempted to make

sanction it; and further, it sets it forth as an evidence of its right to legislate in divine things. The following is a representative question on this point, found in the Catholic catechism called, " Abridgment of Christian Doctrine."

" *Ques.* How prove you that the church hath power to command feasts and holy days ?

" *Ans.* By the very act of changing the Sabbath into Sunday, which Protestants allow of; and therefore they fondly contradict themselves by keeping Sunday strictly, and breaking most other feasts commanded by the same church."

"*Ques.* How prove you that ?

"*Ans.* Because by keeping Sunday they acknowledge the church's power to ordain feasts and command them under sin."

See also Andrews' History of the Sabbath, and the following Catholic works: Treatise of Thirty Controversies, Cath. Catechism of Christian Religion, Catholic Christian Instructed, and Doctrinal Catechism.

That the Catholic power is symbolized by the little horn of Dan. 7, is beyond question. The prophecy said that it should think to change the law of God ; and it steps forth and acknowledges the act. What further evidence can be required ? He who, therefore, with the light before him, and the issue pressed upon him between God and this wicked power, deliberately decides to keep the institution of the beast instead of the commandments of God, worships the beast and receives his mark.

We know the objection which will here immediately fly to the lips of an opponent. He will say,

in the law of God? 89. What questions and answers are found in the Abridgment of Christian Doctrine ? 90. What works give testimony in proof of this position ? 91. How then can a person worship the beast and receive his mark ?

Then all Sunday-keepers, past or present, however eminent as servants of God, have had, or now have, the mark of the beast. And we as quickly answer, Not one. Why? Because they have not kept it, and are not keeping it, with the issue before them presented in the prophecy. They have supposed they were keeping the fourth commandment according to the will of God. But flashes of truth in these closing hours of time are to dispel all such darkness from every honest mind, and show this work in its true light. And this institution, although in itself the mark of the beast, does not become such in any individual case, till such individual adopts it under the pressure of human laws, well knowing it to be a human institution set forth in opposition to the law of God.

Such is the issue against which the third message now warns us. And the message is not premature; for this issue is evidently soon to come. Already an Association including among its officers, State governors, senators, chief justices, presidents of colleges, and any number of doctors of divinity, has been formed to secure by legal enactments the observance of the first day of the week as the Sabbath. They call for a religious amendment to the constitution, of such a nature that "all Christian laws, institutions and usages shall be put upon an undeniable legal basis in the fundamental law of the land."

This movement originated in Xenia, O., in Feb., 1863, in a convention composed of eleven different religious denominations. National conventions have been held in Allegheny, Pa., New York city, Pittsburg, Philadelphia, Chicago, Cincinnati, St. Louis,

92. What objection is urged at this point? 93. How is it answered? 94. What issue is soon to come? 95. What Association is already formed? 96. For what do they call? 97. When and where did this movement originate? 98. On

and other places. At the convention in Pittsburg, Feb. 4, 1874, there were 1,073 delegates present representing 18 States.

Many affect to scout the idea that such a movement will ever succeed, and the arm of persecution be raised in this country to enforce so-called Christian usages under the penalties of law. But the idea that it should now succeed is no more strange than was the idea a few years ago that any such movement would be made as we now see already accomplished. That Sunday-keeping will ever be enforced by law, from any real religious convictions on the part of a majority of the people would be perhaps too much to expect. Even the barbarous institution of slavery did not yield to moral forces, but fell only as a political necessity. So it would be nothing strange nor improbable if circumstances should so shape in the near future that a religio-political compromise should bring forth the Sunday law full fledged. But we need not speculate as to methods. There is the prophecy which cannot be broken. Religious questions are fast entering into the arena of politics, and there is an irrepressible conflict between present Christian usages and the claims of infidelity, which cannot cease till the Constitution shall become wholly infidel or wholly conformed to nominal Christianity. Infidel it can never become so long as a union of Protestants and Catholics can carry any measure upon which they may agree. We therefore look for it to become the instrument of that type of Christianity which the Amendmentists desire to legalize.

With these acts in reference to the image and the mark, the career of this power closes. This is the last conflict into which the people of God are brought.

They are next seen victorious on Mt. Zion with the lamb. And this two-horned beast, as the false prophet, in company with the beast (Catholicism) before which he has wrought his miracles, goes as a living power into the lake of fire, at the great day.

CLASS QUESTIONS ON LESSON IX. WITH ANSWERS.

1. If the Romans crucified Christ, how can it be said that the Jews crucified him ?

ANS. The Romans reserved to themselves the power of inflicting capital punishment. The Jews could try and condemn, but the Romans must have the disposal of the sentence. The Jews showed what they would do by condemning Christ on the conflicting testimony of false witnesses, and clamoring vehemently for his crucifixion. The Romans showed their spirit by giving him up to death, at the same time acknowledging that they were sacrificing an innocent person; for Pilate admitted that there was no cause of death in him. The Jews clamored for his death, because his pure teaching, his unostentatious and holy life condemned their pride, hypocrisy and extortion. The Romans were perhaps the more ready for his death through fear, from a political standpoint, of his claims as king of the Jews. It is evident that great capital had been made out of this point against him ; for even the ignorant and brutal soldiery as soon as he was delivered into their power, went through all the mock ceremonies of royalty. In almost all the representations of the crucifixion, will be seen the banner with the significant letters S. P. Q. R., *Senatus Populusque Romanos*, The Senate and People of

Where are the people of God next seen ? **100.** What is the fate of this beast ?

Rome. This showed Rome's presence, and its sanction of the crucifixion. The Jews might have prevented it; so might the Romans. But both joined in it, and so were both equally responsible, the one to condemn, the other to execute.

2. Are our names written in the book of life at birth, or at conversion?

Ans. Evidently at conversion; otherwise the names of all would at some time be there; but Rev. 17 : 8 speaks of some whose names are never found there. As this book is called "the *Lamb's* book of life," it seems more consistent to suppose that the names of those only are entered there who acquire some interest in the work of Christ as the Lamb of God, or the offering for the world; and that they are entered in the book when they thus make a profession of his name.

3. Some who have heard and understood the Sabbath question, and kept the Sabbath for years, are now keeping Sunday. Have such received the mark of the beast?

Ans. As already explained, the mark of the beast, in the light of the prophecy, can be received only when the issue comes between the claims of God's law, and the institution of the beast, and a person deliberately chooses the latter knowing it to be in opposition to God's requirements. That crisis has not yet come; and hence we do not say that any one now has the mark of the beast. That any one who has ever known the truth and kept the Sabbath, is now conscientiously keeping Sunday, we very much doubt. We venture to assert that it is a matter of policy merely. It does not seem possible to us that it could be otherwise. Still the strange workings of a mind that is enveloped in darkness, wholly deceived, is something we cannot comprehend nor explain.

4. What is meant by receiving the mark in the forehead and in the hand ?

ANS. As the forehead represents the seat of the mind and judgment, receiving the mark there may be explained as giving the assent of the judgment to the institution of the beast and his requirements. Many no doubt will so far fall under the power of deception as to finally enthusiastically endorse the teaching of this anti-Christian power as the truth. The hand is the agent of outward action, and to receive the mark there may indicate compliance by some outward sign, as a matter of policy without compromising the judgment or the affections. The requirements of the truth are more strict. The Lord must have his mark or seal in the forehead and no-where else. He must have the mind and heart; for nothing else is obedience such as he requires. The beast is not so particular; and if a person cannot sincerely endorse his work, and so receive the mark in the forehead, he will be satisfied if he will by yielding a formal compliance, receive it in the hand.

5. Is a person's destiny sealed when he has received the mark of the beast ?

ANS. Undoubtedly. When a person is so far gone either in deception, or a willingness to with-stand the plain requirements of God, to save him-self from persecution, that he will take such a step, he must be beyond recovery. And this is doubtless the turning point with him. The period of proba-tion with the last generation in this country, runs to this issue and terminates. When the worshipers of the beast have received his mark, the servants of God are all sealed with God's seal, Rev. 7 : 1–4 ; 14 : 1, and then the plagues begin to fall, Rev. 16, begin-ning with the very ones, who, in worshiping the beast and receiving his mark, have committed the highest offense against Heaven.

6. Would the Catholic, believing that his church has the right to command sacred days, have the mark of the beast, and the Protestant the mark of the image ?

ANS. The objection against this supposition is that we nowhere read that the image has any mark. All that seems to be done in reference to the image is to worship it. Two powers are involved in this conflict, God and this anti-Christian power symbolized by the beast. There are but two marks to distinguish their respective followers : the mark of the beast and the seal of God. On the one side are the beast, the two-horned beast, and the image ; but one mark, the mark of the beast, is common to them all.

7. Could those who are living outside of this government, and do not regard the first day of the week with any sacredness be said to have the mark ?

ANS. We think not. But the first plague which falls upon those who had the mark of the beast and worshiped his image, will take those in every country who worship the beast and receive his mark, and in this country such as receive the mark and worship the image.

8. When are the beast and the false prophet cast into the lake of fire ? at the beginning or the end of the thousand years ?

ANS. At the beginning. Rev. 19 : 20. The scene described in this chapter from the 11th verse is undoubtedly the second coming of Christ ; and it is at this time that the beast and false prophet are taken and consigned to this doom. This is what Daniel describes, Dan. 7 : 11, when he says that the beast was destroyed and his body given to the burning flame ; and Paul, when he says, 2 Thess. 2 : 8,

that " that wicked," the papacy, shall be consumed
by the spirit of Christ's mouth and destroyed by the
brightness of his coming. The scene at the end of
the thousand years, Rev. 20 : 10, 13–15, seems to
be a repetition, on a larger scale, of that which
occurred at the beginning. The devil, says John,
" was cast into the lake of fire and brimstone where
the beast and false prophet" were cast, as we should
read it according to the literal construction of the
passage. They were cast there a thousand years
before, at the coming of Christ. Thus the same
term is used to describe what takes place at the
beginning of the thousand years, and also at the
close, the destruction of the wicked being largely
due in both cases to the consuming glory of the
presence and power of God; " for our God is a consuming fire" (to the wicked), Heb. 12 : 29; accompanied more or less with the manifestation of literal fire, which at the end of the thousand years is
so hightened and intensified that the elements melt
with fervent heat, 2 Pet. 3 : 10, and the heavens and
the earth flee away from the presence of Him who
sits upon the great white throne, resolved into
their ultimate gases by the intensity of the last
purifying fires. From the elements thus cleansed
from the curse and sin, the new heavens and earth
appear. 2 Pet. 3 : 13.

9. Job 14 : 12 says that man riseth not until the
heavens be no more. Are we to understand by this
that the heavens pass away at Christ's second coming ?

Ans. The word used by the Septuagint in this
passage does not convey the idea of cessation of
existence, as in our English version, but that of
breaking up and dashing together, like the onset of
two armies in battle. The word is defined by Lid-

dell and Scott, "to tear or break up, to dash to pieces." "Passive and intransitive, to break or fall to pieces, to burst out, and crush together." This agrees accurately with the commotion which New Testament writers declare will take place in the heavens when Christ appears. Matthew says, The powers of the heavens shall be shaken," Matt. 24: 29, and John declares that the heavens then depart as a scroll when it is rolled together. Rev. 6:14. What Job affirms is that the dead shall not awake out of their sleep till this breaking up of the heavens takes place; and other writers affirm that this takes place when Christ comes, which is the time for the resurrection of the dead.

LESSON TEN.

THE SABBATH.

As we have seen that the third angel's message brings out a company who are distinguished as keepers of the commandments of God, the inquiry is a natural one in what respect obedience to the message would lead a person to differ with other religionists in his efforts to keep the commandments. The only essential controversy in regard to the commandments among those who hold them to be still binding has reference to that precept which enjoins the Sabbath. If in order to keep the commandments we must keep the seventh day of the week, and almost all professors of religion are keeping the first day of the

1. By what are believers in the third angel's message distinguished? 2. What inquiry does this suggest? 3. On what one of the commandments is there a difference of opin-

week, here is a distinction as marked as the language of the third message would lead us to infer. Thus is our attention called directly to the Sabbath by the third angel's message, as well as by the subject of the sanctuary.

And there is consistency in this; for as the first message brought us to the hour of God's Judgment, or the cleansing of the sanctuary, when the temple of God was opened in Heaven, the ark was seen, and the attention of the people was called to the law contained in the ark, the third message which follows the first, and is the representative of the truth during the period of the cleansing of the sanctuary, ought of consistency to bring out the same fact respecting the law; and we see that it does.

The evidence is now in order, to show that the seventh day is still the Sabbath of the Lord, and must be kept as such. The only command in all the Bible for the observance of the Sabbath is the fourth precept of the decalogue. But the nine other precepts are moral and hence immutable and eternal. Even those who contend for the abolition of the law, would not dare to advocate in any civilized community, that men were not under obligation to do or refrain from doing, just what those commandments say. Is the Sabbath like these others, immutable and perpetual? If not, why was it put in with these as one of them? and again, if not, what reasons can be given to show why and in what respect it is not like them?

---

ion? 4. To what is our attention thus called by the message? 5. To what did the first message bring us? 6. What time is covered by the third message? 7. What truth should we therefore expect it to bring out? 8. What and where is the only commandment in all the Bible for the observance of the Sabbath? 9. What is the nature of the other nine precepts? 10. Is the Sabbath commandment like these? 11.

The Sabbath commandment is the only one in which God has seen fit to set forth the reason why it was given. It is therefore more explicit than the others. Respecting the others we may necessarily infer that they existed from the beignning of the world, but respecting the Sabbath we know that it dates from the beginning, from the record itself. The fourth commandment points back to the creation: "For in six days the Lord made heaven and earth, the sea, and all that in them is, and rested the seventh day; wherefore the Lord blessed the Sabbath day and hallowed it." This day we are to remember and keep holy. It is a marvel that any one should consider this commandment indefinite, enjoining only a seventh part of time, or an institution independent of a day. The act of God in resting had reference to a day. The blessing and sanctification had reference to a day. It is a day that we are required to keep, and it is *the* particular day on which he rested. Let those who call it indefinite tell us how it could be more definite than it is.

Turning to the record to which the fourth commandment points us, Gen. 2 : 2, we read that " on the seventh day God ended his work which he had made. And God blessed the seventh day and sanctified it because that in it he had rested from all his work which God created and made." God performed no part of his work on the seventh day. The fourth commandment says that he made the heavens and the earth and all that in them is in

In what respect is it more explicit than the others ? 12. Which way does the fourth commandment point ? 13. Is there any such thing as a Sabbatic institution independent of a day ? 14. To what did the act of resting, blessing and sanctifying have reference ? 15. How could the commandment be made more definite than it is ? 16. Did God perform any part of his work on the seventh day ? 17. How is this shown

six days, which would not be the case if he made any portion of them on the seventh day. Dr. Clarke says that the Septuagint, Syriac and Samaritan versions read sixth day in Gen. 2:2, instead of seventh day. But such a criticism is unnecessary, and it is not best to plead for a different translation unless there is clear and urgent reason for so doing. The expression in verse 3, "in it he rested" means the same as in verse 2 "on it he ended his work." It means simply that on that day, and during that day, he ceased from his creative work. The entire day was devoted to rest; and this was the first essential act toward the Sabbatic institution. This made it the Lord's rest-day, but laid no obligation on men concerning it. He then blessed it. This did not pertain to the day that was past; for past time cannot be blessed; but it referred to the seventh day for time to come. Every seventh day from that time was a blessed day. This would indicate how it should be regarded; but the next act completed the work: He sanctified it. Sanctify means to set apart to a holy use. This could not pertain to the day that was past, but to the seventh day for time to come. It was not set apart for God's use; for he needs no such day; but Christ said it was made for man. This sanctification was therefore the giving of a command to Adam for its observance. The claim of Sabbath opponents that there is no command in the Bible for the observance of the Sabbath till Sinai,

---

by the fourth commandment? 18. What is the meaning of the expression, "On the seventh day God ended his work"? 19. What was the first essential act toward a Sabbatic institution? 20. What was the second? 21. What completed the edifice? 22. What is the meaning of the word sanctify? 23. To what did this santification pertain? 24. For whose use was the Sabbath made? 25. What was this sanctification? 26. What can be said of the claim that no command existed

falls to the ground; for here is the record that such
a commandment was given. And all the human
race then received that command through Adam
and Eve their representatives. And this sanctification of necessity introduced the weekly cycle;
for Adam must begin to reckon as soon as the commandment was given; and when the next seventh
day was past he must begin his count again, and so
on. The week owes its origin to these facts. It can
be traced to no other.

The Sabbath was not a type; for all types look
forward to a work of redemption, and of course
could not be introduced till redemption was needed,
and till some plan of redemption had been instituted. But the Sabbath was given to Adam before
he sinned, before he needed any redemption, and
before any system of redemption was devised. Had
Adam never sinned, he never would have needed
redemption, and no type would ever have been introduced. But he would still have had the Sabbath
as recorded in Gen. 2:2, 3. The Sabbath, therefore,
was not a type.

The Sabbath not being a type, the commandment
for the Sabbath is not a typical law. There are
plainly two kinds of laws: one class binding on
man before he fell, regulating his duty to God, and
to his fellow-men; the other class, growing out of
the changed condition of man after he had fallen
and the plan of salvation had been introduced. If
man had never fallen, it would have been his duty
just the same to render supreme honor to God, and

before Sinai? 27. Who received that commandment? 28.
What did this sanctification introduce? 29. Why? 30.
Was the Sabbath a type? 31. To what do all types look?
32. When could they be introduced? 33. On this ground
how is it shown that the Sabbath was not a type? 34. What
two kinds of laws are plainly brought to view in the Bible?
35. What would have been man's duty if he had never

to deal justly with his fellow-men. But if he had never fallen, there never would have been any laws regulating ceremonies, sacrifices, offerings, baptism, the Lord's supper, etc. These all grow out of man's necessities in consequence of his fall. The first may be called original or primary laws; and they are, in the very nature of things, immutable and eternal; the others are derived, secondary or typical laws, and are temporary and changeable. No one has any excuse for ignoring or denying a distinction so plain.

The transgression of Adam did not change or abolish any of these primary laws. We are under no less obligation to God and our fellow-men than if we were not sinners. To which of these classes of laws does the Sabbath belong? To the original and primary laws which we should have had even if man never had fallen. It is therefore an immutable and perpetual institution.

The Sabbath is the seventh day of the week as it is reckoned at the present time. The fourth commandment does not, to be sure, use the term week, and say the seventh day of the week; but its appeal to the record of the great facts of creation for its origin, where the week is defined and the seventh day of that week is the one set apart as the Sabbath, makes it just as explicit. To quibble over the absence of the word, week, in the commandment, as we have frequently known ministers to do who even professed to be candid, is the thinnest kind of sophistry, to use no harder term; for of

fallen? 36. Would there then have been any laws of ceremonies and sacrifices? 37. What may the first of these laws be called? 38. What the second? 39. Did Adam's transgression change or abolish any of the primary laws? 40. To which of these classes does the Sabbath belong? 41. What does this prove? 42. Is the Sabbath the seventh day of the week as now reckoned? 43. How does the fourth command-

what is it the seventh day ?   Not the seventh day
of the month, or of the year; not *a* seventh day, nor
every seventh day, allowing us to begin where we
will to reckon ; but *the* seventh day of some definite
cycle of time.   And inasmuch as we have in the
Bible a division of time given us, consisting of just
seven days, the shortest of all which consist of a number of days, to say that the seventh day of the commandment is not the seventh day of this division,
or week, is to go in the clearest manner contrary to
reason.

But it is asked if the reckoning of the week has
not been lost; in other words, can we now tell
which is the true seventh day from creation?
Once admitting that the seventh day in regular
succession is what is required, and there is no difficulty.   It could easily be handed down from
Adam to Abraham, and from Abraham to Moses.
But if anything was out of the way then, God
would have set them right when he gave them a
written copy of his law.   By three distinct miracles
wrought every week for the space of forty years,
God pointed out what day he meant in the
commandment ; and it was the seventh day of the
Jewish week.   From Moses to Christ there was
certainly no derangement in the reckoning.   They
had the true seventh day at that point; and if
there had been any mistake then, Christ, the Son
of God, would have known it and set them right.
But instead of this he endorsed the day they then
observed.   From the days of Christ to the present

ment define the day of the week ?   44. How does it further
appear that it means the seventh day of the week?   45. What
question is next raised ?   46. Was there any danger of losing
the reckoning from Adam to Moses ?   47. How did God then
point out the day of the commandment ?   48. How is it
shown that the true day was preserved to the time of Christ ?

time, the methods of computing time have been too accurate, the custom too wide spread, and the agreement too perfect, to admit for a moment of the idea of any loss of time, or derangement of the week. Therefore the week as we now reckon it, is the same as at the creation, and the seventh day of our week, is the true seventh day from creation down.

It is supposed by some that the change from Old Style to New must have changed the reckoning of the week. A few facts will show that this is a mistake. Old and New Styles are simply methods of reckoning time according to the Julian and Gregorian calendars. Old Style follows the Julian manner of reckoning months and days, or the calendar by Julius Cæsar, in which every fourth year consists of 366 days, and the other years of 365 days. This is something more than 11 minutes too much in the year; and by the time of pope Gregory XIII. in 1582, it had so disarranged the months as to throw the vernal equinox 10 days from where it was at the council of Nice, A. D. 325. To bring it back, 10 days were taken out of October, 1582, and the 5th day of the month was reckoned as the 15th. Gregory then reformed the calendar so that such a derangement would not again occur, by having every year which is divisible by 4, unless divisible by 100 without being divisible by 400, consist of 366 days, and all other years of 365 days. This makes the calendar year coincide so nearly with the solar, that the lapse of centuries makes scarcely any appreciable difference. This is called the Gregorian calendar, and reckoning time by it is called New Style. This change was not adopted by Great Britain till 1751. Then so much time had been gained that to bring the matter right 11 days had

---

49. Has there been any loss of time or derangement of weeks since ? 50. Explain the difference between Old Style and

to be dropped. Therefore in the following year 1752, the 3d of September was reckoned as the 14th; and New Style has since been followed there, and from there brought to America. It will be seen that this simply changed the day of the month but not the day of the week. For instance to-day, May 24, 1877, is Thursday; if we should drop 7 days and call it May 31, it would be Thursday still. Russia still reckons by Old Style, and her week corresponds with ours.

Another attempt is made to nullify the force of the record of Gen. 2 : 2, 3. It is claimed that the seventh day which God blessed was the first day of Adam's existence, and hence the point where the reckoning should commence. If that was the point at which to commence, doubtless Moses, guided by the Spirit of inspiration, would have commenced there. But it so happens that he commenced the reckoning six days before, and has given it to us day by day down to that point. How is it that modern expositors have come to be so wise above what is written ? We can answer : they couldn't oppose the Sabbath in any other way. To make this position of any force, the ground must be taken that Adam's first day was the first day of time. Then all that went before was eternity. God created the world and all things therein, not in the beginning, but in eternity. But time as distinguished from eternity is duration measured, eternity being unmeasured duration ; and these days of creation are measured off to us, and hence belong to time and not to eternity. What blind presumption for men to set a point from which to reckon different from that which the Bible has given us !

But the assumption of this objection is entirely false: the seventh day was not the first day of Adam's existence, nothing of the kind. When was Adam created? On the sixth day. All the animals were then brought to him and he named them, no small amount of work. Then he was put to sleep while Eve was created. After that a marriage ceremony took place. And then followed instruction to Adam and Eve in regard to their manner of life, means of support, extent of dominion, etc., before Moses declares that the evening and the morning were the sixth day. Surely here was enough to occupy the greater part of that day, yet so anxious are people to oppose the Sabbath that they will tell us that the next day was the first day of Adam's existence. What! Adam married before he had an existence! If any, still inclined to urge this ghost of an excuse, should plead that the seventh day of the record was Adam's first complete day, then we ask them why they do not celebrate American independence on July 5 instead of July 4, as July 5, 1776, was the first *complete* day of our independence. This objection cannot be made to stand, however men may try to bolster it up. It is the imbecile offspring of prejudice and folly.

Again it is said that Moses, writing after God had spoken the ten commandments, stated in Gen. 2:2, 3, what was done on the seventh day not at creation, but at Sinai. That is, Gen. 2:2 states what took place on the first seventh day of time, but verse three without any change in the narrative, or any intimation that other than a consecutive order of events is introduced, narrates what took place 2500 years afterward. This view is fabricated

nity? 55. On what day was Adam created? 56. What else was done on that day? 57. What shall be said then of the view that the seventh was Adam's first day? 58. What

by those who claim that the Sabbath originated at Sinai. It is very evident from what source it springs. The wish is father to the thought. To barely state a view which rests so utterly on assumption, and is so contrary to the whole tenor of the narrative, ought to be sufficient. There is not the slightest intimation that God blessed and for the first time set apart the day of the Sabbath at Sinai. The record in Genesis states in the same style of narrative that God rested on the seventh day, and that he blessed and sanctified it. God did not perform the act of resting, certainly, at Sinai; the resting was done at creation; then upon what ground or authority does any one throw in between the sentences of an unbroken narrative a period of 2500 years and make the resting at Sinai, when there is not an item of evidence to show that any resting there took place? It is evident that the resting took place at the creation, and the blessing and sanctification immediately thereafter; and if the day was not to be used till Sinai, we leave with our friends another question: Why was all this done so long beforehand?

There is another objection coming to be urged by a certain class very frequently and with a great deal of assurance; and that is, that the record of God's rest upon the seventh day has nothing to do in fixing a weekly Sabbath; for those days are not literal days but immense periods of time as is proved by geology. And they affect to look with great disdain upon any one who will not acknowledge so notable a scientific fact. It can readily be seen that

---

other objection is now urged? 59. Is there any intimation of such a change in the record? 60. What is the object of this view? 61. Did God rest on the seventh day or bless the day at Sinai? 62. If not to be kept till Sinai, why was the Sabbath blessed so long beforehand? 63. What objection is

this contradicts the Bible; and this many so-called geologists are doubtless very willing to do. But even some professed defenders of the word of God, have been frightened by this bugbear of geology into an admission that these days are great periods, and then gone into a theological St. Vitus' dance to harmonize it with the record. Into a controversy with geology it is not our purpose here to enter further than to deny *in toto* what they call conclusions and we call guess-work, and challenge the proof. In their conclusions geologists assume that the results which modern research has discovered, have been produced in ages past by such agencies only as we see at work at the present time. And right here their theory breaks down; for that is what cannot be proved. The Master Mind in Nature's great laboratory may in remote ages have called into action potent agencies to produce in a short space certain results which by any process now going forward it would take ages to accomplish. To reason from that which is present and known to that which is past and unknown, is illogical. The premise being assumed, the conclusion is but an assumption also. And after all the ludicrous mistakes which geologists have made, attributing a pre-Adamic age to bricks found in the delta of the Nile, which subsequent investigations proved belonged to the age of the later Pharaohs, and dancing with delight over the immense antiquity of a strange piece of wood found in the delta of the Mississippi, which was found upon a little more careful scrutiny to be the gunwale of a Kentucky flat-boat, they ought to be a little modest in their assertions.

It will be enough for Bible believers to test this claim on the age of Adam, and dismiss it. Adam was created on the sixth day, the sixth long period

raised on the authority of geology ? 64. How is it answered ?

the geologist would say. He lived all that period through, his life covering probably the greater part of it. He then lived the seventh day, or entirely through the seventh long period. By this time he must have been many hundred thousand years old. The record then goes on with his history, introducing the birth of Cain, Abel and Seth, and when he came to die, lo, he was all of nine hundred and thirty years old! Where now are the long periods during which he lived? Vanished into the moonshine from which they venture now and then to flaunt themselves.

So far as the record in Gen. 2:2, 3 is concerned, the field is now cleared of every objection. All the raiders upon that citadel of truth are repulsed. The record stands in its native strength and simplicity. The six days of creation were such days as we now have, ruled by the sun, determined by a revolution of the earth upon its axis. The seventh of these was devoted by the Creator to rest. It was set apart to be thus used by man. A command was given to Adam, and through him to all his posterity to keep it. It was not a temporary nor a typical institution, but designed to last through all time, like other primary institutions. These facts are established; and we might rest the whole Sabbath question right here; for if these stand, as they surely do, and will, the Sabbath stands. It was all right in the beginning, gleaming like a coronet on the fair brow of a creation unsullied by sin; and if men had always kept it, the world would have presented a very different moral and religious aspect from what it does to-day; for men never could become idolators so long as they remembered to wor-

65. How does the record of Gen. 2, now stand? 66. Give a synopsis of the facts established. 67. What effect would it have had upon the world if all men had always kept the Sab-

ship the Creator of all things; and we should not, as we do to-day, behold the sad spectacle of seven hundred millions of idolators, whose dark abodes are the habitations of cruelty.

But leaving the creation with its established facts and explicit record, we are willing to follow the Sabbath opponent to all his strongholds, and candidly weigh, and compare with Scripture, his strongest arguments. Taking us to Neh. 9 : 13, 14, he says that the Sabbath was not known nor given to the children of Israel before God spoke it from Sinai; for Nehemiah says: "Thou camest down also upon Mount Sinai, and spakest with them from heaven, and gavest them right judgments, and true laws, good statutes and commandments; and madest known unto them thy holy Sabbath, and commandest them precepts, statutes and laws by the hand of Moses thy servant." The only trouble with the conclusion drawn from this passage is, that it is contradicted by other scriptures. Thus, Ex. 16 gives an account of the Hebrews' having the Sabbath in the second month after their departure from Egypt. When God would prove his people to see whether they would walk in his law or no, he took the Sabbath as the one with which to test their obedience, reproving some who in their unbelief and rebellion went out to gather manna on the Sabbath by saying, "*How long* refuse ye to keep my commandments and my laws." This is not the language that would be used with reference to laws new-made and then for the first time introduced. But this was thirty-three days *before* the law was spoken from Sinai. Therefore the Sabbath was not

bath as God designed ? 68. What position of the Sabbath opponent is next noticed ? Reference. 69. What is the difficulty with his conclusion ? 70. What does Exodus 16 show ? 71. How long was this before the law was spoken on Sinai ? 72.

first made known to them from Sinai, as it is claimed from Neh. 9 : 13, 14. How then shall the statements of Nehemiah be harmonized with the record of Ex. 16 ? Our opponents make a contradiction between these two chapters by giving a wrong meaning to the words " made known " in Neh. 9 : 14. These words do not mean that the Sabbath was then for the first time brought to their knowledge, but only that it was more especially unfolded to them by the commandment's being spoken with the voice of God in their hearing, and a copy of it placed in their hands written with his own finger. In Eze. 20 : 5, God says that he made himself known unto them in the land of Egypt, when he lifted up his hand unto them saying, " I am the Lord your God." This does not mean that they then for the first time received a knowledge of God; for they already knew and revered him. Ex. 1 : 17. It simply means that he then gave a more intimate revelation of himself to them ; and it only means the same in reference to the Sabbath in Neh. 9 : 13, 14.

It is further urged in behalf of the idea that the Sabbath originated at Sinai, that God gave it to the Israelites to commemorate their deliverance from Egypt. Deut. 5 : 15 is quoted to prove this: " And remember that thou wast a servant in the land of Egypt, and that the Lord thy God brought thee out thence through a mighty hand and by a stretched out arm ; therefore the Lord thy God commanded thee to keep the Sabbath day." This is not the original Sabbath commandment, but a rehearsal by

How do our opponents make a contradiction between Ex. 16 and Neh. 9 ? 73. What does the expression "made known," in Nehemiah, mean ? 74. How is it explained by Eze. 20 : 5 ? 75. What is further urged to prove that the Sabbath originated at Sinai ? 76. What text is quoted to prove this ? 77. Is this the original commandment ? 78. How long after God

Moses of God's dealings with that people, as he was
about to leave them. It was 40 years after the law
had been given by the voice of God on Mount Sinai.
Moses intimates as much by referring them back to
the commandment. See verse 12: "Keep the
Sabbath day to sanctify it, as the Lord thy God
hath commanded thee." Why then is this rehearsal
by Moses, forty years after the giving of the law
always quoted by our opponents instead of the
original commandment as found in Ex. 20 : 8–11 ?
The answer is obvious: Because in that original
commandment there is no mention of the coming
out of Egypt, and hence that would not furnish
anything which they could torture into proof that
the Sabbath originated then, and was limited to
that people. But we submit to every candid and
honorable mind whether it is a fair method of reasoning thus to ignore the commandment as spoken
by God, and then endeavor to draw the origin of
the institution from a rehearsal by Moses, forty years
afterward.

But we need not leave the question here. There
are other duties which certainly did not originate
then, and were not confined to that people, but in
reference to which the same language is used. They
were commanded not to pervert judgment, nor
oppress the widow, nor do any unrighteousness, but
to do all the commandments; and in reference to
all these, as in reference to the Sabbath, it is
said, I am the Lord which brought you out of the
land, *therefore* I command you to do this thing.
See Deut. 24 : 18, 22; Lev. 19 : 35–37. Why do

had spoken the commandment, was this rehearsal by Moses?
79. Does Moses refer back to the commandment? 80. Why
do our opponents appeal to Deut. 5 instead of Ex. 20 to show
the origin of the commandment? 81. What other duties are
enjoined for the same reason? References. 82. Why was

they not use this fact in reference to the other commandments as they do in reference to the Sabbath? The answer again is obvious: They do not want it for any except the Sabbath; hence they studiously shut their own eyes, or endeavor to shut the eyes of their readers, to all the others. But the argument will apply to all alike, and hence proves too much for them.

Having shown that there is no proof in the text that the Sabbath was given to that people and confined to them, because they came out of Egypt, since if it proves this, it proves that all the commandments were given for the same reason, we have said all that is demanded of us in this argument. But to clear away all doubt it may be remarked that the reference to the deliverance from Egypt was simply an appeal to their gratitude. They had been in Egyptian bondage, where in all probability the severity of their servitude prevented their worshiping God in keeping his commandments and ordinances. But now they had been delivered from that hard state of bondage into perfect freedom. Should they not therefore, by a ready compliance with his will, show their gratitude to Him who had delivered them? Therefore, in addition to all other obligations, as their great Benefactor he commanded them to keep the Sabbath, not to pervert judgment, nor oppress the widow, but to observe all his commandments.

CLASS QUESTIONS ON LESSON X., WITH ANSWERS.

1. How did God *end* his work on the seventh day? Can one end his work upon a certain day without working a part of that day? What is the meaning of the word end?

---

reference made to the deliverance of Israel from Egypt?

Ans. The expression that God "ended" his work means simply that he ceased from his work. This does not imply that any part of the work was performed on the seventh day, but that the whole of that day was spent in cessation from labor. So it is recorded that God created all that he made, the heavens and the earth and *all* things therein, in six days; and also that he rested the seventh day from *all* his work; neither of which expressions could be harmonized with the idea that he performed any of his work on the seventh day.

2. If Adam was created on the sixth day, then had all the beasts of the field and the fowls of the air to name, then was put to sleep while Eve was created, then was married, and received all the instruction subsequently given, would it not have kept him very busy till the seventh day arrived?

Ans. Yes; so busy that it must be apparent to all that the greater portion of the day would necessarily be taken up with this work; hence the utter falsity and absurdity of calling the seventh day Adam's first day, the first day of his existence.

3. How could it be proved that Adam did not live and die during the sixth great period? Geologists claim that the Bible does not say that he lived any portion of the seventh day.

Ans. This is doing utter violence to the record, and thus refutes itself. After introducing the creation of Adam on the sixth day, the Bible states the events of the seventh day, as events which were, like the acts of the preceding days, accomplished and finished. Then going back to give some of the particulars of Adam's creation, the writer immediately goes *forward* in the world's history to Adam's expulsion from Eden, the introduction of his posterity till the time of his death at the age of 930 years.

Now if this does not take us past the sixth period, and also the seventh, no one can show that the sixth period has ended, or that the seventh has commenced. But this would falsify the record; which is a sufficient objection to the view presented.

4. Some calling themselves scientists, claim that the ancient years were only so many moons; and when the record says that Adam lived 930 years, it only means that he lived 930 months. Is there any evidence that the ancients called months years?

ANS. No. This is one of the instances of a display of that science which is falsely so called, and which is foolishness with God. Why will not these scientists agree? Some will have Adam live immense periods of time, and others, as in this instance, only 930 months, or 77 years and a half. But on this latter supposition we find ourselves involved in some most ridiculous absurdities. For instance, calling the years of the Bible equal to our months, so that twelve of them would be required to make one of our years, it follows that the antediluvians and some of the early patriarchs were most precocious individuals. For instance, on this calculation, Enoch had a son when he was five years and five months of age, Arphaxad, when he was not quite three, and Peleg and many others when they were only two and a half. See Gen. 11. Abraham is spoken of as a man in his "old age" when he was but little over eight years old. Gen. 21: 2. Isaac was married when he was but three years and four months old, Gen. 25: 20, Joseph was out tending his father's flocks when he was one year and five months of age, Gen. 37: 2, and stood before Pharaoh, to interpret his dreams when he was two years and a half old. Gen. 41:46. So we might go on. But this is sufficient. All that need be said of those who indulge in such absurdities, has been said by Paul in Rom. 1: 22.

5. How can it be shown that the Jews could not keep the Sabbath in Egypt?

ANS. There is no positive testimony in the case; but we can reason from the probabilities in the matter. It is not at all reasonable to suppose that persons holding others in such absolute slavery as the Egyptians then held the Israelites, would so far respect their religious views as to allow them to rest one day in seven. As the Egyptians exacted of their Israelitish bondmen the full tale of brick, compelling them to find their own straw, so we may be quite sure they would exact of them seven days of labor out of every week. On this supposition there is force to the reference to their Egyptian servitude, when Moses is exhorting them, after their deliverance, to keep the Sabbath.

6. What is the proof that the Jews came to the wilderness of Sinai on the 15th day of the third month?

ANS. Ex. 16: 1 states that they came to the wilderness of Sin on the 15th day of the *second* month. The first verse of the 19th chapter reads: "In the *third* month when the children of Israel were gone forth out of the land of Egypt, the same day came they into the wilderness of Sinai." Now all depends upon the meaning we give to the expression, "the same day." What else can it mean but the same day of the month in which they came out of Egypt, and the same day of the month in which they came into the wilderness of Sin? If this is its meaning then it was on the 15th day of the third month that they came into the wilderness of Sinai. Three days after this the law was spoken, which was consequently thirty-three days after the experience recorded in Ex. 16, where the Sabbath is so prominently brought to view.

7. How can it be shown in face of Ex. 34: 28, that Moses did not write the ten commandments when the second copy was given, after the first tables had been broken?

ANS. We are not always to take, as the antecedent of a pronoun, that noun which stands nearest to it. In this case the antecedent is the Lord and not Moses. Deut. 10: 2, 4 declares the facts in the case in unmistakable language. Verse 2 states that God promised to write the same words which were on the first table; and verse 4 states that he (God) wrote them. There is therefore nothing in the facts of the giving of the second tables to show any change in the nature or basis of the law, as some claim.

LESSON ELEVEN.

BIBLE VIEW OF THE SABBATH.

WE are accused of going back to Moses and falling from grace, if we now keep the original Sabbath. It is therefore a matter of interest to mark how God formerly regarded that practice of Sabbath-keeping which some now claim that he considers so heinous in his sight. We have seen how the Sabbath was instituted in Eden before sin had entered our world, and how a law was given for its observance which had its place among the primary,

immutable and eternal laws. We have seen how
at the exode God took the Sabbath precept as the
one by which to test Israel's allegiance to himself.
And now we mark, further, that he took the Sabbath to be permanently a sign between himself and
them: "It is a sign between me and you throughout your generations; that ye may know that I am
the Lord that doth sanctify you." Ex. 31 : 13. It
was the pre-eminent institution through which was
to come his acknowledgment of them as his people,
and through which they were to manifest their
recognition of him as their God. This was to
endure throughout their generations. When the
natural branches were broken off, the Gentiles were
grafted in, taking the place of the severed branches,
and keeping the olive tree perfect in all its propor-
tions. Hence the generations of Israel are perpetuated in a spiritual seed, and the Sabbath is still a
sign between God and them. A man who does not
keep the Sabbath cannot show that he is a wor-
shiper of the true God who made the heavens and
the earth.

God further sets forth that his honor is involved
in the keeping of his Sabbath. Isa. 58 : 13 : " If
thou turn away thy foot from the Sabbath, from
doing thy pleasure on my holy day ; and call the
Sabbath a delight, the holy of the Lord, honorable,
and *shalt honor him,* not doing thine one ways, nor
finding thine own pleasure, nor speaking thine own
words ; then shalt thou delight thyself in the Lord,"
&c. Thus the observance of the Sabbath is not
merely for man's necessities and his physical good ;

law then given for its observance? 4. What use did God
make of it at the exode? 5. Where is it declared to be a sign?
6. What is meant by its being a sign? 7. How long was it to
be a sign? 8. How are the generations of Israel still perpetuated? 9. What does Isaiah show· concerning the Sab-

it is to honor God. By keeping it we honor, by disregarding it we dishonor, the Maker of the heavens and the earth.

The Lord further told the people through Jeremiah what he would do for them if they would keep the Sabbath, and what judgments he would bring upon them if they would not regard it: "It shall come to pass, if ye diligently hearken unto me saith the Lord to bring in no burden through the gates of this city on the Sabbath day, but hallow the Sabbath day to do no work therein; then shall there enter into the gates of this city kings and princes sitting upon the throne of David, riding in chariots and on horses, they and their princes, the men of Judah and the inhabitants of Jerusalem; and this city shall remain forever. . . . But if ye will not hearken unto me to hallow the Sabbath day, and not to bear a burden, even entering in at the gates of Jerusalem on the Sabbath day; then will I kindle a fire in the gates thereof, and it shall devour the palaces of Jerusalem, and it shall not be quenched." Jer. 17 : 24, 25, 27. .

And when Jerusalem was overthrown by the Babylonians, the record states that it was to fulfill the word of the Lord by Jeremiah. 2 Chron. 36: 17–21. Nehemiah recognizes the same fact in the restoration. He says: " There dwelt men of Tyre also therein, which brought fish and all manner of ware, and sold on the Sabbath unto the children of Judah and in Jerusalem. Then I contended with the nobles of Judah, and said unto them, What evil thing is this that ye do and profane the Sabbath

bath? Reference. 10. What promise did the Lord by Jeremiah attach to Sabbath-keeping? 11. What calamity did he threaten upon the Jews for its violation? Reference. 12. When Jerusalem was overthrown what prediction did it fulfill? 13. What fact does Nehemiah recognize? 14. What

day? Did not your fathers thus, and did not God bring all this evil upon us, and upon this city? yet ye bring more wrath upon Israel by profaning the Sabbath." Neh. 13 : 16–18.

Here is an explicit acknowledgment that Jerusalem had been destroyed because their fathers had profaned the Sabbath, and that they would bring more wrath upon themselves if they continued in its violation. This is the way the Sabbath stood, the light in which it was held, and the promises and threatenings connected with its observance or violation, from Moses to Christ. And now can we for a moment suppose that such an institution that originated in Eden, that was a test of Israel's loyalty to God, that was declared to be a sign between God and them, and that forever, that was declared to be God's peculiar property, holy to him and honorable, one in the keeping of which his honor was involved, and one which if it had always been kept by that people, Jerusalem would have stood to this day, the pride and joy of that nation, and the ornament of all the earth,—can we suppose that this institution so suddenly changed its position and nature at the coming of Christ that it became at once the symbol of apostasy from God, rejection of Christ, and trust in the flesh? or rather, that God so changed his nature that now he abhors that in which he once took such delight, and pronounces a curse upon that to which he once attached the greatest of blessings? The idea is preposterously absurd. What imperfect ideas of God and

is his testimony? Reference. 15. What does this testimony acknowledge? 16. How long was the Sabbath held in this high regard? 17. What is the general view of it in the Old Testament? 18. If the Jews had always properly kept the Sabbath, what would have been the condition of Jerusalem to-day? 19. In supposing that we now fall from grace

his plans, must they have who can entertain such a thought.

In all the prophecies given in the former dispensation concerning the present one, and setting forth the position of the law and Sabbath under this new covenant, and the relation of Christ to these institutions, and the effect of his work upon them, the perpetuity of the law and the continuance of the Sabbath is in the strongest manner affirmed. Thus in the prophecy of the new covenant, Jer. 31 : 31–34, God promises to write his law in the hearts and minds of his people. Instead of being abolished, it would thus be enshrined in their inmost affections.

Again, in the prophecy concerning Christ, it is said that he should "magnify the law and make it honorable." Isa. 42 : 21. This could not be said of any law which he had to take out of the way by nailing it to his cross. And when Christ came into the world, his motives and purpose of action were set forth in the following language: "I delight to do thy will, O my God; yea, thy law is within my heart." Ps. 40 : 8; Heb. 10 : 6, 7.

There is one prophecy of a change of the law; but the power that was to change it, or rather think to change it (for that was all he would be able to do) was not Christ, but the little horn of the fourth beast of Dan. 7, the blasphemous papal power which was to speak great words against the Most High, wear out the saints of the Most High, and think

by keeping this institution, what absurdity is involved? 20. What position do the prophecies of the former dispensation assign to the Sabbath in this dispensation? 21. What place does the law occupy under the new covenant? Reference. 22. What does Isaiah say that Christ would do to the law? Reference. 23. Could this be said of the ceremonial law, and why not? 24. What is the language of Christ respecting the law when he came into the world? 25. Is there any prophecy of the change of the law? 26. What power was to

to change times and laws. The secular history of the Sabbath will show how this has been attempted, and that this prophecy can have been fulfilled in nothing but the change of the Sabbath. The feast days, new moons and ceremonial sabbaths which as shadows were to cease at the cross, God declared that he would take away. Hos. 2 : 11.

Thus we are brought to the time of Christ; and in his first recorded sermon he speaks thus definitely in regard to the law: "Think not that I am come to destroy the law or the prophets; I am not come to destroy but to fulfill. For verily I say unto you, Till heaven and earth pass, one jot or one tittle shall in no wise pass from the law, till all be fulfilled." Matt. 5 : 17, 18. Here is some law the perpetuity of which is affirmed in the strongest terms till the end of time; till all things spoken by the prophets are fulfilled. This certainly is not the law of ordinances and ceremonies, which he took out of the way, nailing it to his cross within less than three years and a half of the time when these words were spoken. Eph. 2 : 15; Col. 2 : 14. The law of which Christ speaks and declares that not a jot or tittle shall pass from it to the end of all things, is that law which determines the degree of our righteousness. Matt. 5 : 20. But man was to be righteous from the beginning, and all laws regulating that were primary laws applicable to him before the fall. The Sabbath law, as we have seen, was one of this kind. The perpetuity of the Sab-

change it? 27. What does the prophet say of the yearly sabbaths of the Jews? Reference. 28. In Christ's first recorded sermon, how does he speak of the law? Reference. 29. What does this text affirm? 30. Why cannot this refer to the ceremonial law? 31. What scriptures speak of the taking away of the ceremonial law? 32. How does Matt. 5 : 20 show what law our Lord refers to? 33. How does this show that the Sabbath is of perpetual obligation? 34. What

bath, therefore, throughout this dispensation is most expressly affirmed in this passage. For whatever is affirmed of a code of laws as a whole, is equally affirmed of every precept composing that code. Hence the solemn admonition which Christ utters, not to the Jews as such, but to his disciples, that whosoever should break one of these least commandments, and teach men so, he should be called least in the kingdom of Heaven, and the blessed promise to all who should both do and teach them, to be called great in the kingdom of Heaven.

In his ministry, our Lord seems to take especial pains to rescue the Sabbath from the burden of Jewish traditions. He declared that it was made for man, for his good, for Christians as well as Jews. It was not among those laws and requirements which were against us, and contrary to us, and which therefore were taken out of the way. He recognized the Sabbath law by repeatedly declaring that what he did, though contrary to the traditions of the Jews, was *lawful* to be done on that day. By all his teachings in reference to the law, and in all his life here upon the earth, declaring its holiness and perpetuity, and rendering perfect obedience to it, he magnified it and made it honorable, as the prophet declared he would do. By his death upon the cross he infinitely magnified and made it honorable. There he demonstrated its immutability and perpetuity by showing that nothing less than the death of God's divine Son interposed could release men from its inexorable claims.

may be said of the whole and its parts? 35. What admonition does Christ give to his disciples? 36. How did Christ treat the Sabbath in his ministry? 37. What did he recogn:ze by showing what was lawful on the Sabbath? 38. How did he magnify and make honorable the law? 39. What was shown by his death respecting the law? 40. After Christ's

The apostles took up the subject, and we hear Paul declaring that the law, the law of which the Sabbath is a part, is not made void by faith in Christ, but is established, confirmed, by such faith. Rom. 3:31. This cannot by any possibility refer to the typical law; for the moment we have faith in Christ, we set that law aside as an inevitable consequence. They frequently bring the Sabbath to view showing that they were accustomed to worship on it, Acts 17:2, that they knew of no other Sabbath but the seventh day then in existence, Acts 15:21, and that that was the day they took upon which to preach not to the Jews merely but also to the Gentiles. Acts 13:42, 44. The Sabbath is mentioned in the New Testament fifty-nine times, always in a way to show its still binding obligation.

Finally prophecies were given of a great Sabbath reform to take place just before the coming of Christ. Isa. 56:1, 2: "Thus saith the Lord, Keep ye judgment and do justice; for my salvation is near to come, and my righteousness to be revealed. Blessed is the man that doeth this, and the son of man that layeth hold on it; that keepeth the Sabbath from polluting it, and keepeth his hand from doing any evil." The Lord's salvation is near when the coming of Christ is near; for it is then brought to us. Heb. 9:28; 1 Pet. 1:5. And at that time

death what did Paul say of the law? Reference. 41. What text shows the custom of the apostles respecting the Sabbath? 42. What passage shows that they knew no other Sabbath but the seventh day? 43. What reference shows that they took that day to preach to the Gentiles as well as to the Jews? 44. How many times is the Sabbath mentioned in the New Testament? 45. What prophet, and where, points out a great Sabbath reform before the Lord comes? 46. What is meant by the Lord's salvation being near to come? 47. What passages in the New Testament

a blessing is pronounced upon those who lay hold on the Sabbath. The third angel's message, Rev. 14, brings out a company distinguished as commandment-keepers, by their observance of the Sabbath, just before the coming of Christ. The remnant, or last generation, of the church are distinguished in the same way. Rev. 12 : 17. And when in the closing testimony of the book, the Lord declares that he is coming quickly, he pauses to pronounce a blessing upon those who at that time are found keeping the commandments of God, and to promise them an abundant entrance into the city and free access to the tree of life. And even there the Sabbath attends them as a day of joy and worship; for about 800 years before this, the Lord, by the pen of Isaiah, had put this promise on record : " For as the new heavens and the new earth, which I will make shall remain before me, saith the Lord, so shall your seed and your name remain. And it shall come to pass that from one new moon to another, and from one Sabbath to another, shall all flesh come to worship before me saith the Lord." Isa. 66 : 22, 23.

Thus the Sabbath comes to view in Paradise restored, as it stood at first in Paradise lost; and in all the world's dark history between these two bright periods, it has been the golden clasp to bind earth to Heaven, and man to his Creator.

The Sabbath and the first day of the week in the New Testament will be the subject of a separate lesson.

_____

point out the same reform ?   48. What distinguishes the last generation of Christians ?   49. What promise is given to the commandment-keepers who are waiting for the coming of Christ ?   50. What is said of the Sabbath in the new earth ? 51. What is its office between paradise lost and paradise restored ?

CLASS QUESTIONS ON LESSON XI., WITH ANSWERS.

1. How long after the disappointment in 1844, was it before the sanctuary question was brought out, and the Sabbath adopted by the Adventists?

ANS. The Sabbath began to be observed among Adventists in that same year, 1844. Almost the entire church at Washington, N. H., besides several Adventist ministers, commenced its observance during that year. The subject of the sanctuary, as now held by us, was first written upon by O. R. L. Crozier in 1846.

2. Is there positive proof that Paul kept 78 Sabbaths at Corinth? It says that he reasoned in the synagogue every Sabbath; but after a short time he left the synagogue and went into Justus' house and "continued there a year and six months." Acts 18.

ANS. The regular time of Paul's meeting is at first particularly mentioned. It was every Sabbath. His object was to persuade, not the Jews alone, but the Greeks also. His change of place, verse 7, was not a change of city, nor even of his own lodgings, but only of his place of preaching; he left the synagogue, and continued his meetings in the house of one Justus, who lived close by the synagogue, but still in Corinth. His object and work was the same there, to teach the word of God among them. And the chief ruler of the synagogue, Crispus and all his house and many Corinthians were brought over. And this went on for the space of a year and six months, 78 weeks. Now where is there the first shadow of a reason to suppose that Paul did not use every Sabbath of this time as the day for religious gatherings and instruction, according to the manner in which he commenced? There is none. He says, indeed, verse 6, "Henceforth I will go unto the Gentiles." But we have found him a little before preaching to the Gentiles at their own request, but doing it on the very day that meetings were held in the synagogue, namely, the seventh-day Sabbath. Acts 13 : 42, 44. We have no right to presume a change of circumstances which have been once fairly described, unless some necessity for a change can be shown, or some testimony proving a change can be produced. But in this case the only change mentioned is the place of preaching and the class to whom he directed his efforts; no change in the nature of his preaching, nor in the *time* of his preaching. Therefore we consider the testimony positive that Paul kept 78 consecutive Sabbaths in Corinth.

3. On what day of the week did the 15th of Abib occur?

ANS. On all days of the week. The 15th of Abib was simply the 15th day of the month, and a day of the month comes on different days of the week from year to year.

4. Will the Sabbath be observed by the saints during the thousand years they are in Heaven? If so, what will mark the succession of days, which are here determined by the revolution of the earth?

ANS. Inasmuch as the Sabbath is binding upon us here till the end of time, and the prophet presents the fact that it will be observed after the close of the thousand years, when we come into possession of the new earth, we see no reason why there should be any break in the observance during the thousand years. And if we can there measure and determine the succession of years, as the record makes it sure that we can, we can also determine that of months and weeks,

5. Do angels keep the Sabbath day?

ANS. On this question we can do little more than conjecture, or perhaps draw a fair inference. We read in Ps. 103 : 20, that the angels "do his commandments, hearkening unto the voice of his word." And our Lord taught his disciples to pray, "Thy will be done in earth as it is in Heaven." Matt. 6 : 10. From this we infer that when earth is brought into harmony with Heaven, God's will will be carried out in the same manner, and by the same worship, in both places. Hence we may reason from what we know would be carrying out God's will here, to what it is there. But here God has ordained that we keep the Sabbath in honor of himself; hence we infer that the higher orders of his intelligences keep the Sabbath also. Indeed it seems to us a consistent and beautiful idea to suppose that all God's creative work has been so performed with reference to periods of rest, that the Sabbath of each of his creatures will be the Sabbath of all the rest, so that all will observe the same period together for the same purpose.

6. Would it be right for a person to go to his place of business before the Sabbath had ended with the intention of doing business *after* it had ended, if he had to walk or ride some distance to reach it?

ANS. The commandment forbids our doing any of our own work or business on the Sabbath day. Going to or from our place of business is certainly a part of our work. It plainly is not God's work and should not be performed on his time.

7. Are the tables on which the commandments were written and the ark which contained them still in existence? Where in Bible history are they last mentioned?

Ans. The ark is last mentioned historically, we believe, in 1 Kings 8 : 4–9, when it was brought with great pomp and rejoicing and placed in the temple which Solomon had built, according to Usher's chronology, B. C. 1005. Here it remained till the destruction of this temple by Nebuchadnezzar, B. C. 588. What then became of it is not positively known. A passage in the book of Maccabees leads some to suppose that it was concealed by Jeremiah the prophet, and will be discovered again before the end. The passage reads as follows : Jeremy the prophet, " being warned of God, commanded the tabernacle and the ark to go with him, as he went forth into the mountain where Moses climbed up, and saw the heritage of God. And when Jeremy came thither he found a hollow cave, wherein he laid the tabernacle and the ark, and the altar of incense, and so stopped the door. And some of those that followed him, came to mark the way, but they could not find it ; which, when Jeremy perceived, he blamed them saying, As for this place it shall be unknown until the time that God gather his people again together and receive them unto mercy." 2 Mac. 2 : 4–7.

LESSON TWELVE.

THE SABBATH THEORY OF AKERS, JENNINGS, MEDE AND FULLER.

A theory of the Sabbath, not newly invented, but an old theory newly modified, and now generally known as Akers' Theory, has come to be received quite largely with a certain denomination,

REVIEW QUESTIONS ON LESSON TWELVE.

1. What is the theory generally known as Akers' Theory?

and is therefore here presented in a separate lesson. This theory, briefly stated, is, that the day now known as the first day of the week, and kept as the Sabbath, is the day which God originally blessed and gave to Adam as the Sabbath; so that in keeping the first day of the week, we are keeping the original seventh day according to the commandment. This would be a splendid way out of the Sabbath difficulty if it could be sustained; and multitudes have been made to hope that Mr. A. would confirm them in their practice of Sunday sabbatizing, which they are so unwilling to abandon.

We find objections to this position in two directions: first, in the fact that in many particulars it contradicts the positive testimony of the Scriptures, and secondly, in the self-contradictions and absurdities involved in the theory itself.

It is certain that if we are now keeping the original seventh day, by keeping Sunday, the Jews did not keep that original seventh day; for they did not keep Sunday, but the day before. It follows, therefore, from this position, that there have been, to the present time, two changes of the Sabbath; first, from the Adamic to the Mosaic or Jewish Sabbath; secondly, from the Jewish to the present, or Christian Sabbath. We have supposed that the necessity of proving one change was a sufficient burden for the first-day Sabbath. That is a bold, and we shall find it a reckless and presumptuous one, which advocates two. To see how they do this, we will look at the position which each one of these men has taken.

First in point of time comes Mr. Joseph Mede, who early in the seventeenth century announced to

2. In what respect are there objections to this theory? 3. According to this theory, how many changes of the Sabbath have there been? 4. Who first in point of time suggested

the world a wonderful discovery, namely, that the Hebrew people did not have the original Sabbath which had been binding from creation to Moses, but that Saturday was given them in place of the original Sabbath, because on this day God overthrew Pharaoh in the Red Sea. Mr. M. was very sure the Sabbath was thus changed at this time, but what day it was changed from he could not tell. See Jennings' Jewish Antiquities, pp. 329, 330.

This theory is too indefinite to be more than simply stated. But the seed had been dropped which was after two hundred years to spring up and bear baleful fruit. If it could only be shown that the Jews had a changed Sabbath and we have the original, that would suit much better than the idea that they had the original Sabbath, and we have the one that is changed. So a hundred years from the days of Mr. Mede, Dr. Jennings arises and responds, virtually, "That is a splendid idea of yours, Bro. Mede, that the Sabbath was changed for the Jews at the commencement of their dispensation, but you are altogether wrong in the time when it occurred, and you are wrong in reference to the place where it occurred, and you are wrong in the arguments you adduce to sustain it; but your idea is nevertheless all right and true! However, the overthrow of Pharaoh had nothing to do with this change; it did not take place at the crossing of the Red Sea, but at a later point, when the manna was given."

Dr. Jennings' theory recognizes the institution of the Sabbath at the close of the work of creation, and binding from that time to Moses. But there

this theory? 5. What was Mede's theory? 6. How long after Mede did Jennings appear? 7. According to Jennings how far was Mede wrong? 8. Where does Dr. J.'s theory

he contends for a change; and to be a little more definite than Mr. Mede, he proposes to tell what day the Sabbath was changed from when a new one was given to the Hebrews. So he undertakes to "make it appear to be probable" that "the Jewish Sabbath was appointed to be kept the day before the patriarchal Sabbath." Antiquities, p. 320. That is to say, the Sabbath was set back one day for the Jews to Saturday, and the Sabbath in regular succession of seventh days from the creation would come the day following, on Sunday. His principal argument for this position is the following: The manna fell for six days, and was withheld on the seventh, this seventh day was Saturday, and was ever after to be observed as the Sabbath by the Hebrews. As the manna had fallen six days before this Saturday on which it was withheld, it began to fall on Sunday; and the day before it began to fall, or Saturday, was spent by the Israelites journeying from Elim to Sin.

This argument stands on three legs, every one of which breaks down when we bring the pressure of examination upon it. For, first, it cannot be proved that the journey from Elim to Sin was on Saturday; and even Dr. Akers, who labors strenuously to reach the same point Dr. Jennings is trying to prove, denies that this journey was on Saturday, declaring that it took place on Monday. Secondly, it cannot be proved that one or more days did not elapse after Israel arrived at Sin, before the manna began to fall. Thirdly, it cannot be proved that the manna fell six days before the Sabbath spoken of in connection therewith in Ex. 16; as the sixth day there mentioned is the sixth day of the week, and

place the institution of the Sabbath? 9. What change was made at the exodus? 10. What is his argument from the manna? 11. In what respects does this argument fail?

has no reference to the number of days upon which
the manna had fallen. These assumptions constituting the warp and woof of his position, when
these are taken away nothing is left.

With a glance at the monstrous absurdities into
which this theory explodes like a rocket, and disap-
pears, we leave it: 1. We have the original Sabbath
abolished for them five days before the new Sabbath was instituted.   2. We have a period of
twelve days without any Sabbath at all; and 3. We
have the providence of God in the giving of the
manna requiring them to violate the Sabbath, when
it was to prove their willingness to keep the Sabbath, that the manna was given. Thus, according
to Dr. J., the 15th of Abib, on which they journeyed
from Elim to Sin, was Saturday. The next day,
Sunday, the 16th, which had been the Sabbath
from Eden down to that point, the manna began to
fall, and they had to go out and gather it, which
showed they were no longer to regard that day as
the Sabbath. The manna fell six days to the 22d
of Abib, when the people rested. And this was
the first rest they had had since Sunday the 9th of
Abib, thirteen days before. For the Saturday
before, the 15th, had not then been instituted as the
Sabbath; if it had been, says Dr. J., they would not
have journeyed from Elim to Sin; and the Sunday
before, the 16th, had ceased to be the Sabbath for
that people, if it had not, the manna would not
have begun to fall then, causing the people to go
out and engage in their secular labor by gathering
it. We have, consequently, a period of twelve full
days from the 9th to the 22d of Abib without any
Sabbath; we have the original Sabbath abolished
on the 16th of Abib, five days before the new was

12. In what absurdities does this theory end? 13. How
long a period does he give us without a Sabbath? 14. Who

instituted on the 22d; we have God saying, I will rain bread from heaven to prove you whether you will walk in my law or no; and lo! the very day that bread begins to fall, it happens to be the original Sabbath, and they are obliged to violate it by going out to gather their food. Thus in following the providence of God in the giving of the manna, they are obliged to break the law of God in disregarding his Sabbath. And what is remarkable the people express no surprise that they are obliged, without any previous instruction, to violate the original Sabbath, and ready as they were to complain and rebel at the slightest grievances, they close up one week's labor with the march from Elim to Sin, and immediately enter upon a second week of labor in gathering the manna, without a murmur.

Something more than another hundred years elapse, and there appears that prodigy among chronologists, Dr. Akers. In 1855 he gave to the world the result of his lucubrations. He seizes upon the idea that the Sabbath was changed for the Hebrews in the days of Moses as one too good to be lost, but one which unfortunately had not down to his day been sustained by any adequate proof. But he will remedy this matter, and will retain the kernel of this nut for Sabbatarians, though he does not consider that the efforts of Mede or Jennings, in their attempts to sustain this idea, amount to respectable shucks. He therefore places the change at a different point of time from either of the others, namely, not at the fall of the manna, nor at the passage of the Red Sea, but on the 15th of Abib,

---

came to the rescue of this theory next after Jennings? 15. How long? 16. In what year was Akers' work published? 17. In what respect according to Akers, is Jennings' theory wrong? 18. What is Akers' method of argument? 19. What change does Akers make at the exode? 20.

when the children of Israel started on their exodus
from Egypt. And how does he attempt to show that
this was Saturday the sixth day of the original
week, and should be kept by that people as the
Sabbath instead of the day following, which was
the Edenic Sabbath, and which had been kept down
to that time? He takes his stand at the crucifixion
of Christ, which he places on the 28th of March A.
D. 28, in the year of the world 5573. From this
point he reckons back to the rest-day of the Lord
at the close of creation week, and finds just 290,767
weeks, from which he claims that the *seventh* day
of Gen. 2, is the *first* day of Matt. 28 : 1 ; and that
the creation was begun on Monday, Sept. 15. From
this point he then reckons down to the day Israel
left Egypt, and finds the 15th of Abib to be the sixth
day of the week. Here he has to re-arrange matters generally ; and under cover of the institution of
the sacred year at this point, slips in a new week,
jogging the reckoning back one day, making the
last day of the previous week the first day of the
new, and the sixth day of the old week the seventh
day of the new. And this day that people were to
regard as the Sabbath. Having thus re-adjusted
his machine, it runs first-rate down to the resurrection of Christ, but there it comes to a dead stop,
being entirely out of joint with the arrangement
that follows. Here that peculiarly Jewish arrangement of Sabbaths and weeks should disappear, and
the patriarchal arrangement revive. The Sabbath
should go back to its original day, Sunday, and the
week should resume its old order, which would
make Sunday its seventh day. He has no hesi-
tancy in claiming that the Sabbath went back to
Sunday ; but lo, the week refuses to change ; for

What change does this make necessary at the cross ? 21.
Will his week change back there ? 22. What shows this ?

the Sunday following the Jewish seventh day, four
of the inspired writers call plainly the *first day* of
the week. But what does it matter if the inspired
writers have inadvertently called this the first day,
has not Dr. A. proved by actual count from creation
that it is the true *seventh* day, and is that *count* to
be set aside by the simple fact that the evangelists
happen to use the word in this manner!!

On what authority then does Dr. A.'s count rest?
He adopts the chronology of the Septuagint, a
Greek translation of the Old Testament reputed to
have been made at Alexandria in Egypt, about 280
years before Christ, though this is disputed by some.
This chronology gives us, between the creation and
the exodus, 1386 years more than the Hebrew
Scriptures, and down to the Christian era, 1426
years more. Dr. A. therefore by adopting the Septuagint, sets aside the Hebrew as entirely unreliable.
But is the Septuagint of such undoubted authority
in this particular? Dr. A. himself confesses that it
sometimes needs correcting. For instance it makes
Methuselah survive the flood some fourteen years;
and he corrects this strange error only by following
those copies of the Septuagint which *in this particular case* conform to the numbers given in the
Hebrew. Thus the doctor shows himself adequate
to the task of meeting every difficulty, first by
adopting the Septuagint, and rejecting the Hebrew
as wholly unreliable, then falling back upon the Hebrew to correct some of the glaring and notorious

23. With what is Dr. A.'s count thus brought into direct
conflict? 24 Upon what authority does his computation
rest? 25. What is the Septuagint translation and when
was it made? 26. How does this differ in chronology from
the Hebrew? 27. What does Dr. A. himself confess in
regard to the Septuagint? 28. Where does this chronology
place the death of Methuselah? 29. How does Dr. A. get
over this difficulty? 30. What does he have to do further

errors of the Septuagint, and lastly by correcting the Septuagint in other particulars by such authorities as he may judge to be reliable. But what is a chronology good for, the value of which depends upon its accuracy even to a day, that rests upon such palpable uncertainties? A more unreasonable claim could scarcely be put forth than this which pretends to give the exact number of days from creation to the present time. Dr. E. O. Haven, formerly president of the University of Michigan, and likewise a Methodist clergyman, whose name overtops that of Dr. A. as the cedar of Lebanon towers above the bramble, pronounces such an effort at chronology a complete failure.

Again, Dr. A. places the creation on Sept. 15, but the Rabbins on Oct. 7, yet he takes up their reckoning to show that Sunday was the original seventh day. But if his date is right theirs is wrong, and *vice versa*. But besides this difference of 22 days, the two systems of chronology differ 1785 years to the exodus, yet the doctor has so wonderful a system of chronology that he can prove himself right by either. Whether the world was created Sept. 15 or Oct. 7, some 1785 years later, it is all the same to him. He can show in either case that Sunday is the true seventh day any way. What further proof is needed that his method of reasoning is altogether sophistical and deceptive.

But how does Dr. A. help the matter? Let us see what he asks us to believe: 1. That the first day of time was Monday. 2. That God gave up

to make his theory stand? 31. What may and must be said of that claim which professes to give the exact number of days in the age of the world? 32. What is Dr. Haven's testimony? 33. Where does Dr. A. place the creation? 34. Where do the Rabbins place it? 35. How does their chronology differ from Dr. A.'s? 36. Yet what does Dr. A. prove by their chronology? 37. What is the first point we must

his own rest-day to be desecrated by his chosen people during the whole period of their separate existence, giving them in its stead only a ceremonial Sabbath which they were to sacredly observe. 3. That God gave them a new week made up of the seventh day of one of his weeks, and the first six days of the following. 4. That here was a genuine week, with only six days in it. 5. That when that arrangement ceased, the week refused to go back, and God's seventh day is now our first day. 6. That the sixth day, with which the new week given to Israel closed, was made into a new Sabbath. 7. That this sixth day was then made into the seventh. And 8. That at Christ's resurrection two Sabbaths came together.

It is not to be greatly wondered at that such a tissue of confusion should not be suffered long to remain without some one making an effort to tinker it into greater consistency. So some ten years after the publication of Dr. Akers' book, the Rev. E. Q. Fuller tried his hand at this very desirable, but yet unaccomplished job. He likes the main idea which they are trying to establish. He likes Akers' reckoning of time even to days, and he thinks Akers has fixed the time and place of the change all right, but does not rightly state the change. He will have it that the Sabbath was changed at the exode, not from the seventh day to the sixth, as Dr. A. asserts, but from the first day to the seventh. And this he brings about in this way. The first six days of creation belong to eternity, not time. The seventh day was Adam's first day,

and there time began, and the week began with its
first day as a Sabbath.   At the exode the Sabbath
was set back from this first day of the week to the
seventh; but the week was not changed as Dr. A.
asserts.   This went on to the resurrection of Christ
when this seventh day Sabbath was abolished, leaving the first day Sabbath in all its glory.   Thus Fuller
gives us a week at the exode with two Sabbaths in
it, and one at the resurrection of Christ, with no
Sabbath in it.   It will be seen at once how he contradicts Akers in some of his most essential particulars.   But what is most remarkable, he depends
on Akers' count of the days; yet he begins with
the seventh day, six days later than Dr. A. and
proceeding on the same count, comes out exactly
the same!   Where is all this putty and India-
rubber?   In these men's hearts, or in their heads?

We have said but little by way of comparing the
theories of these men with the Bible; nor is it necessary to speak particularly on that point.   Read the
record of Gen. 2, and the fourth commandment.   If
the Sabbath given in that commandment is not the
very day upon which God rested and which he
blessed in the beginning, it is a deception.   For an
exhaustive examination of the theories of these
men and an exposure of the wicked course of the
later writers on this subject, the reader is referred
to the pamphlet entitled, "Sunday Seventh-day
Examined.   A Refutation of the teachings of Mede,
Jennings, Akers and Fuller, by Eld. J. N. Andrews."

Fuller's theory?   48.   What kind of a week does Fuller
give us at the exode?   49.   What kind at the crucifixion?
50.   What is remarkable about his use of Dr. A.'s count of
the days?   51.   What day is enjoined as the Sabbath in the
commandment?   52.   Where and by whom are these theories
fully exposed?

LESSON THIRTEEN.

SABBATH AND SUNDAY——SECULAR HISTORY.

THOUSANDS upon thousands suppose that history shows a unanimous and uninterrupted observance of Sunday on the part of Christians from the days of Christ, and that just as unanimously and continually, the seventh day which had been the Sabbath to that time, was disregarded by them. Many innocently hold this view in ignorance; others assert it who know better than to believe it.

The popular Sunday view is well expressed in these words of Mosheim: "All Christians were unanimous in setting apart the first day of the week, on which the triumphant Saviour arose from the dead, for the solemn celebration of public worship. This pious custom which was derived from the church of Jerusalem, was founded upon the express appointment of the apostles, who consecrated that day to the same sacred purposes, and was observed universally throughout the Christian churches, as appears from the united testimonies of the most credible writers."

This reads very much to the mind of the Sunday-keeper; but lo! in the following century another historian, equally worthy of credit, arises and says: "The festival of Sunday, like all other festivals, was always only a human ordinance, and it was far from the intentions of the apostles to establish a divine command in this respect; far from them, and from the early apostolic church, to transfer the laws of

---

1. What historian states the Sunday view? 2. What is his language? 3. What historian makes a counter statement? 4. What is his language? 5. When did these his-

the Sabbath to Sunday. Perhaps at the end of the second century a false application of this kind had begun to take place; for men appear by that time to have considered laboring on Sunday as a sin." *Neander's Ch. Hist., as translated by H. J. Rose, p. 186.*

Mosheim was a writer of the 18th, Neander of the 19th, century. From what source did they obtain the information they give us respecting Sunday? No one lived from apostolic times to their day to tell them how it was and had been. They were dependent on the records which have come down from that time. We have the same, and can thus test the truthfulness of their assertions. Mosheim, indeed, declares that it was founded upon the express appointment of the apostles. Where is that appointment? It is not in the New Testament. Mosheim's assertion avails nothing, therefore, for Protestants; for it can be used only by departing from the Protestant ground of "the Bible and the Bible alone," and adopting the Romanist position, "the Bible and tradition."

The whole question sums itself up in this one proposition: that Sunday was called the Lord's day in the days of John, and from that time onward; and that such a title showed that it was the Sabbath of this dispensation. This proposition we deny, and shall now examine.

John in Rev. 1:10 does not mean the first day of the week by the term Lord's day; for he twice afterward speaks of that day, but calls it simply first day of the week. John 20:1, 19. John's gospel

---

torians respectively flourish? 6. Where are they therefore obliged to go for their authority? 7. What rule would Mosheim's statement compel us to adopt? 8. What proposition is the sum of the whole Sunday question? 9. What does John mean by the term "Lord's day" in Rev. 1:10?

was written in A. D. 98, two years after the book of
Revelation. He must mean by that term that day
which the Lord has claimed as his, which is the seventh day of the week. Ex. 20 : 10, Isa. 58 : 13, and
in the New Testament, we have testimony to show
that the day which Christ is Lord of is the Sabbath,
the seventh day. "The Son of man is Lord even of
the Sabbath day," the seventh day. Matt. 12: 8;
Mark 2: 27.

We now notice all the writers who are claimed to
have applied the title of Lord's day to Sunday, down
to the close of the second century.

First. Ignatius is quoted, in his epistle to the
Magnesians. But the reader will find history sustaining the following facts in regard to this matter:
1. No epistle was written by Ignatius, the disciple of
John, to the Magnesians. That epistle is a forgery.
2. Even that forgery does not say anything about
the Lord's day. That has been added by the additional fraud of some subsequent writer. 3. The
term, Lord's day, does not occur in the entire writings of this father, either in the spurious, or those
which are supposed to be genuine.

Secondly. Pliny, A. D. 104, is quoted as saying
that this question was put to the martyrs: "Have
you kept the Lord's day?" and the answer was, "I am
a Christian, I cannot omit it." What splendid testimony this would be, if it was only true. And how
many have been confirmed in their false practice by
this quotation. The testimony professes to come from
a work entitled, *Acta Martyrum*, or The Acts of the

References. 10. What father is first quoted as calling Sunday the Lord's day? 11. In what epistle? 12. What is the
nature of that epistle? ·13. Does that forged epistle say anything about the Lord's day? 14. Does the term, Lord's day,
occur in the entire writings of Ignatius? 15. What writer
is referred to as the second authority? 16. What is the
claim urged from Pliny's writing? 17. From what work

Martyrs. But the testimony of Mosheim on this work, is that it is of no authority whatever; and even if it was it contains no such expression as is here ascribed to it. Gilfillan, unwilling to lose the testimony, refers for authority to Baronius. But what Baronius speaks of, is the martyrdom of Saturninus and his four sons, in Northern Africa; but this was in A. D. 303, not in the time of Pliny, two hundred years before; and the question put was not "Have you kept the Lord's day?" but "Have you celebrated the Lord's supper?" Thus vanishes another famous falsehood put forth in behalf of Sunday.

Thirdly. Justin Martyr, A. D. 140, is quoted as calling Sunday the Lord's day. But Justin gives no such title to Sunday, nor any other title whatever. He simply says, "On the day called Sunday, all who live in cities or in the country, gather together to one place, and the memoirs of the apostles, or the writings of the prophets are read as long as time permits," etc. Justin Martyr's First Apology, chap. LXVII. But some one, wishing his testimony, has deliberately put in "the Lord's day," instead of Sunday, and added, "because that is the day of our Lord's resurrection." Thus Justin is made to testify in behalf of Sunday as the Lord's day only by fraud.

Fourthly. Theophilus, A. D. 162, is introduced as a witness in behalf of Sunday. Justin Edwards' Sabbath Manual, p. 114, presents this case as follows:—

---

does this claim to be taken? 18. What is the nature of the *Acta Martyrum*? 19. Does any such expression occur in that work? 20. What authority does Gilfillan refer to? 21. When did the event referred to by Baronius take place? 22. What was the questions then put to the martyrs? 23. Who next is quoted? 24. Does Justin Martyr ever give the title of Lord's day, or any other title, to Sunday? 25. Who is the fourth writer quoted? 26. What is the quotation

"Theophilus, bishop of Antioch, about A. D. 162, says: 'Both custom and reason challenge from us that we should honor *the Lord's day*, seeing on that day it was that our Lord Jesus completed his resurrection from the dead.'"

We have presented the quotation in full because we have the curious fact that nothing of the kind whatever can be found in the writings of Theophilus. He does not once use the term Lord's day; he does not even speak of the first day of the week. It is astonishing beyond expression that testimony can be thus manufactured from nothing and be deliberately ascribed to these early fathers.

Fifthly. Dionysius of Corinth, A. D. 170, is quoted. Dionysius does use the term, Lord's day, or rather, "the Lord's holy day," but he makes no application of it to any day of the week. He says nothing to show what day of the week he means. Having found the first four witnesses for Sunday inexcusable frauds, it cannot be claimed that this was the familiar name for Sunday and did not need to be defined. And no writer, for a long time after Dionysius, applies such a title as "Lord's *holy* day" to Sunday. But this was the title of the Sabbath of the Lord; and at this very time, in Greece, the country of Dionysius, the Sabbath was extensively observed as an act of obedience to the fourth commandment. All the probabilities in his testimony, therefore, point to the Sabbath instead of Sunday.

Sixthly. Melito of Sardis, A. D. 177, is brought forward as the sixth witness. His testimony is

given from him? 27. Is anything of this kind to be found in the writings of Theophilus? 28. Who is the fifth father quoted? 29. What term does Dionysius use? 30. Does he tell what day of the week he means? 31. From what country was Dionysius? 32. How was the Sabbath regarded in that country at that time? 33. Who is the sixth writer

made to do service on this wise: He wrote several
books of which only the titles have been preserved
to us.   One of these, as given in the English version
of Eusebius, is, "On the Lord's Day."   This of course
is claimed to be a treatise on Sunday, though it cannot be shown that any writer down to this point
calls Sunday by that name.   But the most remarkable
thing about it is that the essential word "day" is not
found in the original.   So it was simply a discourse
about something pertaining to the Lord; and it may
have been, and doubtless was, a treatise on the life
of Christ, as Eusebius uses the expression "Lord's
life," *kuriakeen zoeen*, in connection.

Seventhly.   Irenæus is quoted by Justin Edwards
as follows: "On the Lord's day every one of us
Christians keeps the Sabbath, meditating on the
law, and rejoicing in the works of God."   The great
reason why this is not good testimony for Sunday
is that not a word of the kind can be found in
Irenæus.   The term "Lord's day" is not to be found
in any of his writings, nor in any fragments of his
writings preserved in other authors.

These are the seven witnesses through whom the
Romish church, copied by Protestants, trace their
Lord's day back to, and identify it with, the Lord's
day of the Bible.   But the first, second, third,
fourth, and seventh of these, are inexcusable frauds;
the fifth speaks of the Lord's day, but does not tell
us what day it is, and the sixth writes something
about the Lord, but tells us nothing about a day.

A little later, Clement of Alexandria, A. D. 194,
uses the title with reference to the eighth day; but

quoted?   34. What is the testimony drawn from him?   35.
Does the word, day occur in the title of his last book?   36.
What was his treatise then probably concerning?   37. Who
is the seventh witness?   38. What is the objection to this
testimony from Irenæus?   39. How and when does Clement

in his explanation he makes this to signify, not the first day of the week, but Heaven itself.

The next writer who uses the term is Tertullian, A. D. 200; and he applies it definitely to the day of Christ's resurrection. This, says Kitto, is the first authentic application of this kind; and this was 104 years after John wrote the book of Revelation, and 169 years after the resurrection of Christ. This sustains the statement of Neander, that perhaps at the end of the second century men had begun to make a false application of the laws of the Sabbath to Sunday; "for men appear," he says, "by that time to have considered laboring on Sunday a sin."

Origen, A. D. 231, is the third writer who calls the "eighth day" the Lord's day. But he uses it in two senses: 1. For a natural day, in which sense it ranks with the Preparation day, the Passover, and the Pentecost; and 2. For a mystical day, as did Clement, in which sense it stands for the whole Christian life.

We have thus traced the Lord's day as far as it is needful. This Lord's day as it now exists, first appears in the early apostasy of the church; but between that and the days of the apostles there is a fatal break, which men have endeavored to bridge over by a series of fearful frauds. An honest mind will desert any institution which is obliged to depend on such support.

Two more quotations only remain to be noticed before we come to the time of Constantine, A. D. 321. The first is the so-called epistle of Barnabas, which says, "We observe the eighth day with glad-

of Alexandria use the term? 40. Where and when do we find the first authentic application of Lord's day to the first day of the week? 41. How long was this after the resurrection of Christ? and how long after John wrote the Revelation? 42. How and when does Origen use the term? 43.

ness, in which Jesus arose from the dead." This was not an epistle from Barnabas, the companion of Paul. Mosheim, Neander, Stuart, Dr. Killen, Prof. Hackett, Milner, Kitto, Encyclopedia of Religious Knowledge, Eusebius, Domville and Coleman, all unite in declaring it a forgery, the production of a Jew of mean abilities, who lived at a much later period than that of the true Barnabas. The second is a quotation from Pliny, stating that the Christians were wont to meet together on a "stated day." It is claimed that this stated day was Sunday. But how do they know? The essential link in the evidence is wanting; for he does not say what day of the week it was.

In A. D. 321 a new era dawned upon the Sunday institution. In that year Constantine, on the throne of the Roman empire, enacted a law in behalf of the "venerable day of the sun," from which it soon came to be the venerable day in the church. Of the effect of this law Mosheim thus speaks:—

"The first day of the week, which was the ordinary and stated time for the public assemblies of the Christians, was in consequence of a peculiar law enacted by Constantine, observed with greater solemnity than it had formerly been."

What, then, did Constantine's law require? It read as follows:—

"Let all the judges and town people, and the occupation of all trades rest on the venerable day of the sun; but let those who are situated in the country, freely and at full liberty attend to the business of agriculture; because it often happens that no

What is to be said of the Epistle of Barnabas? 44. Name the authors who condemn it. 45. What can be said of Pliny's "stated day"? 46. What took place in A. D. 321? 47. What did this law of Constantine's provide? 48. What does Mosheim say of the effect of this law? 49. What fol-

other day is so fit for sowing corn and planting
vines; lest the critical moment being let slip, men
should lose the commodities granted by Heaven."

It follows, therefore, according to the testimony
of Mosheim, that if this law, restraining only town
people and trades, caused Sunday to be observed more
strictly than formerly, no restraint had previously
been laid upon any class from working on that day.

Constantine's law, it will be noticed, speaks not
of the Lord's day, or the Christian Sabbath, but of
"the venerable day of the sun." This was the
heathen, not the Christian, name of that day.
And this law was in behalf of Sunday as a
heathen, not a Christian, institution. This will
appear by comparing dates. The law was dated
A. D. 321. Constantine did not experience his so-
called conversion to Christianity till A. D. 323, two
years afterward. The day following his Sunday
law, he enacted another, regulating the work of the
soothsayers who foretold future events by examin-
ing the entrails of beasts offered in sacrifice to the
gods; fitting companion to the preceding.

But how did this heathen law come to have a
bearing upon Sunday as a Christian observance?
The pope of Rome cheerfully looked after that
matter. When Constantine professed Christianity,
his Sunday law was left on the statute book unre-
pealed; and Sylvester, bishop of Rome, since called
pope, took advantage of this fact, and giving the
day the imposing title of Lord's day, by his apostolic authority, enforced it upon the church as a
Christian institution. Constantine also, then deem-

lows from this statement? 50. What was the nature of
Constantine's law? 51. When was it enacted? 52. When
was Constantine nominally converted to Christianity? 53.
What law did he enact the day following his Sunday law?
54. How did this come to be a Christian law? 55. What

ing himself as much the head of the church as the pope, took upon himself to elevate it still further, by church authority, as a Christian observance, taking "upon him," says Heylyn, not only "to command the day, but also to prescribe the service."

The parts which paganism and the papacy have acted in the elevation of Sunday are now plain to be seen. From the earliest times, the first day of the week, in the religion of idolatry, was dedicated to the worship of the sun; so that when Christianity came into contact with that false system, Sunday was a venerable day throughout all the heathen world.

In the Christian church, being the day of Christ's resurrection, it appeared as a festival, observed in the same manner, and for the same reason that they observed the day of the crucifixion, the day of the ascension, etc. But as heathenism and Christianity approached each other, and illustrious pagans became half converts to the gospel, seeking to engraft their Gnostic notions upon the Christian scheme, the question of expediency suggested that it would tend to conciliate their heathen neighbors, and also to promote the spread of Christianity among them, for Christians to pay more especial honors to their great festival day.   They could do it as Christians, and please them as pagans.

In the days of Constantine so near had the two systems come together that it was not difficult to transfer institutions from one to the other.   Sunday had heretofore run on the pagan track; now it could be switched off upon the Christian. *Pope Sylvester turned the switch*; and henceforth Sunday is a palace sleeping car upon the Christian track, and not upon the heathen.

---

are the parts paganism and the papacy have played in this matter?   56. What is the testimony of Roman Catholic cate-

We need not trace it any further. Roman Catholic catechisms tell us the place it occupies in that church, and the claims they base upon it. They hesitate not to acknowledge that the church has changed the Sabbath from the seventh day to the first day of the week, without any sanction from the Scriptures, or any outward command from God. And they boast of this as an evidence of their power to legislate in sacred things. Says the "Abridgment of Christian Doctrine" (Catholic catechism):—

"*Ques.* How prove you that the church hath power to command feasts and holy days?

"*Ans.* By the very act of changing the Sabbath into Sunday, which Protestants allow of; and therefore they fondly contradict themselves by keeping Sunday strictly, and breaking most other feasts commanded by the same church."

In the latter part of the 16th century a controversy broke out between the Presbyterians and the Episcopalians, which brought the Sunday question on Protestant grounds to an issue. The Episcopalians were for retaining all the feasts commanded by the church. The Presbyterians were for rejecting them, as being but popish leaven and superstition; yet they retained Sunday. The Episcopalians retorted that if they gave up the others they must give up the Sunday, or if they kept that they must keep all the others, to be consistent, for they all rested on the same foundation, namely, the authority of the church. Then it was that, driven to find some support from the Scriptures, the "Rev. Nicholas Bound, D. D.," A. D. 1595, invented the seventh part of time fallacy, which is even to this day, with many theologians, their stock in trade on the Sunday question.

The limits of this lesson will not permit a further notice of the Sabbath, historically, than merely to say that Sabbath-keepers can be traced in an unbroken succession all through the gospel dispensation, from the church of Jerusalem to the present time.

For the historical facts above stated, we are indebted to " The History of the Sabbath " by Eld. J. N. Andrews, a work of extensive and exhaustive research on this question, unanswered and unanswerable. To this we refer the reader and all others who desire reliable information on this subject.

CLASS QUESTIONS ON LESSON XIII., WITH ANSWERS.

1. WAS the true church observing the seventh day at the time it passed into the wilderness?

ANS. Yes. The church went into the wilderness by being overborne by the apostasies and corruptions of the times. When the great apostate church had arisen and overshadowed Christendom, the true church, the real people of God, were crowded into obscurity. It was a gradual work. So the coming out from that wilderness state is a gradual work; but before the Lord comes, the church will be fully out, and keeping the Sabbath, as it was before it went into the wilderness. This is the secret of the great Sabbath reform now going forth under the last message.

2. Is it true that Christ was raised from the dead on the first day of the week?

ANS. We think it is. But even if we thought

---

it was not, we should never raise any controversy over the point; for more would be lost than gained by it. The idea is firmly planted in the public mind that the resurrection of Christ did occur on the first day of the week. And if we contest that point, they will inevitably interpret it as a concession on our part to the idea that if the resurrection did occur on that day, it proves that day to be the Christian Sabbath; if not, they will say, why labor so hard to disprove it ? And it will take ten times more effort to make people believe that the resurrection did not occur on the first day of the week, than it will to convince them that even if it did occur then, it has no bearing whatever on the Sabbath question. Spend no time discussing doubtful or unessential points. Take issue on vital questions, and then make your positions very clear and strong.

3. Isa. 56 : 12. Is "this day" the day of the Sabbath, so frequently referred to all through the chapter, and the "to-morrow," the day following, or Sunday ?

ANS. We think the passage can have no application of this kind. And while nothing would be gained by applying it so, it would be considered fanciful, and hence would be objectionable. The same may be said of the question whether Hos. 6 : 7 does not prove that Adam had the law of God in his day.

4. Please state how the "round world theory" is used as an objection to the Sabbath, and give the answer.

ANS. The objection proceeds on the assumption that those who keep the Sabbath, must keep the same absolute, not relative, time; and, as time differs at different points east and west, this cannot be done. Therefore the Sabbath cannot be kept around the world. And this objection, strange to say, almost invariably comes from those who are great sticklers for Sunday, and who believe it should be kept in every essential particular just as we claim for the Sabbath. If they can find the first day of the week around the world, why cannot we find the seventh, which is just the day before? It is a fact which few are so unreasonable as to deny, that the day, by means of those operations of nature which God has ordained to govern the lapse of time, travels around the earth from east to west. On every spot of the earth, therefore, the days in their proper order commence and end. We are to keep the days as they come to us. At whatever places we can ascertain the beginning and the close of the day, we can keep it.

From this idea that days travel around the world, it follows that somewhere on the earth there must be a starting point for all days, or a day line, in crossing which we must change our reckoning according to the direction in which we are traveling. Where is this day line? Experience shows that if we start from the western coast of America, and travel eastward to the eastern coast of Asia, we have no change to make; or, if we reverse it, and travel from the east coast of Asia to the west coast of America, it is the same; our reckoning agrees with that of every country through which we pass. The day line is not, therefore, anywhere on that part of the earth's surface. But when we cross the Pacific ocean from San Francisco to Pekin, taking California time with us, we find ourselves one day behind the people of China; or, if we come from Pekin to San Francisco, bringing Pekin time with us, we find ourselves one day in advance of the people of California. Thus it is demonstrated that the day line runs through the Pacific ocean. And it seems to be a providential fact that a line can be run from the north pole to the south, through Behring's straits, and touch no appreciable body of land. Hence the confusion is avoided that must exist if this line passed through a thickly populated land. All a person has to do, therefore, is, in sailing east across the Pacific to drop back a day in his reckoning, and in sailing west, to go forward a day in his calendar, in crossing this day line; and no other change is required the earth around. Navigators understand this and act accordingly.

But it is thought that even this arrangement might sometimes interfere with Sabbath observance. The following supposable case was suggested in the class:—

"A, who was sailing in the Pacific ocean, found by observation on Friday that he was five miles *east* of the day line; and being desirous that his crew should observe the Sabbath as soon as the sun went down, he made everything ready. But just as the sun went down he was drifted *west* of the line, and found that it was already Sunday there, and therefore kept no Sabbath. Was he right in so doing?"

We answer, No. He should have kept his old reckoning till he had observed the Sabbath. For a person on shipboard is not obliged to change on just such a degree of longitude. While some definite line must be fixed so that permanent locations on either side of the line may have a uniform reckoning, all that a person on the water need to do is to adjust his reckoning before he touches land, or meets passing ships, so that his reckoning will agree with those he meets. It will thus be seen that a person need never interfere with the Sabbath in adding or dropping his day in crossing the day line. This is a very simple matter and no difficulty at all is involved in it respecting the Sabbath.

Another difficulty is urged from the great length of days and nights in high northern latitudes. How, it is asked, can the Sabbath be kept in countries where in summer the days are several months in length, and in winter the nights are of equal duration? We reply, There is no difficulty whatever; for the revolution of the earth is marked, in summer by the sun, in winter by the stars, just as accurately as it is in any other quarter of the earth; and the point corresponding to sunset in lower latitudes, can be just as definitely determined even at the north pole, if men could reach it, as sunset itself in other places.   And this is all that is necessary to know, to be able to keep the Sabbath according to the commandment.   All the difficulties that are raised in the way of Sabbath-keeping are purely imaginary; and the more the subject is examined, the more clearly it is seen that that God who in infinite wisdom gave a Sabbath for all men to keep in all places of the earth, has not by any wayward providence, or any fatal necessity in the operation of his laws, made it impossible for them to do so.   For a full exposition of the subject of the Sabbath on a round world, the day line, etc., the reader is referred to a tract by Eld. J. N. Andrews, entitled, "The Definite Seventh Day."

A word as to the revelations of the Bible on this point. These are sufficient to show that no objection really exists. For instance, in the land of Palestine itself, there is a little difference of time between its eastern and western boundaries; and if the Sabbath could be kept on its eastern border, and at the same time on its western, distant a little over two degrees of longitude, and involving a difference in time of about ten minutes, it could be kept as much further west, and so on.   Consequently in the extensive travels of Paul we read of his keeping the

Sabbath far distant from Jerusalem. He kept at least seventy-eight of them in Corinth, Acts 18; and Corinth was thirteen degrees from Jerusalem, involving a difference in time of fifty-two minutes; that is, the Sabbath commenced in Corinth nearly an hour later than in Jerusalem; yet Paul had no difficulty in keeping it there. He pushed on to Rome, and found many Jews there. Acts 28 : 17. Do you suppose those Jews were living in violation of the Sabbath ? By no means. Did Paul keep the Sabbath there? There is not a shadow of reason to suppose that he did not. But what is the difference in time from Jerusalem? Two hours and sixteen minutes. And Paul in writing to the Romans dwelt much on the perpetuity of the law, and assured them that they did not make it void by faith in Christ; Rom. 3 : 31; but he ought to have added, according to our opponents, "Nevertheless you poor Romans will have to make void the Sabbath commandment, you are so far west. There is a difference in time, between your place and Jerusalem, of two hours and sixteen minutes; and with that difference you can't keep the Sabbath, so you needn't try." Paul would laugh at the manufactured perplexities of modern anti-sabbatarians; or, rather, he would wither them with some of his righteous invectives.

LESSON FOURTEEN.

NATURE AND DESTINY OF MAN.

THE long digression through which we have passed on the Sabbath question, should not cause us to forget that the subject still under consideration is the third angel's message of Rev. 14. We have been led to an examination of the Sabbath question from the fact that that message brings out a class distinguished as commandment-keepers; and we have found that to be thus distinguished we must keep all the commandments of God, besides the faith of Jesus; for while we can be commandment-breakers, if we break only one of them, to be commandment-keepers we must keep them all. There being no controversy on any point but the Sabbath, that must be the distinguishing commandment. And such in our investigation we have found it to be; for it is an institution which had its origin in the beginning, and from its very nature must exist without change to the end; and the fourth commandment of the decalogue confines us to the seventh day of the week as the Sabbath. The great Sabbath reform is borne upon the front of the message; and it is bringing out a people of whom it can truly be said, "Here are they that keep the commandments of God and the faith of Jesus."

The message also brings to view the punishment of those who reject the message, and practice the

---

1. What is the subject still under investigation? 2. In what way is the Sabbath connected with this message? 3. What have we found in our investigation of the Sabbath question? 4. What else does this message bring to view?

sins against which it warns us; and this will, therefore, next engage our attention. It says of those
who worship the beast and receive his mark, that
they "shall drink of the wine of the wrath of God,
which is poured out without mixture into the cup
of his indignation;" and they "shall be tormented
with fire and brimstone in the presence of the holy
angels and in the presence of the Lamb; and the
smoke of their torment ascendeth up forever and
ever; and they have no rest day nor night who
worship the beast and his image, and whosoever
receiveth the mark of his name."

This is considered one of the strong texts to
prove the eternal misery of the lost, and consequently the immortality of the soul. The whole
question, therefore, of the nature of man, the condition of the dead, and the destiny of the wicked,
comes up for examination.

Is the soul immmortal? What saith the Scripture? The word "immortal" occurs but once in the
English version of the Scriptures; 1 Tim. 1 : 17;
and there it is applied, not to man nor any part of
man, but, to God. The original word, however,
from which this comes, *aphthartos*, occurs seven
times in the New Testament; and in the six other
instances of its use it is rendered incorruptible, but
is never applied to man. Its entire use is as follows, the rendering of the word being in italics :—

Rom. 1 : 23, the glory of the *uncorruptible* God.
1 Cor. 9 : 25, crown; but we an *incorruptible*.

---

5. In what terms is this threatening of punishment expressed?
6. What is this supposed to prove? 7. What question does
this therefore bring up? 8. How many times is the word
"immortal" used in the English version of the Scriptures?
9. To whom is it then applied? 10. What is the original
word from which immortal is translated? 11. How many
times is that word used in the New Testament? 12. Give

Chap. 15 : 52, dead shall be raised *incorruptible*.
1 Tim. 1 : 17, unto the King, eternal, *immortal*.
1 Pet. 1 : 4, to an inheritance *incorruptible*.
Verse 23, *incorruptible*, by the word of God.
Chap. 3 : 4, that which is *not corruptible*.

It will thus be seen that in Rom. 1 : 23, it is applied to God; in 1 Cor. 9 : 25, to the crown of immortality which we seek; in 1 Cor. 15 : 52, to the incorruptible bodies we receive in the resurrection; in 1 Pet. 1 : 4, to the future inheritance of the saints; in verse 23; to the principle by which conversion is wrought in us; and in 1 Pet. 3 : 4, to the ornament of a meek and quiet spirit which we put on through Christ.

But, although man is nowhere called immortal, is not the equivalent declaration somewhere made that he has immortality? The word immortality occurs in the English Scriptures but five times; but it comes from two words in the Greek, and these occur in the aggregate eleven times. The first of these, *athanasia*, occurs but three times, and is every time rendered immortality as follows:—

1 Cor. 15 : 53, this mortal must put on *immortality*.
Verse 54, shall have put on *immortality*.
1 Tim. 6 : 16, who only hath *immortality*.

In these instances the word is applied to what we are to put on in the resurrection, and to God, who, it is declared, is the only one who by nature

---

the texts of its occurrence. 13. By what word is it usually rendered? 14. To what is it applied? 15. How many times is the word "immortality" found in the English Scriptures? 16. From how many Greek words is "immortality" translated? 17. How many times do these occur in the aggregate? 18. What is the first of these? 19. How many times does this word occur? 20. Name the texts. 21. How is it every time rendered? 22. To what is it applied? 23. What

hath it. The other word, *aphtharsia,* occurs eight times as follows :—

Rom. 2 : 7, glory and honor and *immortality.*

1 Cor. 15 : 42, it is raised in *incorruption.*

Verse 50, doth corruption inherit *incorruption.*

Verse 53, must put on *incorruption,* and

Verse 54, shall have put on *incorruption.*

Eph. 6 : 24, love our Lord Jesus Christ in *sincerity.*

2 Tim. 1 : 10, brought life and *immortality* to

Titus 2 : 7, uncorruptness, gravity, *sincerity.*

In all these instances it will be seen that the word is not once applied to man, but to that for which we are to *seek,* to that which we obtain by the resurrection, to our love to Christ, to what Christ has brought to light, and to the doctrine we are to cherish. The way in which these words are used is very significant, and should have great weight in deciding this question.

There is another fact perhaps more stupendous still. The words, soul and spirit, so often in modern theological parlance joined with the words, immortal, deathless, and never-dying, come from two words in the Hebrew, *nephesh* and *ruach,* and two corresponding words in the Greek, *psuche* and *pneuma*; and these words are used in the aggregate in the Old and New Testaments seventeen hundred times, and yet not once are the terms immortal, deathless or never-dying, applied to them, or any other term which would convey the idea of an imperishable nature or continued existence in either the soul or spirit.

---

is the other word which is rendered immortality? 24. How many times does it occur? 25. Name the texts of its occurrence. 26. To what is it applied? 27. What should we conclude from the fact that man is never called immortal, nor is once said to have immortality? 28. What other stupendous fact is discovered in the Bible? 29. What claim is

But man was made "in the image of God," Gen. 1:26, therefore, say our popular theologians, he was made immortal. But this image did not consist in immortality any more than it did in omnipotence, omniscience, omnipresence, or any other attribute of God. It had reference only to outward shape and form; for God is a person and has a form. Phil. 2:6; Heb. 1:3; Rev. 5:1; Dan. 7:9; Ex. 24:10; 33:20-23. Where the word image is used in a figurative sense, it is applied to something which we do not possess by nature, but which we must put on. Col. 3:10, explained by Eph. 4:23, 24.

It is further said that when God created man, he breathed into his nostrils the breath of life, or, as it is interpreted, imparted to him a deathless spirit, or immortal nature. Gen. 2:7. But this breath of life cannot denote an immortal soul, unless we admit that immortality is also an attribute of the brute creation; for all animals have the same breath of life. Gen. 7:22. If it be urged that the word life in Gen. 2:7 is plural, "breath of *lives*," from which some attempt to argue both the animal life and immortality, we reply that the word is also plural in Gen. 7:22, and in Gen. 2:9.

But man became a "living soul," which proves that he was endowed with an immortal soul. We answer, not unless we are willing to grant the same to all the lower animals; for they are all called by the same Hebrew terms. In Gen. 1:22-24, the

based on Gen. 1:26? 30. If image there means immortality, what else does it mean? 31. To what has it reference? 32. Has God a form? Proof. 33. To what is the word image applied in a figurative sense? References. 34. What is the breath of life, in Gen. 2:7, supposed to mean? 35. If we admit this of man what must we admit of the brute creation? 36. Where is the word in the plural? 37. What argument is based on the term living soul? 38. To what else is this term applied besides man? References. 39.

"living creature" is from the same Hebrew words that are translated "living soul" in Gen. 2:7. And in verse 20, the word "life" is from the Hebrew "soul," margin, and in Rev. 16:3 we read about "living souls" in the sea.

Gen. 35:18: "And it came to pass as her soul was in departing; for she died." The word here rendered soul, *nephesh*, is sometimes rendered breath, and Parkhurst, the distinguished lexicographer, says that it should be so translated here. A parallel case is found in 1 Kings 17:17–24. "The soul of the child came into him again." Verse 22. We are told in verse 17 what it was that had left the child. It was his breath; and this, the breath of life, returned, and he lived again.

Eccl. 3:21: "Who knoweth the spirit of man that goeth upward, and the spirit of the beast that goeth downward to the earth?" Solomon does not here assert that there is a difference between the spirit of man and beast, for he had just said that they all have one breath, verse 19, which is the same word that is here rendered spirit. But, properly translated, his words are interrogative: "Who knoweth that the spirit of man goeth upward," &c. So Milton, the Douay Bible, Septuagint, Vulgate, Chaldee Paraphrase, and Syriac version, render it.

Eccl. 12:7: "The spirit shall return unto God who gave it." Very well, what is this spirit, or what did God give to man? The only record we have of

What is the word for soul in Gen. 35:18? 40. How does Parkhurst say that it should be translated? 41. What is, then, the explanation of this passage? 42. What parallel case is found and how explained? 43. What does Solomon assert in Eccl. 3:21? 44. Is the word breath in verse 19, from the same Hebrew that is translated spirit in verse 21? 45. What is the proper translation of verse 21? 46. What authorities sustain such a translation? 47. What expression is found in Eccl. 12:7? 48. What is this supposed to prove?

man's creation says that God gave him the "breath
of life." How could the breath of life go to God?
It could go to him in the same sense in which it
could come from him. But if we say, according to
the popular view, that the spirit goes to God as a
separate conscious, intelligent entity, it commits us
to the doctrine of the pre-existence of souls; for, on
that ground, it must have come from him in the
same condition.

Samuel and the witch of Endor, 1 Sam. 28 : 3–20.
It was not Samuel's immortal soul which appeared
on this occasion; because it was an old man covered with a mantle that came up; and immortal
souls are not of that age or form, nor clothed in that
manner. Again this old man came up out of the
earth, but immortal souls are not down there, they're
up in Heaven, we are told. Moreover it is not probable that God, having prohibited necromancy, this
pretended communicating with the dead, and having
forsaken Saul so that he would not answer him by
prophets, nor in any legitimate way, should now
permit this abandoned woman to summon at will
the soul of his servant Samuel from the upper
spheres. The whole transaction was simply a piece
of ancient spiritism, Satanic deception played off
upon God-forsaken Saul.

Matt. 10: 28: "Fear not them which kill the
body, but are not able to kill the soul; but rather
fear him who is able to destroy both soul and body
in hell." Because the term soul is used here, and it

49. What did God give man in the beginning? 50. How
could the breath of life go to God? 51. If the spirit goes to
God as a conscious, intelligent entity, what conclusion are we
compelled to admit? 52. Where is found the record of Samuel and the witch of Endor? 53. Was it Samuel's immortal
soul that appeared on that occasion? 54. What reasons can
be given for saying that it was not? 55. What was this ex-
hibition? 56. What conclusion is drawn from our Lord's

is said that it cannot be killed, the conclusion is at once drawn that here is an immortal part of man that lives right on in death. But this text is conclusive against the immortality of the soul, whatever it is, inasmuch as it is a declaration that God will destroy in hell the souls of all those who do not fear and serve him. And it does not necessarily prove an intermediate conscious state; for the word soul here is from *psuche*, which is forty times rendered life in the New Testament, and the word to kill, may be rendered to destroy. Now what has the Christian which man cannot destroy? Man can destroy the body, he can deprive us of our life here; but he cannot deprive us of our future life, which we have by the promise of the Son of God. "And this is the record, that God hath given to us eternal life, and this life is in his Son." 1 John 5: 11. "Ye are dead, and your life is hid with Christ in God." Col. 3: 3. This life men cannot touch, this soul they cannot destroy. Matt. 10: 39, furnishes an excellent comment on Matt. 10: 28. Thus, "He that findeth his life shall lose it; and he that loseth his life for my sake shall find it." The word here rendered life is *psuche*, the same that is rendered soul in verse 28. He that findeth his *psuche*, life, shall lose his *psuche*, life. What does this mean? Simply this: He that seeks, at the expense of truth and moral integrity, to save his life, *psuche*, here, shall lose his life, *psuche*, in the world to come; but he who is willing to lose his life, *psuche*, here, willing that men should destroy it, for the sake of

---

words in Matt. 10:28? 57. What does this text prove respecting the immortality of the soul? 58. What is the Greek word here translated soul? 59. How many times is this rendered life in the New Testament? 60. How may the word kill be rendered? 61. What has the Christian which man cannot destroy? References. 62. What bearing has Matt. 10:39 on verse 28? 63. What is meant by losing

Christ and his truth, shall find his life, *psuche*, in the world to come. Here is the *psuche*, life, soul, which man cannot destroy, and therefore we are not to fear him, for our present life is of no account compared with the eternal life of Heaven; but God can deprive us of this future life, and him we are therefore to fear, instead of fearing men. There is therefore no conscious state brought to view here between death and the resurrection.

The transfiguration. Matt. 17: 1–9. On the mount of transfiguration Moses and Elias appeared with Christ. Moses had died hundreds of years before this; hence it is claimed here was his immortal soul. But this will not do; for this was a representation of the kingdom of God, 2 Pet. 1: 16–18, and there will be no disembodied immortal souls there. We claim that Moses had been raised from the dead, and was there in his resurrected body, as a representative of all those who will be raised from the dead, as Elias was a representative of those who will be translated without seeing death. Dr. Clarke, and other commentators, admit this. The allusion to the body of Moses in Jude 9, proves this. The only objection to it is that Christ was to be the first to rise from the dead. But the reader will find those passages which speak of Christ as the first fruits, 1 Cor. 15: 20, 23, or the first begotten, Heb. 1: 6; Rev. 1: 5, or the first born among many brethren, Rom. 8: 29; Col. 1: 15, 18, to refer to his office

and finding one's life? 64. Is there, then, any conscious intermediate state brought to view in Matt. 10: 28? 65. Where is an account given of the transfiguration? 66. How is this used to prove the immortality of the soul? 67. What did this scene represent? Reference. 68. What class did Moses represent? 69. What does Dr. Clarke admit in reference to Moses? 70. How does Jude 9 prove the resurrection of Moses? 71. What objection is urged against this? 72. What texts speak of Christ as first fruits, first begotten,

as antitype, or to his position as head or chief, the one upon whom all depended. While the passage in Acts 26:23 asserts, not that he should be absolutely the first to rise from the dead, for we have the record of six instances before his, but simply that he first by a resurrection from the dead should show light to the Gentiles. The scene of the transfiguration to be accounted for, demands the resurrection of Moses. And the objections all being removed, that hypothesis stands.

CLASS QUESTIONS ON LESSON XIV., WITH ANSWERS.

1. Does not the word soul in Gen. 2:7, mean the whole man, and could Adam be said to be a dead soul before the breath of life was breathed into him?

Ans. The antithesis in Gen. 2:7 turns on the word "living," beyond all question. It does not say that in place of something else Adam became a soul when the breath of life was breathed into him; but, in place of being a soul in some other condition, he became, after the breath of life was breathed into him, a *living* soul. He was a soul before, but not a living soul. The question asked is, then, simply, whether it would be proper to apply the term dead to him before his life. As this term is usually employed to denote something which has previously had life, which was not the case with Adam, we think it would be better to use the term "lifeless," instead of "dead." But the terms dead soul are applied to those who have once lived. In Num. 6:6, dead body is literally, says the Hebrew Concordance, "dead soul."

---

etc.? 73. To what do they refer? 74. How is the scene of the transfiguration, then, explained?

2. In what way is God everywhere present?

ANS. By his representative, his Holy Spirit. Ps. 139 : 7.

3. What is the Holy Spirit?

ANS. Any attempt to answer this question is venturing upon holy ground. It is something which is common to the Father and the Son: the Spirit of God, the Spirit of Christ. It is something to which the expressions, " poured out," " shed abroad," " descended," etc., are applied. It was breathed by Christ upon his disciples. John 20 : 22. It was an agent in the creation of the world. Gen. 1 : 2. But it would be useless to try to enumerate all the methods and varieties of its manifestations. In a word it may, perhaps, best be described as a mysterious influence emanating from the Father and the Son, their representative and the medium of their power.

4. In the case of Samuel and the witch of Endor, did Satan produce a real substance, or simply hold the mind of the woman under mesmeric influence?

ANS. Probably the latter. It does not appear that Saul saw the apparition at all; but " perceived " from the woman's description that it was Samuel. A mesmeric influence exercised upon the woman, would therefore be all that was required in the case.

5. Spiritualists sometimes quote 2 Chron. 21 : 12–15 as proof that the spirit of man exists after death and can communicate with the living. What is the most direct way of showing the absurdity of this claim?

ANS. If Elijah had died, and it could be shown that he wrote his epistle to Jehoram *after* his death then the Spiritualists would have some show for their claim. But when we stop a moment and consider that Elijah did not die but was translated, the use Spiritualists make of the case shows either their thoughtlessness or their ignorance. Whatever Elijah translated and alive in the unseen world might do, it would have no bearing on the question whether or not man has a spirit which can exist consciously after the body has gone into the grave.

6. Does the word "vision" in Matt. 17 : 9 and Luke 24 : 23, come from the same word in the Greek?

Ans. It does not. The word for vision in Matthew is *horama*, and in Luke *hoptasia*. This question has reference to the transfiguration; and because Jesus said, "Tell the *vision* to no man," some have endeavored to explain it on the ground that it was not a real appearance, but simply a vision on the part of the disciples. The use of the two words quoted above which are translated "vision," disproves this idea. Thus the word in Luke refers to the angels which the women saw when they came to the sepulcher of Christ, which was beyond question a real appearance. But this is a weaker word than the one Matthew uses in reference to the transfiguration. The word Luke uses is defined, "a vision, supernatural appearance, apparition;" while the word Matthew uses is defined, "a thing seen, sight, appearance," and secondly, "a supernatural appearance, vision." We must therefore conclude that what the disciples saw on the mount of transfiguration was not simply a mental picture, but a reality. The language of Peter confirms this view, when he says, We were *eye-witnesses* of his majesty. 2 Pet. 1 : 16–18.

LESSON FIFTEEN.

NATURE AND DESTINY OF MAN—(CONTINUED).

CHRIST and the Sadducees. Matt. 22 : 23–32. " I am the God of Abraham, and the God of Isaac, and the God of Jacob. God is not the God of the dead but of the living." From this it is claimed that Abraham, Isaac and Jacob, though their bodies had been laid in the grave ages before, were still alive when Christ spoke these words, and it must have been as disembodied spirits in the spirit world. But hold, this was not the point under discussion. The question up was the resurrection which Christ taught and the Sadducees denied. They bring up the case of the woman who had had seven husbands, and inquire whose wife she shall be (not whose wife she now is in the spirit world, but whose she shall be) in the resurrection when she is raised, and all the seven men who had been her husbands here, are raised also. Christ first nullifies their objection by telling them that in the resurrection we are raised to a higher state of being, and the marriage relation no longer exists. Then he appeals to a source of authority which they acknowledged, the writings of Moses, to show that their doctrine of no resurrection, and consequently no future existence, was contrary to their own scriptures. " But as touching the *resurrection of the dead* [that is, that the dead will be raised, which you deny] have ye not read that which was spoken unto you by God,

---

REVIEW QUESTIONS ON LESSON FIFTEEN.

1. What is claimed from the words of Christ to the Sadducees? 2. What was the question under consideration ? 3. What was the difficulty the Sadducees presented ? 4. How does Christ answer their difficulty ? 5. To what does he then

saying, I am the God of Abraham, and the God of Isaac, and the God of Jacob." These words are found in Ex. 3 : 6; and let it be marked that they were not spoken while Abraham, Isaac and Jacob were living, but to Moses, long after they were dead. Now if they were forever dead, as the Sadducees believed, then God called himself the God of something which did not exist, which would be an impeachment of his wisdom and power. But if they were to have a resurrection and future existence, God could still call himself their God; for he to whom both past and future are an eternal present, can speak of "those things that are not" (but are to be) "as though they were." Rom. 4 : 17. These words of God respecting Abraham, Isaac and Jacob, were therefore, under the circumstances, conclusive proof that they will live again; and if they, then all the righteous dead; and hence the doctrine of Christ against the Sadducees was maintained. But no conscious intermediate state is here taught.

The rich man and Lazarus. Luke 16 : 19-31. "The rich man also died, and was buried; and in hell he lifted up his eyes, being in torments." With the utmost confidence it is claimed that this was the rich man's soul; but the narrative says nothing about his soul. The word rendered "hell" is *hades*, but *hades* is not the place of punishment, not the hell, *gehenna*, of the wicked. It is simply the place of the dead, where all alike go, both righteous and wicked. The narrative says nothing about the

appeal ? 6. Where are the words found which Christ quotes? 7. When were they spoken ? 8. How did these words disprove the doctrine of the Sadducees ? 9. What is the case of the rich man and Lazarus supposed to prove ? 10. Does the narrative say anything about the soul of either the rich man or Lazarus ? 11. From what word in the Greek is the word "hell" here translated ? 12. Is *hades* the place of punishment ? 13. What is the place of punishment ? 14. What

soul of Lazarus, but says that *he* was carried by the angels into Abraham's bosom. When do the angels carry the saints into the kingdom of God? At the second coming of Christ, but not before. As literal events, this scene must have its location beyond the resurrection, and hence proves nothing respecting the intermediate state. But if it is not a literal narrative, it is simply a parable; and then it proves nothing for consciousness in death; for in a parable language is used figuratively, and life and intelligence are attributed to inanimate objects; and no doctrine can be based on parables; it must have the most literal and explicit language.

The narrative of the rich man and Lazarus is a parable; for it stands in connection with a notable list of narratives which are all acknowledged to be parables. Its object was to rebuke the Pharisees for their covetousness, verse 14, and to correct their false idea, that riches in this world were a mark of God's favor, and a sure passport to bliss hereafter. And having represented the rich man as awaking from his terrible delusion, and desiring that his brethren might be informed, it is shown that Abraham does not send one raised from the dead to instruct them, but refers them to Moses and the prophets. While the Jews were thus referred to Moses and the prophets more especially in reference to future reward and punishment, modern theology needs to go to Moses and the prophets for instruction respecting the place, *hades*, where this scene is located.

---

is *hades?* 15. What was carried into Abraham's bosom? 16. When are the saints carried by the angels into the kingdom? 17. If this narrative is literal, where must the scene be located? 18. What then does it prove concerning the intermediate state? 19. If it is not literal, what is it? 20. What does it then prove? 21. Is it literal or a parable? 22. What shows it to be a parable? 23. What was its object? 24. To what are they referred for instruction? 25. What is

What have these inspired writers told us about *hades*, and the condition of those who go there? The word in Hebrew which corresponds to the Greek word *hades*, and means the same thing, is *sheol*. This word is used sixty-five times in the Old Testament, and is translated hell and grave thirty-one times each, and pit three times; and we are taught respecting it, 1. That all alike go there. Num. 16 : 30, 33; Ps. 89 : 48. 2. That the whole man goes there. Gen. 42 : 38; Ps. 30 : 2, 3; Acts 2 : 27, 31. 3. That it holds dominion till the second coming of Christ. 1 Cor. 15 : 51–55. 4. That it is located in the earth beneath. Eze. 31 : 15–18. 5. That the righteous dead do not praise the Lord there. Ps. 6 : 5; 146 : 1–4; Isa. 38 : 10–19. 6. That the wicked are all silent there. Ps. 31 : 17; 1 Sam. 2 : 9. 7. That it is a place of silence, secrecy, sleep, rest, darkness, corruption and worms, in which there is no work, device, wisdom or knowledge. Job 4 : 11–19; 17 : 13–16; Eccl. 9 : 4–6, 10.

We have also in the Old Testament, representations precisely similar to this in Luke 16, respecting the inhabitants of *sheol*. Multitudes who have gone down to the grave through the oppression of tyrannical kings, are represented as lying with their swords under their heads, and worms covering them, and yet as rising up and paying mock obeisance to their oppressors when they come into *sheol*, and

the Hebrew word corresponding to *hades?* 26. How many times is this word used in the Old Testament? 27. How is it translated? 28. Who go into *sheol?* References. 29. In what condition do we go there? References. 30. How long does it hold dominion over its subjects? References. 31. Where is it located? References. 32. What is the condition of the righteous there? References. 33. What is the condition of the wicked there? References. 34. What is its general character? References. 35. What other representations have we in the Old Testament on this point?

taunting them with becoming weak as themselves.
See the address to the king of Babylon in Isa. 14:
9–11, and the lamentation for Egypt in Eze. 32:18–
32. So in the case of the rich man and Lazarus.
The rich man in *hades*, where, as they were fully
instructed, there was no knowledge, consciousness,
nor life, is nevertheless represented by the figure of
personification, as living and acting as there represented. And the object was to show that the next
state of being after the present (passing over the
intermediate unconscious state) will be one of torment and suffering to the ungodly, covetous rich
man, but one of happiness and bliss to the righteous
poor. With the language of the Old Testament
before them respecting *sheol*, and the parables
respecting the kings of Babylon and Egypt, the
Jews would readily understand it. It was not
given to show the nature of *hades*, nor the condition
of those who go there, and hence is not to be used
for that purpose.

The thief on the cross. Luke 23: 39–43, is supposed to contain another strong proof of the conscious state of the dead, in the words of Christ to
the thief on the cross. The thief's request was,
" Lord, remember me when thou comest into thy
kingdom." To which Christ made answer, " Verily
I say unto thee, To-day shalt thou be with me in
paradise." How could the thief be with Christ in
paradise that day, it is triumphantly asked, unless
by means of a disembodied conscious spirit ? If he
was to be with him in paradise that very day, it
must have been in the form of an immortal soul,

References. 36. How do these explain the parable of the
rich man and Lazarus ? 37. Where is found the record of
Christ's words to the thief on the cross ? 38. What are these
words supposed to prove ? 39. What was the thief's request ? 40. What was Christ's answer ? 41. How is the

unless he had been raised from the dead, or been translated. But there are two objections to the common view of this matter: the first is that Christ did not go to paradise that day, and the second is that the thief did not die that day, so that his immortal soul did not leave his body. Either of these propositions established, destroys entirely the popular view of the passage; and we know that one of them is true; that Christ did not go to paradise that day; because he told Mary, on the day of his resurrection, three days after his crucifixion, that he had not yet ascended to his Father. But where his Father was there was paradise. 2 Cor. 12:2, 4; Rev. 2:7; 22:1, 2. He had not therefore at that time been to paradise; and consequently the thief could not have been with him in paradise on the day of his crucifixion.

In regard to the second proposition, that the thief did not die that day, we have a strong inference if not absolute proof in this fact: When the Jews desired that the bodies might be taken down from the cross just before the Sabbath, because no bodies could remain there over the Sabbath, the soldiers broke the legs of the two thieves, but coming to Christ and seeing that he was dead already they brake not his legs. The thieves therefore were not dead. Now the breaking of their legs must have been for one of two purposes, either to hasten their death, or to prevent their escape, after being released from the cross. But their immediate death was not the object sought. It was only to get them off from the cross; and inasmuch as persons on the cross are said to live from three to eight days, it is not at all probable that breaking their legs near the close of the day would cause them to die before the day ended.

If, then, the Lord did not go to paradise that day, and the thief did not die, and so he did not go, how can the passage be explained? Place the comma after to-day, instead of before it, and all is clear. With this change, Christ does not say to him that he shall be with him that day in paradise, but he simply says to him that day that he shall be with him in paradise when he comes in his kingdom, and this is just what the thief requested. As to the punctuation, we have a right to make this change, if the sense demands it; for the punctuation of the Bible is but the work of men and of comparatively recent origin, the comma in its present form not having been invented till the year 1790. A parallel expression is found in Zech. 9 : 12. Some Greek manuscripts, according to Griesbach, place the comma after to-day, in Luke 23 : 43. Thus punctuated it is consistent with itself and with other scriptures.

Absent from the body. In 2 Cor. 5 : 8 Paul says: " We are confident, I say, and willing rather, to be absent from the body, and to be present with the Lord." This text is urged with great assurance as proving a conscious intermediate state. But the

---

thief did not die that day? 47. How then is the passage to be explained? 48. Have we a right to make such changes in the punctuation? 49. When? 50. What is the comparative date when punctuation was first used? 51. When was the comma in its present form invented? 52. Where do we find a parallel expression? 53. What is Griesbach's testimony? 54. Punctuated in this manner, does this text prove anything in regard to the intermediate state? 55. Where does Paul speak about being absent from the body? 56. What is this supposed to prove? 57. What is lacking

essential point in the argument is lacking; for Paul does not say that we are present with the Lord just as soon as we leave the body. Granting that by absence from the body he means our condition in death, he does not tell us how long it is after we are thus absent from the body that we are present with the Lord. The first part of the chapter explains this verse. In our earthly house of this tabernacle, in this present mortal state, we groan, desiring, not to be unclothed, as we are in death, but to be clothed upon with our house from Heaven, or to reach the eternal immortal state promised to the believer. And when we reach this, "mortality is swallowed up of life." Verse 4. But when is mortality swallowed up of life? When all that there is mortal is made immortal. Paul had written to the Corinthian church very plainly on this subject in his first epistle. He had spoken about this mortal being made immortal, and this corruptible being made incorruptible, which is the same thing as mortality being swallowed up of life. And when is this? Not when we die, but at the last trump, when Christ appears, and the dead are raised. 1 Cor. 15 : 52–55. Then is the time when we are present with the Lord, not before, nor by any other means. John 14 : 3; 1 Thess. 4 : 17.

In the body and out. In 2 Cor. 12 : 2–4, Paul speaks of a man, " in the body or out," he could not tell which, caught up to paradise, &c. Here, it is said, such a condition is recognized as " out of the

---

in this proof? 58. Where is this verse explained? 59. What does Paul mean by our earthly house? 60. What does he mean by being unclothed? 61. What, by our house from Heaven? 62. When we reach this, what happens? 63. When is mortality swallowed up of life? References. 64. By what means are we brought into the presence of the Lord? References. 65. Where does Paul speak of being in the body and out? 66. What do believers in natural im-

body." Very well, what does it mean? Believers
in the immortality of the soul say that it means
that the soul or spirit is separated from the body.
But what condition is a person then in? According
to popular theology, the person is dead when he is
out of the body; for the separation of soul and
body is death. Now what is Paul's subject? Visions. Verse 1. He here describes the visions with
which he had been favored; and while he was in
vision he did not know whether he was in the body
or out. If he was out of the body, according to our
friends, he was dead; and when he came into the
body again he had a resurrection. Do they believe
that Paul, when he had a vision, died, and was
raised from the dead when he came out of vision,
or that he designed to teach that such a condition
of things was possible? They must accept this
absurdity, or surrender this text.

Departing and being with Christ. Phil. 1 : 21–
24 : "For I am in a strait betwixt two, having a
desire to depart and to be with Christ, which is far
better." The only way in which this text can be
made to do service in behalf of the conscious
intermediate state is to connect the being with
Christ immediately with the departing. But Paul
does not so connect them. The next thing of which
the person is conscious after departing is being with
Christ. But this does not preclude the idea that a
long space might be passed over in unconsciousness.
And such a period the apostle would of necessity

mortality say this means? 67. What is, in popular parlance,
the separation of soul and body? 68. What is Paul's
subject here? 69. What absurdity is involved in the common view of this passage? 70. What famous expression is
found in Phil. 1: 21–24? 71. How is this text made to serve
the popular cause? 72. Does Paul make this connection?
73. Of what is the Christian next conscious after death?
74. Does this preclude the idea of a period of unconscious

pass over in silence, as it is an utter blank to the individual, and the change from one state to the other seems to him to be instantaneous. Bishop Law says: "The Scriptures, in speaking of the connection between our present and future being, do not take into the account our *intermediate state in death;* no more than we, in describing the course of any man's actions, take into account the time *he sleeps.* Therefore the Scriptures (to be consistent with themselves) must affirm an immediate connection between death and the Judgment."

Paul has in other places told us very definitely when we go to be with Christ. Rom. 8:23; 1 Cor. 15:51–54; Phil. 3:20, 21; Col. 3:4; 1 Thess. 4:16, 17; 2 Thess. 1:7; 2 Tim. 4:8; Heb. 11:39, 40. His testimony in Phil. 1:23, must not therefore be interpreted in such a way as to contradict these statements. Hence it cannot be used in support of the theory of the conscious intermediate state.

Spirits of just men made perfect. Paul uses this expression in Heb. 12:23; and this is supposed by some to be a confirmation of the idea of the separate conscious existence of the spirit of man. But Paul speaks of no such thing. He does not speak of *spirits* made perfect, but of *men* made perfect. And when are men made perfect? If we take it in the absolute sense, it is not till after the resurrection, when the body is redeemed, and mortality is clothed with immortality. Rom. 8:23, 1 Cor. 15:51–54; Phil. 3:21; 1 John 3:2. If it is in an accommodated sense, then it must refer to the

rest in the grave? 75. What is Bishop Law's testimony? 76. What has Paul told us in other places? References. 77. What do these scriptures teach? 78. How, then, must we treat Paul's testimony in Phil. 1:23? 79. What use is made of Paul's testimony in Heb. 12:23? 80. What does Paul speak of here? 81. When are men made perfect?

perfection of Christian character we are able to acquire under the gospel, through the offering of Christ. Many, following Dr. Clarke, think it refers to this, as Paul is here setting forth the superiority of the blessings and advantages we enjoy under the gospel, over those enjoyed under the former dispensation. But in either case this scripture would have no bearing on the question of consciousness in death. It is either fulfilled entirely in the present state, or it has its application beyond the resurrection.

The spirits in prison. 1 Pet. 3:19. "By which also he went and preached unto the spirits in prison." This is supposed to be a strong text in favor of the intermediate conscious state of the dead; for here were spirits in prison, supposed to mean in the grave, or in death, and they must have been conscious and intelligent, because they were preached to. We inquire who these spirits were? The following verse says: "Which sometime were disobedient, when once the long suffering of God waited in the days of Noah, while the ark was a preparing."

The persons meant by the word spirits are therefore the wicked antediluvians. But what is meant by their being in prison? In Isaiah 61: 1 is found a prophecy concerning the work of Christ, and it is said that he should proclaim liberty to the captives and the opening of the prison to them that are bound. This prophecy is quoted by our Lord himself in Luke 4:18 and an application made of it to his own work. The situation of the antediluvians

References. 82. What is Dr. Clarke's admission on this passage? 83. What is Paul here setting forth? 84. What two conditions are the only ones referred to? 85. What bearing then has it on the intermediate state? 86. What testimony is found in 1 Pet. 3:19? 87. What is this supposed to mean? 88. Who were these spirits? 89. What is meant by their being in prison? 90. When and by whom

while Noah was preaching to them was similar to
that of those to whom Christ preached. They were
in darkness and error and under the condemnation
of death. Therefore the antediluvians may likewise
have been said to be in prison, while Noah was
preaching to them.

We inquire further who it was that preached to
these spirits? It was Christ. When did he preach?
In the days of Noah while the ark was preparing.
Through whom did he preach? Through Noah.
Dr. Adam Clarke takes the same view of this pas-
sage, that the preaching was done by the spirit of
Christ in Noah. It therefore has no bearing upon
this question of the intermediate state of the dead.

There are some absurdities connected with the
common view which deserve to be noticed. If these
spirits were the spirits of the wicked antediluvians,
and the preaching was done by the spirit of Christ
while his body lay in the grave, these spirits were
then in hell; and we inquire, Why should the spirit
of Christ go down into hell to preach to the antediluvians? Could they be benefited by it? No.
Then what was the object of it? Here is a difficulty which popular theologians are not able to
solve.

But further, before the preaching is spoken of,
the quickening or resurrection of Christ is brought
to view, verse 18, therefore it could not have been
by the disembodied spirit of Christ that this preaching was done while he lay in the grave.

The souls under the altar. Rev. 6:9. "And
when he had opened the fifth seal I saw under the

were they preached to? 91. How could Christ preach
through Noah? 92. What is Dr. Adam Clarke's view of this
passage? 93. What absurdity attaches itself to the common
interpretation of this passage? 94. If the preaching was
done by Christ personally, when was it done? 95. What

altar the souls of them that were slain for the word
of God and for their testimony which they held."
Here it is claimed are souls brought to view in a
disembodied state, conscious, and active, crying unto
God for vengeance. These souls were seen under
the altar. What altar? Evidently the altar of sacrifice where they were slain. Is there such an altar
as that in Heaven? and are the saints there shut
up under such an altar? Dr. Clarke says this altar
was upon the earth, and that these souls were the
victims of papal persecution; and they are represented as having fallen down by the altar where
they were slain. But if they are not conscious in
Heaven, it is asked, how could they cry to God for
vengeance? We answer, By the figure of personification, just as Abel's blood is represented as crying
to God, or the stone out of the wall, and the beam
out of the timber, spoken of by Habakkuk 2:11,
or as the wages of the laborers spoken of by James
5:4. These souls cried for their blood to be avenged;
but do immortal souls have blood? And who were
those upon whom they called for vengeance? Their
persecutors. And where were these persecutors?
If dead, according to the popular view, they were in
hell. And as that view further represents, they
were right before the face and eyes of those saints
in Heaven. This, it is claimed is taught by the
parable of the rich man and Lazarus. How then
could they call for vengeance upon them? Was it
not vengeance enough for them to be tormented in
the flames of hell? How amiable does this make

claim is made on Rev. 6:9? 96. What altar is brought to
view? 97. Is there such an altar in Heaven? 98. Is it consistent to suppose that souls are shut up under an altar in
heaven? 99. What is Dr. Clarke's view of this matter? 100.
If not conscious, how can they cry for vengeance? References.
101. What is the first absurdity involved in the common

these righteous souls appear! And if we say that those persecutors were not then dead, in the natural course of things they would soon be in hell, tormented, it would seem, as fiercely as any one could wish. Such is the absurdity that is attached to the popular view of this text.

But how, it is asked further, could white robes be given unto them? We answer, those were given in the Reformation when the characters of these martyrs were vindicated from the aspersions of their Romish executioners. We find, therefore, in this testimony no evidence for the doctrine of the conscious state of the dead.

In Rev. 19:10 and 22:9 John fell down to worship at the feet of the angel who was employed in giving him his revelation. In restraining him, the angel said, "See that thou do it not, for I am thy fellow servant and of thy brethren, the prophets." Here it is claimed that the angel asserted that he was one of the old prophets, of course communicating with John in his disembodied state. But the angel does not say this. He says simply, "I am thy fellow servant and the fellow servant of thy brethren, the prophets." He had been employed in imparting to them divine revelations as he was now doing to John.

We notice one more text that is supposed to teach the conscious intermediate state of the dead. Gen. 25: 8: "Then Abraham gave up the ghost, and died in a good old age, an old man and full of years, and was gathered to his people." It is said that Abraham was not buried where his fathers were buried, therefore,

view? 102. What is the second? 103. How could white robes be given them? 104. What argument for consciousness in death is drawn from Rev. 19:10; 22:9? 105. What did the angel mean by the language he addressed to John? 106. What is said in Gen. 25:8? 107. What argument is

this could not apply to his body, but it must be that his spirit went to be with the spirits of his fathers in the spirit world. We therefore inquire where his fathers were? We learn from Joshua 24:2 that his fathers were idolaters and died such. They were consequently according to the popular view in hell. Now if the spirit of Abraham went to be with the spirits of his fathers, he went, according to this view, inevitably to hell. But the theory which leads to such absurdity must be abandoned. We have a parallel expression in the case of David. Paul says in Acts 13:36, that David was laid unto his fathers —which of course means the same as being gathered to his people; but Paul continues—after he was thus gathered unto his fathers, he saw corruption. This explodes the idea of the conscious existence of the soul in the spirit world.

LESSON SIXTEEN.

DESTINY OF THE WICKED.

WE have now examined all the more important texts that are supposed to teach the consciousness of the dead between death and the resurrection, or such as are used as objections to the view that man has not by nature an immortal soul. With a brief examination of the positive testimony of the Scriptures on this point we shall pass to the other branch of the subject, namely, the destiny of the wicked.

The sentence which God pronounced upon trans-

drawn from this? 108. Where were Abraham's fathers? 109. How does this argument inevitably dispose of Abraham? 110. What must be done with such an argument? 111. Where do we find a parallel expression? 112. What does the testimony show?

gression in the garden of Eden was death. "In the day that thou eatest thereof, thou shalt surely die." After Adam had sinned and the sentence was to be put into execution, God addressed Adam thus: "In the sweat of thy face shalt thou eat bread, till thou return unto the ground; for out of it wast thou taken; for dust thou art and unto dust shalt thou return."

What part of Adam was addressed by this language? Was it the body or the soul? We are told that the soul is the intelligent, responsible part of man, that incurs guilt by transgression and is entitled to reward for obedience. But that part which did transgress was addressed in this sentence; and the personal pronouns, *thou* and *thy*, are five times used in addressing this sentence to Adam. Certainly this must have been the intelligent, responsible man, and the sentence pronounced upon it was, "*Dust* thou art and unto *dust* shalt thou return."

If it is said that this refers simply to the body, then we ask if the same personal pronoun *thou* used by Christ in his address to the thief on the cross, meant simply his body. If it did not there, it does not here. Our friends must be consistent in their interpretation of the Scriptures.

The penalty pronounced upon Adam, in which we are all involved, can therefore be understood in no

---

REVIEW QUESTIONS ON LESSON SIXTEEN.

1. What sentence did God pronounce upon transgression in Eden? 2. When God explained the sentence to Adam what language did he use? 3. What part of Adam was addressed by this language? 4. What part of man is the soul said to be? 5. Was the part which did transgress addressed in the sentence? 6. How many times were the personal pronouns *thou* and *thy* used in presenting this sentence to Adam? 7. To what did these pronouns refer? 8. What is shown by the same pronoun in Christ's words to the thief on the cross? 9. What therefore was the penalty pro-

other way than as meaning the reduction of the real responsible man to the dust of the ground, to a condition of utter unconsciousness.

There is another doctrine taught in the Scriptures which has an important bearing upon this question, and that is the resurrection of the dead. It is over and over again stated in the word of God, that there is to be a resurrection of the dead. But what need is there of this, if the soul exists in a conscious, intelligent condition without the body?

William Tyndale says: "And ye in putting them (souls) in heaven, hell and purgatory, destroy the argument wherewith Christ and Paul prove the resurrection."

Andrew Carmichael (*Theology of the Scripture,* Vol. 2, p. 315) says: "It cannot be too often repeated: If there be an immortal soul, there is no resurrection; and if there be any resurrection, there is no immortal soul."

Dr. Muller (*Christian Doctrine of Sin,* p. 318) says: "The Christian faith in immortality is indissolubly connected with a promise of a future resurrection of the dead."

Again, death is compared to sleep, and there must be some analogy between the state of sleep and the state of death. And this analogy must pertain to that which renders sleep a peculiar condition. Our condition in sleep differs from our condition when awake simply in this, that when we are soundly asleep we are entirely unconscious. In this respect,

nounced upon Adam? 10. What other doctrine of the Scriptures has an important bearing upon this question? 11. What is stated over and over again in the word of God? 12. What need is there of a resurrection if the soul is conscious in death? 13. What does Tyndale say? 14. What are the words of Carmichael? 15. What does Dr. Muller testify on this point? 16. To what is death compared? 17. What is the analogy between death and sleep? 18. What

then, death is like sleep, that is, the dead are unconscious, and without the resurrection they will forever remain so.

Speaking of the dead man Job says, 14: 21 : " His sons come to honor and he knoweth it not, and they are brought low and he perceiveth it not of them." David says, Psalm 146: 4: " His breath goeth forth, he returneth to his earth; in that very day his thoughts perish." Solomon spoke to the same effect as his father David, Ecclesiastes 9: 5, 6: "For the living know that they shall die; but the dead know not anything; also their love, and their hatred, and their envy, is now perished; neither have they any more a portion forever in anything that is done under the sun." Verse 10 : "There is no work nor device, nor knowledge, nor wisdom in the grave, whither thou goest." Evidence like this can neither be mistaken nor evaded. It is vain for the immaterialist to claim that this applies to the body only in distinction from the soul, for they do not hold that the body of itself thinks or has knowledge while the person lives. Therefore, without a resurrection the dead will forever remain without knowledge.

The dead are not in Heaven nor in hell, but in the dust of the earth. Job. 17:13–16; 14:14; Isa. 26:19.

The dead have no remembrance of God, and do not, while dead, render him praise and thanksgiving; Proof: Ps. 6:5; 115:17; Isa. 38: 18, 19.

does this show concerning our condition in death? 19. What does Job say in chapter 14: 21? 20. What is the testimony of Psalm 146: 4? 21. How and where does Solomon speak of this question? 22. How is evidence like this to be treated? 23. May not this refer to the body only? 24. Without a resurrection, therefore, what would result? 25. Where are the dead? Reference. 26. Have the dead any remembrance of God? Reference. 27. Have they ascended

The dead have not yet ascended to Heaven. Acts 2 : 29, 34, 35.

And finally Paul, in his masterly argument on the resurrection, 1 Cor. 15 : 18, makes this conclusive statement: "If the dead rise not, then is not Christ raised; and if Christ be not raised, your faith is vain; ye are yet in your sins. Then they also which are fallen asleep in Christ *are perished*." If the souls of the dead live right on are they perished? What! perished and yet alive in a larger sphere? Perished? and yet enjoying the attendant blessings of everlasting life in Heaven? Perished? and yet at God's right hand, where there is fullness of joy and pleasures forevermore?

Bishop Law says:—

"I proceed to consider what account the Scriptures give of that state to which death reduces us; and this we find represented by sleep; by a negation of all life and action; by rest, resting-place, or home, silence, oblivion, darkness, destruction and corruption."

Christ says, John 6 : 39, that of all that was given him, he would lose nothing, but would raise it up at the last day, showing again that it was lost unless it should be raised up at the last day.

It is thus seen that the two doctrines of the immortality of the soul and the resurrection of the dead cannot exist together; but the Bible does sustain the resurrection of the dead, and, as we may therefore expect, gives no countenance to the other.

There is still another doctrine of the Scriptures

to heaven? Reference. 28. What does Paul say in 1 Cor. 15 : 18? 29. Can this be reconciled with the idea that the soul lives right on after the death of the body? 30. What is Bishop Law's testimony? 31. What are the words of Christ in John 6 : 39? 32. Can the two doctrines of the immortality of the soul and the resurrection of the dead exist together? 33. What other doctrine has a decisive bearing

which has as decisive a bearing upon this question as the preceding, and that is the doctrine of a future Judgment for man. If men when they die go directly to Heaven or hell, accordingly as they have lived righteous or wicked lives, it follows that they are all judged at death. Then we ask, What necessity is there for this general future Judgment which is made so prominent a doctrine of the Bible? Is it for the purpose of correcting mistakes that may have been made in the first judgment? Can it be supposed that some have been in hell who ought to have been in Heaven, and some in Heaven who ought to have been in hell, and that this Judgment is to correct these mistakes? If not, why have this Judgment at all? And if so, what guarantee have we that mistakes will not be made in this final Judgment, and some be sent to hell for all eternity who should be in Heaven, and some retained in Heaven who are deserving of the punishment of hell? Such must be our conclusion if we hold to the doctrine of the immortality of the soul; but such a conclusion is a libel upon the government of God and an insult to the justice of Heaven.

Luke 24: 39. "For a spirit hath not flesh and bones, as ye see me have."

From this definition of a spirit by Christ, it is concluded that a spirit cannot be a real, tangible being, and hence must exist in the disembodied state, as popularly supposed. But to what did Christ have reference by the term spirit? What did the apostles suppose they had seen? The 37th

upon this question? 34. If men go directly to Heaven or hell at death when are they judged? 35. Then what necessity is there for a future general Judgment? 36. In what light does this place the government and justice of God? 37. What does Christ say respecting the spirit in Luke 24 : 39? 38. What argument is based on this definition?

verse says they were affrighted and supposed they
had seen a spirit.   On this verse Griesbach puts for
the word spirit, *phantasma;* but the meaning of
phantasma is an apparition, a ghost.   It is evident
that Christ used the term spirit in the same sense.
Not that there was any spirit of that kind, but he
wanted to show them that such a spirit as they
conceived of was not then present before them; for
such a spirit had not flesh and bones as they saw
him have.   The word *pneuma,* to be sure, is here
used; but this has a great variety of meanings and
while it may be employed, perhaps, to express such
a conception as the disciples had then in mind, we
are not to understand that the word cannot be used
to describe bodies like that which Christ then possessed.   Bloomfield on this verse says: "It may be
added that our Lord meant not to countenance these
notions, but to show his hearers that, according to
their *own* notions of spirits, he was not one."

Acts 23:8.   "For the Sadducees say that there
is no resurrection, neither angel, nor spirit; but the
Pharisees confess both."   Paul declared himself in
verse 6 to be a Pharisee, and in telling what they
believed, in verse 8, it is claimed that Paul ranged
himself on the side of those who believe in the separate, conscious existence of the spirit of man.   But
does this text say that the Pharisees believed in
such a thing?   Three terms are here used in ex-
pressing what the Sadducees did not believe; namely,
"resurrection, angel and spirit."   But when the

---

39. To what kind of a spirit did Christ have reference ?   40.
What proves this ?   41. How then did Christ use the term
spirit ?   42. Did he mean to teach that there was anything of
that kind ?   43. What word is here used for *spirit* ?   44. Could it
ever be used to signify a spirit such as they then had in mind ?
45. What is Bloomfield's testimony ?   46. What objection
is raised on Acts 23:8 to our view ?   47. How many terms
are used to express what the Sadducees did not believe ?

faith of the Pharisees is stated, these *three* terms are reduced to *two*: the Pharisees confess *both*. *Both* means only *two*, not three. Now what two of the three terms before employed unite to express one branch of the faith of the Pharisees? The word *angel* could not be one, for the angels are a distinct race of beings from the human family. Then we have left, resurrection and spirit. The Pharisees believe in angels, and in the resurrection. Then, all the spirit they believed in, according to this testimony, is what is connected with the resurrection, and that, of course, is the spiritual body with which we are endowed. If any who say that the word *both* sometimes means more than two, and quote Acts 1:13 as proof, we reply, that the word *both* in Acts 1:13 is not the same word translated both in Acts 23:8. The word *both* here means just two, no more nor less.

CLASS QUESTIONS ON LESSON XVI., WITH ANSWERS.

1. Ecclesiastes 9:5. "The dead know not anything, neither have they any more a reward. How do you reconcile this with the scripture that says that "the righteous shall be recompensed in the earth, much more the wicked and the sinner?" Prov. 11:31.

ANS. Ecclesiastes 9:5 does not refer to the time of future rewards and punishments, but to this present dispensation. The dead know not anything and have no reward during this state of being, till the close of probation; but the passage quoted from Proverbs does have reference to the future reward and punishment of the righteous and

---

48. How many to express the faith of the Pharisees? 49. What is meant by this word, both? 50. Is the word here translated both, the same as that used in Acts 1:13?

the wicked after probation is closed. Hence there is no discrepancy between these passages.

2. In 1 Thess. 5 : 23, are the words "soul and spirit" identical?

ANS. We think not. The expression "body, soul and spirit" is to be taken as a description of the whole man, with his physical, mental and emotional natures, soul and spirit in this instance signifying the mental and emotional part of man's nature. But how would the immaterialist explain this? According to his vocabulary the soul means the immortal part of man, and spirit also means the immortal part. Has man two immortal parts in his nature?

3. What became of those saints that came out of their graves after Christ's resurrection, as recorded in Matt. 27 : 52, 53?

ANS. The only definite record we have of them is that they went into the holy city and appeared unto many; but Paul makes use of an expression from which we infer that they ascended to Heaven with Christ. For, speaking of his ascension in Ephesians 4 : 8, he says : "When he ascended up on high, he led captivity captive, and gave gifts unto men." The margin reads, "a multitude of captives." Who could these captives be except those who came out of their graves after the resurrection of Christ? We therefore conclude that they are now with Christ in Heaven, represented by the four living creatures and the four and twenty elders of the book of Revelation; for they declare that they have been redeemed from the earth. Rev. 5 : 9.

4. Is the word *grave* in Ecclesiastes 9 : 10 from *sheol*?

ANS. Yes.

5. How do you reconcile Matt. 22 : 32 with Rom. 14 : 9 ?

ANS. Matt. 22 : 32 reads, "God is not the God of the dead, but of the living," and Rom. 14 : 9 reads, "For to this end Christ both died, and rose, and revived, that he might be Lord both of the dead and of the living." There is nothing here to reconcile, because the passages refer to different things. Matthew has reference to the future living again of those who are in their graves; while Romans speaks of that work of Christ which enables him to bring salvation to the dead as well as to the living; and in that sense he is Lord of both.

6. Does Romans 5 : 14 prove that the reign of death was broken at the resurrection of Moses ?

ANS. The passage reads as follows: "Nevertheless death reigned from Adam to Moses;" but death was not the subject upon which Paul was here speaking, but the existence of law and the effects of law. "Sin is not imputed," he says, "when there is no law; nevertheless death reigned from Adam to Moses;" proving thereby that the law was in existence, and mankind were held amenable to it. Therefore the obligations of the moral law, or ten commandments, were not introduced with the Mosaic dispensation; for their existence is proved even from the time of Adam.

7. Did Christ have "life in himself" before he came down from Heaven ? If so, how could an immortal being die ?

ANS. We think he did. An immortal being is one which is exempt from death. Such was Christ before his advent to this world; but he could lay off his immortality, and take upon him our nature. How he could do this, is not for us to try to explain;

for this is one of those mysteries of godliness of which Paul speaks, which are beyond the comprehension of man.   1 Tim. 3 : 16. ·

8. 1 John 3 : 15 seems to contain an inference that some have eternal life abiding in them which contradicts Rom. 2 : 7, and Col. 3 : 3, 4. Please harmonize the above.

ANS. The eternal life which we now have abiding in us, we have by faith. John, in his first epistle, 5 : 11, confirms this. He says, "And this is the record, that God hath given to us eternal life." And where is this life? Is it now in us? Do we yet have it in possession? No; but John adds, "This life is in his Son." Now, Rom. 2 : 7, and Col. 3 : 3, 4, do not contradict this; for they speak of that absolute possession of eternal life which we will have beyond the resurrection.

9. Acts 17 : 28. "For in him we live, and move, and have our being." How do we live, and move, and have our being in God? Can it not here be claimed that the soul is a part of God, and hence immortal?

ANS. Paul speaks here of our relation to God as created beings; for, to confirm this declaration which he makes, that we live, move, and have our being in him, he immediately adds, "For we are also his offspring." That is to say, all the life which we have, even our present, temporal, immortal life, we have from God; but this has no bearing upon the question whether we have a principle within us that can never die.

10. Please explain Rev. 6 : 11. What is meant by their waiting a little season after the white robes were given them?

ANS. Although the spirit of persecution was

restrained by the work of Reformation which gave white robes to those martyrs, yet it was not entirely suppressed. In many countries, especially in England, as the Catholic party occasionally gained the ascendency in the nation, terrible persecutions were the result, and many were put to death. But this was to last only for a little season, and we are now happily beyond that period when men are put to death on account of their faith.

11. 1 Pet. 3 : 20. "Which sometime were disobedient." Shall we understand by this that they were disobedient only at times?

ANS. The word is "sometime," and not *sometimes;* and it does not mean at different intervals of time, but at that particular time. They were at that time disobedient, that is while Noah was preaching to them.

12. 1 Pet. 3 : 19. Is not the prison here referred to, the prison-house of the grave?

ANS. We think not, inasmuch as the scripture seems to represent that the preaching was done to those spirits while they were in prison; hence they could not have been in their graves; but the time referred to must be while they were yet alive; therefore we take the word "prison" in this instance, to refer to their peculiar condition, they being shut up under the wrath of God, and their days limited to a hundred and twenty years.

13. Spiritualists, who claim that there is a part of God in everything, sometimes quote 1 Cor. 15 : 38, basing all on the pronoun *his.*

ANS. The passage reads, "But God giveth it a body as it hath pleased him, and to every seed his own body." This does not mean that God has given to every seed a part of his (God's) own body, but the pronoun "his" there refers to the seed, and might be rendered *its* own body, or the body belonging to it, as peculiarly its own, in distinction from the body of other seeds.

14. "Does not the Jew believe in an intermediate state, that is entered on immediately at death? and do they not call it Paradise? If so, would not the words of Christ addressed to the thief leave the impression on the minds of those that heard him, that that was the Paradise to which he referred?"

We have another question involving so nearly the same point that we present them together. It is this:—

"Is it not true that the Jews believed in the conscious state of the dead? If so, did not Christ give assent to the doctrine by his silence on the subject in the parable of the rich man and Lazarus?

Ans. On the point involved in these two questions which is chiefly, What did the Jews believe on these questions, we offer the following thoughts from Eld. J. H. Waggoner:—

"The question is almost always put thus, Do the Jews believe? &c., but an answer to this question is of no interest so far as the subject is concerned. The truth is the Jews now believe almost everything. The "Reform" Jews, as they call themselves, are infidels; they have no belief in the Bible. The orthodox Jews of the present day are restorationists, believing in the ultimate salvation of all. But they believe in a hell or purgatory where the righteous are confined four weeks, and the wicked eleven months, before their restoration. They also believe in the transmigration of souls, with many other vagaries. These beliefs are the outgrowth of their traditions, which are gathered from various sources. There are few people more superstitious than the Jews of the present day.

"We are convinced that it is not possible to ascertain at this day what traditional views the Jews held in the time of the Saviour. The best informed Jews do not pretend to know; they do not think it can be known. They have but one *reliable* source of information on such subjects, namely, the sacred Scriptures. Outside of these they may have imbibed other views from the nations with which they held intercourse, but of them we cannot be certain, and they must have been as vague as we know the fancies of the heathen nations were.

"The searcher for truth on this subject is shut up to the writings of the prophets or writers of the Hebrew Scriptures. These were the models of the Jewish faith, so far as they had any tangible faith. And we have the confession of the most eminent men, both Jews and Christians, that the writings of the Old Testament give no countenance to the Platonic idea of the soul, or the heathen notions of *hades*. It is true the confession is not greatly needed, for every reader must be struck with the fact. Both Jesus and his apostles always appealed to "the Scriptures" as the source and ground of belief, and we think it is safe to conclude that what the Scriptures did not contain they did not enforce or sanction.

"The Hebrew *sheol* and the Greek *hades* represented a state of death, of darkness and silence, from which the resurrection alone was expected to deliver man. When Christ the Son of God died, we learn that his soul was not left in *sheol*, Ps. 16:10; *hades*, Acts 2:31; *hell*, Eng. version. Now if the soul of the Saviour went to Paradise at death we are forced to conclude that Paradise is no other than the *sheol* of the Old Testament, the *hades* of the New, or the *hell* of our English rendering; and if so, then Paradise is a place of darkness, and silence, of no knowledge, for in this our Saviour's soul was not left, nor did his body see corruption, the resurrection rescuing him therefrom.

"'What say the Scriptures?' 'How readest thou?' Here is our only source of light and truth. Now if the Saviour's words can be explained in harmony with the teachings of the Scriptures we need look no further. We confidently say they can, and therefore rest without conjecturing what somebody else *may have* believed."

LESSON SEVENTEEN.

DESTINY OF THE WICKED—(CONTINUED).

WE have now examined briefly the testimony of the Bible in regard to the nature of man and his condition in death. The only remaining branch of the subject, namely, his destiny beyond the resurrection, next claims attention. From the evidence already presented, it is clear that the final doom of the wicked cannot be endless suffering, because we have seen that man has no immortal element in his nature. It only remains therefore that we take up those passages which are supposed to teach eternal suffering and see if they can be harmonized with the scriptures already examined.

It may be remarked first, that the immortality of the soul leads to some very grave conclusions. For instance, the punishment of the sinner is set forth as being eternal; and if the soul cannot cease

---

REVIEW QUESTIONS ON LESSON SEVENTEEN.

1. What is shown by the testimony already examined? 2. What then remains to be done? 3. To what contradictory conclusions does the doctrine of the immortality of

DESTINY OF THE WICKED.

to be conscious, the doctrine of eternal misery inevitably follows. On the other hand we read of a time when every intelligence in the universe will be ascribing honor, blessing and praise to God. And if the soul is immortal, we are just as clearly taught by this, the universal restoration of all the race. Christ says, speaking of the wicked, "These shall go away into everlasting punishment," but he adds immediately concerning the righteous, "but the righteous into life eternal." Here the same word is used in reference to the punishment of the wicked that is used to measure the life of the righteous. The punishment of the wicked therefore is eternal; and this overthrows universalism and the restoration view of Origen. How then can this scripture be harmonized with the declaration just quoted, that all living intelligences shall finally bless and praise the God of Heaven? The harmony is found in the nature of the punishment. This the Scriptures show to be death; and this view overthrows alike the restoration view of Origen and the eternal hell of Augustine.

We will now examine those passages of scripture which are put forth as evidence that the punishment threatened to the wicked is eternal misery.

1. Dan. 12:2. "But many of them that sleep in the dust of the earth shall awake, some to everlasting life and some to shame and everlasting contempt." The objector couples the shame with the contempt and makes both to be everlasting; but the

the soul lead? 4. In what terms does Christ describe the final destiny of the righteous and the wicked? 5. How long is the punishment of the wicked to be? 6. What doctrines does this overthrow? 7. How can this be harmonized with Rev. 5:13? 8. What is the punishment of the wicked? 9. What doctrines does this overthrow? 10. What

Scripture does not so express it. It is the contempt and that only that is said to be everlasting. The contempt is an emotion exercised not by the wicked, but by the righteous. The Syriac reads, "some to shame and the eternal contempt of their companions." The shame they will feel for themselves, which shows that they are raised to consciousness; but the contempt is exercised by the righteous so long as they hold them in remembrance at all. This text therefore furnishes no proof of the eternal suffering of the wicked.

2. Matt. 25 : 41. "Depart from me, ye cursed, into everlasting fire, prepared for the devil and his angels." Wicked men are not said in this text to be everlasting; and this destroys all the force of the passage for the popular view. Not even the devil is said to be everlasting; but only the fire. And in what respect is this everlasting? Not in its process of burning, but in its effects. Just as we read in Heb. 5 : 9 of eternal salvation; in Heb. 6 : 2 of eternal Judgment; in Heb. 9 : 12 of eternal redemption. Not a salvation Judgment and redemption that are forever going forward, but never accomplished, but such as are eternal in their effects.

3. Matt. 25 : 46. "And these shall go away into everlasting punishment, but the righteous into life eternal." As we have said, the punishment and the life mentioned in this text are of equal duration. But what is this punishment? The Greek word here used for punishment is *kolasis*, which is defined

objection is based on Dan 12 : 2? 11. What is here said to be everlasting? 12. By whom is the contempt spoken of, exercised? 13. How does the Syriac read? 14. In Matt. 25 : 41, what is said to be everlasting? 15. Why is the fire here called everlasting? 16. What parallel passages explain this? 17. What is the punishment spoken of in Matt. 25 : 46? 18. What is the Greek word here used for punishment? 19.

a *curtailing,* or *pruning.* The idea of "cutting off" is the prominent idea. The righteous go into everlasting life, but the wicked go into an everlasting "cutting off" from something. What is that? Happiness? No, but life or existence such as is given to the righteous.

But how, it will be asked, can death be an everlasting punishment? It is well understood that death is considered the highest punishment that can be inflicted in this world. And why? Because it deprives the individual of all the blessings of life which he might have enjoyed had he lived. So in the case of the wicked at the final Judgment. They are cut off from the eternal blessings of life in the kingdom of God which the righteous enjoy; and hence it is to them an everlasting punishment.

4. Mark 9:43, 44. "And if thy hand offend thee, cut it off; it is better for thee to enter into life maimed, than having two hands to go into hell, into the fire that never shall be quenched; where their worm dieth not and their fire is not quenched." Twice in verses 46 and 48 our Lord repeats this solemn sentence against the wicked. The word here used for hell is *gehenna,* a word used to designate the valley of Hinnom, near Jerusalem. The use of this word throws much light upon the passage before us; for in this valley fires were kept constantly burning to consume the bodies of malefactors and the filth of the city, which were cast into it, and what the fire failed to consume, the

What is its primary signification? 20. How does this apply to the wicked? 21. From what are the wicked cut off? 22. Is death a punishment? 23. How can it be called everlasting punishment in the cases of the wicked? 24. What is the language used in Mark 9:43, 44? 25. What is the word here translated hell? 26. What was it used to designate? 27. What was the peculiarity of this valley of Hinnom? 28.

worms preyed upon and destroyed. The figure then to which Christ called the minds of his hearers was that of complete and utter destruction.

With such language and such figures the Jews were familiar. Isaiah and Jeremiah frequently used them. The Lord, in Jeremiah 17 : 27, said that he would kindle a fire in the gates of Jerusalem which should not be quenched. 2 Chron. 36 : 19, 21 records the fulfillment of this. It was simply a fire which burned until it had entirely consumed the gates of Jerusalem. Psalm 37 : 20 says that the wicked shall consume into smoke. Malachi 4 : 3 says that they shall be ashes under the feet of the righteous. Ezekiel in chap. 20 : 47, 48 speaks of unquenchable fire in a similar manner.

But our Lord, in the passage under consideration, undoubtedly borrows the language he uses from Isa. 66 : 24. But here in Isaiah those that are subject to the unquenchable fire and the undying worm are not living persons but dead bodies. So the Jews would understand Christ by these terms to threaten complete and utter destruction against the wicked. Eusebius even uses the same terms, unquenchable fire, in reference to the martyrdom of Christians.

5. Jude 7. "Even as Sodom and Gomorrah and

What, then, would be suggested to the minds of Christ's hearers by these terms? 29. Were the Jews familiar with such imagery? 30. What is said in Jer. 17:27? 31. Was this unquenchable fire? 32. Where is the fulfillment of this threatening recorded? 33. What did this unquenchable fire do? 34. What is the meaning, then, of unquenchable, in this instance? 35. What does David say in Ps. 37:20? 36. What does Malachi say in 4:3? 37. Where does Ezekiel use the term unquenchable in a similar manner? 38. Where is the language found from which Mark 9:43, 44, was borrowed? 39. What does Isaiah represent the unquenchable fire as preying upon? 40. How does Eusebius use the term? 41. What is the next passage quoted to prove eternal misery?

the cities about them in like manner, giving themselves over to fornication, and going after strange flesh, are set forth for an example, suffering the vengeance of eternal fire." What is said to be eternal in this text? Not the people, not the suffering, but only the fire. And why is this called eternal? Simply because it is eternal in its effects. Sodom and Gomorrah will never recover themselves from that destruction. 2 Peter 2: 6 says, "And turning the cities of Sodom and Gomorrah into ashes condemned them with an overthrow, making them an ensample unto those that after should live ungodly." This text therefore proves, not that the wicked will be punished with eternal conscious suffering, but with an utter consumption, even as Sodom was consumed.

6. But two or more texts remain which are urged in favor of the doctrine of the eternal torment of the wicked. These both are found in the book of Revelation. The first is in Rev. 14:11, being a part of the third angel's message which is now under consideration: "And the smoke of their torment ascendeth up forever and ever; and they have no rest day nor night, who worship the beast and his image, and whosoever receiveth the mark of his name."

We first inquire of whom this is spoken? It is only of a particular class, those "who worship the beast and his image." This, therefore, is not decisive relative to the punishment of the wicked in general. But we inquire further, Does it mean eternal torment for those of whom it is spoken? As was said of the language quoted from Mark 10, so it may be of this. It is not original with the New

---

42. What is said to be eternal here? 43. Why is it called eternal? 44. How does 2 Pet. 2:6 explain this? 45. What is the next passage? 46. Of whom is this spoken? 47. Is

Testament, but is borrowed from the Old. In Isa.
34:9, 10 the prophet, speaking of Idumea, says,
"And the streams thereof shall be turned into
pitch, and the dust thereof into brimstone, and the
land thereof shall become burning pitch. It shall
not be quenched night nor day; the smoke thereof
shall go up forever: from generation to generation
it shall lie waste; none shall pass through it forever
and ever."

There are but two ways in which this language can
be understood, and in one of these ways it must be
understood. It refers either to the literal land of
Edom, east and south of Judea, or it is a figure to
represent the whole world in the day of final
conflagration. But in either case the meaning of
the language is evident. If the literal land of
Idumea is meant, and the language has reference to
the desolations which have fallen upon it, then
certainly no eternity of duration is implied in the
declaration that "the smoke thereof shall go up
forever;" for the judgments that fell upon that
land have long since ceased. But if it refers to the
fires of the last day, when the elements shall melt
with fervent heat, and the earth also, and the works
therein shall be burned up, even then, the terms
must be understood as denoting only limited duration; for from the ashes of the old earth, after a
suitable lapse of time, through the working of Him
who maketh all things new, there shall come forth
a new heavens and a new earth according to the
declaration of Peter, which shall be the eternal
abode of the righteous.

this language original with the New Testament? 48. From
what is it borrowed? 49. What does Isa. 34:9, 10, say of
Idumea? 50. What are the only two ways in which this can
be understood? 51. If it refers to the literal land of Idumea,
what conclusion are we led to? 52. If it is a figure representing the general conflagration of the last day, what is the

As we thus see that the terms as used in the Bible denote limited duration, we inquire if the lexicons define them in the same manner? The terms used are *aion* and *aionios*. *Aion* is defined by Greenfield, Schrevelius, Liddell and Scott, Parkhurst, Robinson, Schleusner, Wahl and Cruden, as meaning finite duration as well as infinite. The term seems to imply primarily, simply duration or the flow of time; but the extent of that must be defined by other terms. When it is applied to objects which we are told will endure absolutely without end, as God, Christ, angels, the saints' inheritance, and immortal beings, it means unlimited duration; but when it is applied to objects which we know will come to an end, it then covers only the length of time during which those things exist. Dr. Clarke in his closing remarks on 2 Kings, 5th chapter, gives us this rule for the interpretation of the words *forever and ever*. He says they "take in the whole extent or duration of the things to which they are applied." If, therefore, we find other declarations stating positively that the wicked will come to an end, and we do find multitudes of such, then this term forever, or forever and ever, applied to them, must signify only the length of time during which they exist.

The second word, *aionios*, is subject in all respects to the same definition and rule which is noticed above in reference to *aion*.

The second passage, Rev. 20:10, being exactly parallel to the one found in Revelation 14, is

conclusion still? 53. What do the terms forever and ever as used in the Bible represent? 54. What are the Greek terms employed for these words? 55. What is the meaning of these terms? 56. What lexicographers give this among the significations of these terms? 57. What is Dr. Clarke's rule, and where found? 58. What may be said of *aionios?* 59. How is Rev. 20:10 explained? 60. When does Rev.

explained in the same manner. Rev. 14:11 doubtless applies at the beginning of the thousand years,
when the *beast* and the *false prophet* are cast into
the lake of fire burning with brimstone, as stated
in Rev. 19:20; while the passage in Rev. 20:10
refers to a similar scene of destruction visited upon
Satan and all his hosts at the end of the thousand
years.

7. Having now examined all the texts supposed
to teach eternal misery, and having found that all
are easily harmonized with the view of the destruction of the wicked, and that some are even the
strongest testimony *for* that doctrine, we now look
at a few of the passages of the Bible which speak
positively of the doom of the lost:—

Eze. 18:26: "When a righteous man turneth
away from his righteousness, and committeth iniquity, and dieth in them; for his iniquity that he
hath done shall he die." Here two deaths are
brought to view: the first, a death *in* sin, and the
other a consequence following that, a death *for* sin.
We have seen that the first death, leaves a man
unconscious in the grave; and the second must
leave him in the same condition, with no promise
of a resurrection.

Paul says in Rom. 6:23, "The wages of sin is
death;" and James (1:15) corroborates this testimony in saying, "Sin, when it is finished, bringeth
forth death." Death cannot, by any proper definition, be made to mean continuance in life. "The
death that never dies" is a contradiction of terms.

Here are some of the declarations of the Bible
respecting the wicked: They shall be destroyed,
Ps. 145:20; they shall perish, John. 3:16; they

14:11, doubtless apply? 61. When, Rev. 20:10? 62. What
is taught in Eze. 18:26? 63. What texts sustain this view?
64. What does **Ps. 145:20,** say of the wicked? 65. John

shall go to perdition, Heb. 10:39; they shall come to an end, and be as though they had not been, Ps. 37:10, Obad. 16; they are compared to the most inflammable and perishable substances, as a potter's vessel, Ps. 2:9; beasts that perish, Ps. 49:20; a whirlwind that passeth away, Ps. 68:2; a water-less garden, Isa. 1:30; garments consumed by the moth, Isa. 51:8; thistle down scattered by the whirlwind, Isa. 17:13; the fat of lambs consumed in the fire, Ps. 37:20; ashes, Mal. 4:3; wax, Ps. 68:2; tow, Is. 1:31; thorns, Is. 34:12; exhausted waters, Ps. 58:7.

In the New Testament they are likened to chaff which is to be burned entirely up, Matt. 3:12; tares to be consumed, Matt. 13:40; withered branches to be burned, John. 15:6; bad fish cast away to corruption, Matt. 13:47, 48; a house thrown down, Luke 6:49; the old world destroyed by water, Luke 17:29; the Sodomites destroyed by fire, 2 Pet. 2:5, 6; natural brute beasts that perish in their own corruption, 2 Pet. 2:12.

Finally, the teaching of the Bible on this subject may be summed up in this proposition: The wicked shall be consumed and devoured by fire, Isa. 5:20–24, Ps. 37:20, Rev. 20:9. The word, in this last reference rendered devoured, says Prof. Stuart, "is intensive, so that it denotes utter excision."

In the light of these testimonies from the Script-ures we can readily understand how it is that the wicked are to be recompensed in the earth. Prov.

3:16, what? 66. Heb. 10:39, what? 67. Ps. 37:10, and Obad. 16, what? 68. To what kind of substances are the wicked compared? 69. Name the texts and tell how they speak of them? 70. What are the New Testament representations? 71. What general proposition covers the teaching of the Bible on this question? 72. What is Prof. Stuart's definition of devour in Rev. 20:9? 73. What bearing have these testimonies on Prov. 11:31? 74. How

11:31. Coming up in the second resurrection at the end of the thousand years, they surround the beloved city, New Jerusalem, then descended from Heaven, and their fearful retribution then overtakes them. This is the day of Judgment and perdition of ungodly men, described by Peter. 2 Pet. 3:10, 12; and this is the fire that melts the earth and the elements with fervent heat.

We can also understand how the righteous are recompensed in the earth according to the same passage in Proverbs; for they, after the destruction of the wicked, go forth and take possession of the earth made new as their eternal inheritance.

We can also understand how and when Rev. 5:13 is to be fulfilled; for now we have a universe clean and pure. Satan and all his followers are destroyed, the last taints of the curse and the least stains of sin are all wiped away, and all creatures raise their voices in the glad anthem of universal jubilee, ascribing "blessing and honor and glory and power unto Him that sitteth on the throne, and unto the Lamb forever."

There is something most dishonorable to God in the idea that sin, introduced contrary to his will, must continue to all eternity. Its origin and its temporary continuance we can explain on Scriptural and rational principles; but its eternity, never.

With this view of eternal misery there is the most fearful discrepancy between the sins of this finite life and the eternal suffering visited upon them; hence divines are driven to say that the sins will continue in hell. Benson says that they, (sinners) "must be perpetually swelling their enor-

does the doctrine of the eternity of sin affect our views of the character of God? 75. How can sin and the punishment be balanced on the ground of eternal misery? 76. What does Benson say? 77. How does this represent the sinner? 78.

mous sums of guilt and still running deeper, immensely deeper in debt to divine and infinite justice." This represents the sinner as being able to accumulate his load of guilt faster than God can devise terrors and judgments adequate to their punishment. But the Bible says that we are to give an account for the deeds done in the body, or in this life only, and be rewarded according to our works here. God has made no provision for the eternity of sin, but has devised the most effectual means to prevent it.

The philosophical objections, resting on the ground of immateriality, and that matter cannot think, the capacities of the soul, and the analogies of nature are disproved by an examination of the powers and capacities of the brute creation. It is said that immortality is assumed in the Bible; or as Bishop Tillotson says, "taken for granted." But it cannot be taken for granted any more than the immortality of Jehovah; and that is expressly revealed.

It is said again, that annihilation is impossible. We answer, True, in reference to matter, as matter, (that is, we have no evidence that God will annihilate matter, though he could do so if he chose), but not in reference to intelligent and conscious beings. And we claim that the wicked are to cease to be, only in this respect.

It is said that this doctrine has an evil tendency. If so, let the objector show us the infidels, criminals, profane, wicked and corrupt persons in the ranks of the friends of this doctrine. The truth is just

---

What does the Bible say we are to be punished for? 79. Does God provide for the eternity of sin? 80. How are some of the objections of Philosophy disproved? 81. What may be said about annihilation? 82. What about the charge that this doctrine has an evil tendency?

the opposite of this. Multitudes in the light of this teaching are able for the first time to exclaim that they can harmonize the ways of God with reason and revelation; and therefore can believe the Bible to be his word.

LESSON EIGHTEEN.

THE SEVEN LAST PLAGUES.

THE subject of the seven last plagues is another theme that demands examination in connection with the third angel's message; for they are brought to view in the message itself, and are intimately connected with it according to other prophecies, following immediately its close. The threatening which this message utters is expressed in these words: "The same shall drink of the wine of the wrath of God which is poured out without mixture into the cup of his indignation." The first verse of chapter 15, speaks of judgments in which " is filled up the wrath of God." This must certainly mean the same as the unmixed wrath threatened in the message. But here it is plainly said to be the seven last plagues.

This is still further proved by the chronology of these plagues. They are still future; for they cannot be poured out till the work in the sanctuary is finished. John says in Rev. 15:5–8 that the temple

---

REVIEW QUESTIONS ON LESSON EIGHTEEN.

1. What other subject is connected with the third angel's message? 2. Where are the seven last plagues brought to view? 3. In what language is the threatening expressed? 4. What expression is used in Rev. 15:1? 5. What must this be equivalent to? 6. What is the judgment of Rev. 15: 1, called? 7. Can these plagues be poured out till the work in the sanctuary is closed? 8. How is this proved? 9.

of the tabernacle in Heaven was opened. This brings
to view the work of Christ in the most holy place.
From that temple then came forth seven angels with
the seven last plagues, and while they were pouring
them out, the temple was filled with the glory of
the Lord so that no one was able to enter therein,
till the seven plagues of the seven angels were fulfilled. This brings us to the time when the priesthood of Christ has closed; for till then there will
be some one ministering in that temple. Being
thus future they must be that unmixed wrath
threatened in the third message, which is the last
judgment to be inflicted on men before the Lord
appears.

The chronology of these plagues is shown more
fully still by the language of the first plague itself.
Rev. 16:1. This first messenger of wrath pours out
his vial upon the earth, and there falls a noisome
and grievous sore upon those who have the mark of
the beast, and upon those who worship his image.
But this reception of the mark and worship of the
image, is the very thing against which the
third angel's message warns us. These plagues,
therefore, do not fall till the third angel's message is
concluded.

Now if we say that these plagues have been
poured out in the past, ages in the past as some contend, or that they even commenced to be poured out
then, it follows that the third angel's message
accomplished its work ages in the past. But the
third message warns us against two antecedent
powers brought to view in Rev. 13: the leopard

Upon whom does the first plague fall? 10. By what are we
warned against receiving the mark, &c.? 11. What is the
chronology of these plagues, therefore, as compared with the
message? 12. If we throw the beginning of these plagues
ages in the past as some demand, where must we put the
message? 13. What then becomes of the leopard beast and

beast and the two-horned beast. These could not have existed and acted later than the message which warned against them.

But if, in order to have the first plague poured out ages in the past, we place the third message there, we throw the second and first still further back. But the first message, identical with the angel of Rev. 10, is based upon the fulfillment of the prophetic periods. Hence we thus throw all prophetic interpretation ages away from our own time, where it is having its fulfillment. But we have shown that the two-horned beast is now on the stage of action, preparing to perform his last work, and that the third angel's message is now going forth, and beginning to be heard in power. The plagues which follow it are therefore future, the last manifestation of God's wrath upon the last generation of men, after the third angel has ceased his warning, and the work in the sanctuary is ended, and a mediator no longer stands between God and men to stay from them the vials of his indignation.

These plagues will be literal. A parallel is found in the plagues inflicted upon the Egyptians, as recorded in Ex. chaps. 7–10, which no one thinks of regarding other than literal. The terrible nature of these judgments is sufficiently learned from the record given us in Rev. 16.

As the result of the first plague, a terrible and

---

two-horned beast of Rev. 13? 14. And how are the first and second messages affected by this view? 15. With what is the first message of Rev. 14, identical? 16. Upon what is it based? 17. Then how is all prophetic interpretation affected by such an application? 18. What has already been proved? 19. What do all these arguments show in reference to the plagues? 20. Will the plagues be literal 21. What parallel plagues are brought to view in the Bible? 22. Where is the record of these plagues? 23. What is the result of the

grievous sore breaks out upon the men which have the mark of the beast.

As the result of the second plague, the sea becomes as the blood of a dead man, the most infectious and deadly substance known. If the sea here means the oceans of our globe, as it probably does, we leave the reader to imagine as far as he can the terrible effects of this plague. It is no wonder that John says that every living soul died in the sea.

At the pouring out of the third vial, the rivers and fountains of waters become blood. This touches the human family in a still more vital point. Probably these two plagues will be of short duration; for otherwise it would seem that all flesh must perish from the face of the earth. John heard the angel say, as this plague was poured out, Thou art righteous, O Lord; for they have shed the blood of saints and prophets, and thou hast given them blood to drink. The query may arise how the last generation of the wicked, who are not permitted to slay the saints, can be said to have shed the blood of saints and prophets. The answer is, They designed to do it, determined to do it, tried to do it, Rev. 13:15–17, and are therefore just as guilty as if they had done it. It is no virtue in them that God restrains them from their evil intentions, and they meet the just fate of the actual transgressor.

The fourth angel pours out his vial upon the sun, and it scorches the earth with unwonted heat, thus most fearfully intensifying the effects of the preceding plagues. In the result of this plague we doubtless find a fulfillment of Joel 1:14–20.

first vial? 24. Of the second? 25. Of the third? 26. How can it be said of men at this time that they have shed the blood of saints and prophets? 27. What is the effect of the fourth vial? 28. What prophecy is fulfilled in this? 29.

The fifth angel pours out his vial upon the seat of the beast, and darkness like that which overspread Egypt pervades his kingdom. This judgment is inflicted especially upon the papacy, the seat of the beast being Rome, and his kingdom being his subjects wherever they are found. In the description of this plague we find an expression which shows that all these plagues fall upon the same generation; for it says that they blasphemed God, because of their pains and their sores. These sores must be the ones brought to view under the first plague. Those upon whom the first vial was poured, many of them at least, are thus shown to be still living under the fifth plague, and still suffering from the effects of the first plague.

The sixth angel pours out his vial upon the great river Euphrates. This is a symbol of the Ottoman empire, and the drying up of its waters denotes the utter consumption and overthrow of that power. And the way seems to be even now preparing for that consummation. Under this plague three unclean spirits go forth from the dragon, beast and false prophet, that is, Paganism, the Papacy, and apostate Protestantism. In this we behold the work of spiritualism which has already made such headway in the world. Some have even concluded that we are already under this sixth plague because of the decline of the Turkish power, and the work of

Upon what locality is the fifth plague poured? 30. What is the seat of the beast? 31. What is his kingdom? 32. What proof is found here that these plagues fall upon the same generation of men? 33. Upon what is the sixth vial poured? 34. What is here symbolized by the river Euphrates? 35. What is meant by the drying up of its waters? 36. What further development takes place under this plague? 37. What is meant by the dragon, beast and false prophet? 38. What is denoted by these spirits? 39. What conclusion have some come to from the condition of Turkey and the

THE SEVEN LAST PLAGUES.

spiritualism. But before the Euphrates can be entirely consumed, there must be a process of the drying up of its waters, and before the spirits can go out of the *mouth* of the dragon, beast and false prophet, they must win their way into the hearts of these powers. We now see the preparatory work going forward: the strength, resources, influence of the Turkish power are growing less and less, and the spirits of devils are making their way into the high places of the earth. Under this plague we behold the completion of this work; and it cannot, from present indications be far distant.

The work of the spirits when they thus go forth with authority is to gather the kings of the earth and of the whole world to the battle of the great day of God Almighty which is then impending. They are gathered into a place called Armageddon. The spirits gather them there. In our English version it reads, "*he* gathered them;" but in the Greek a neuter plural subject can regularly take a verb in the singular number; and the subject of the singular verb " gathered " in verse 16, is the neuter plural spirits (*pneumata*) of verse 14.

The seventh angel pours out his vial into the air. The effect of this is all-pervading. A great earthquake such as never before was known rends the earth from center to circumference. The cities of the nations fall. Great Babylon receives her cup of wrath. The islands and mountains flee away; and great hailstones, about the weight of a talent (57 lbs.) each, fall upon men. Here are seen the treasures of

work of spiritualism? 40. How is this explained? 41. What is the object of the work of these spirits? 42. Who gathers the nations? 43. What criticism is made on the singular verb of verse 16? 44. Where is the seventh and last vial poured out? 45. What then takes place? 46. What is the weight of the hailstones that then fall? 47.

hail which God has reserved against this day of
trouble and battle and war. Job 28:22, 23. This
plague brings us into scenes which are intimately
connected with the coming of Christ. See Rev.
6:14–17. Christ soon appears; and those who have
survived through all these judgments, are slain by
the spirit of his mouth and the brightness of his
coming. Rev. 19:21; 2 Thess. 2:8.

For some of the gracious promises which are given
to the people of God during this time of fearful
trouble, a time of trouble on the nations, such as
never was, Dan. 12:1, read the 91st psalm.

CLASS QUESTIONS ON LESSON XVIII., WITH ANSWERS.

1. The plagues mentioned in Rev. 16:1, are to
fall on those who have the mark of the beast. Will
not those lands where they do not have the mark
be exempt?

ANS. It is only the first plague which is said to
fall especially upon those who have the mark of the
beast, and who worship his image; and such persons
seem to be the only ones involved in it. Of course
it will fall upon them in whatever country they are;
and those countries where there are none of this
class will be exempt from this plague; but other
plagues are more extensive in their application, and
the whole earth is finally involved in the judgments
threatened.

What Old Testament declaration is then fulfilled? 48. Into
what scenes does this plague bring us? 49. How are those
who survive the plagues finally slain? References. 50. To
what does the time of trouble such as never was, mentioned
in Dan. 12:1, apply? (This trouble coming on the nations
is not to be confounded with the tribulation such as never
was, Matt. 24:21, which comes upon the church.) 51.
What promises have the saints during this time of trouble?

2. Rev. 16:12. Who are the kings (plural) of the east, and from what stand-point do we reckon?

Ans. The great river Euphrates is dried up that the way of the kings of the east might be prepared. The objective point to which the nations are gathered together under this plague is Armageddon, or Mount Megiddo, overlooking the plain in the half tribe of Manasseh. This is probably the same as the "valley of Jehoshaphat," to which the heathen will be gathered; as declared in Joel 3:12. In Jerusalem, therefore, or the land of Palestine, is the stand-point from which we are to determine the points of the compass. The principal nationality lying east of Palestine is Persia; but there are other petty tribes, sovereignties and nationalities, described in Joel as the heathen, who are more or less intimately connected with Persia in all her interests and movements; and who, with Persia, doubtless constitute the kings of the east here spoken of.

It may be asked further, for what the way of these kings is prepared by the drying up of the Euphrates? and the answer is, The way is prepared for them to come up to the battle of the great day of God Almighty. Persia claims a personal interest in the land of Palestine, regarding it as rightfully belonging to her dominion, dating from the conquest of Cyrus. The Greek Church, or the Russians, and the Catholic Church, both claim a right there, because there are the holy sepulchers. This is the great bone of contention. Yet, so long as the integrity of the Ottoman empire is maintained, which now controls that land, these other parties cannot go in to claim what they call their rights. But as soon as the Euphrates, or the Ottoman Empire, is dried up, then nothing will prevent these powers from coming into collision at Jerusalem in behalf of the interests which they there consider that they have at stake.

3. Please explain James 5:7. What is meant by the latter rain? or what relation does it hold to the third angel's message?

ANS. The early and the latter rain spoken of in this verse is doubtless taken as a figure to represent special blessings to come down upon the church at the beginning and close of this dispensation.

The early, or the former rain, is applied to the outpouring of the Spirit on the day of Pentecost; and the latter rain will be a still greater outpouring of God's Spirit as the dispensation closes. It is, therefore, very intimately connected with the third angel's message, and will doubtless be experienced when that message goes in its greatest power.

There are many scriptures which speak of the great outpouring of the Spirit upon the church to take place at this time, to a few of which we here refer: Rev. 3:20; 2 Pet. 1:19; Rev. 12:17; 19:10; 18:1; Dan. 12:1.

The latter rain which literally came down upon the husbandman ripened the grain for the harvest; so the outpouring of the Spirit in the last days ripens the saints for the heavenly garner. Rev. 14:15, 16. And the coming of the Lord is at the door when James introduces this figure of the early and the latter rain.

LESSON NINETEEN.

THE ONE HUNDRED AND FORTY-FOUR THOUSAND.

As we investigate the third angel's message, we naturally feel an interest to know if the prophecies anywhere intimate what the effect of this message will be; or what measure of success will attend it. We think we find this clearly indicated in the seventh chapter of Revelation. We have shown that the angel ascending with the seal of the living God here brought to view is the same as the third angel of Rev. 14. And as the result of this work, in Rev. 7, it is declared that 144,000 were sealed as the servants of God.

But says one, the 144,000 cannot belong to the present generation, or be gathered in the gospel dispensation; for they were sealed out of the twelve tribes of the children of Israel. A sufficient answer to this is found in the testimony of James. He, writing in A. D. 60, to Christians, and for the benefit of Christians, and carrying us down even to the coming of Christ, addresses his epistle to the twelve tribes scattered abroad. It is evident, therefore, that Christians are counted as belonging to the twelve tribes.

In what sense are they so considered? for there are no genealogies of tribes preserved in this dis-

---

REVIEW QUESTIONS ON LESSON NINETEEN.

1. What scripture indicates the result of the third angel's message? 2. With what is the sealing angel of Rev. 7, identical? 3. What is the result of the sealing work of Rev. 7? 4. From whom are the 144,000 gathered? 5. What do some conclude from this? 6. Where do we find an answer? 7. When did James write? 8. For whom and to whom did he write? 9. Under what title does he address them? 10. What does this prove? 11. Where and by what

pensation. Paul illustrates this by a beautiful figure in the eleventh chapter of Romans. He sets forth the people of God in the former dispensation, the literal Israel, under the figure of an olive tree with twelve branches. These branches represented the twelve tribes of the children of Israel. These branches were broken off, which signified that the Jews by rejecting Christ ceased to be God's people.

The Gentiles, who accepted Christ, were taken by the Lord as his people; and Paul represents this movement by branches of a wild olive grafted into the tame. Where the natural branches, the Jews, were broken off, there the wild olive, the Gentiles, were grafted in. Now, how did this effect the tree? There were, at first, twelve branches, representing the twelve tribes of the children of Israel; and after they were broken off, and grafts were inserted from the Gentiles, or Christians, there are still twelve branches, or tribes, in the household of faith

These are not the literal seed, but spiritual; because they are brought in by faith. So we hear Paul saying in Rom. 2:28, 29, "He is not a Jew, which is one outwardly; neither is that circumcision, which is outward in the flesh; but he is a Jew, which is one inwardly; and circumcision is that of the heart, in the spirit, and not in the letter." Again, Paul says, Rom. 9:6-8, "They are not all Israel which are of Israel; neither, because they are the seed of Abraham, are they all children; but, In Isaac shall thy seed be called. That is, They which are

figure does Paul illustrate this matter? 12. By what are the people of God in the former dispensation represented? 13. What did the twelve branches signify? 14. What became of these branches? 15. What did this illustrate? 16. What then was done? 17. When the Gentiles are grafted in, what is the condition of the tree? 18. What kind of a seed are these Gentiles? 19. Name and explain, the texts which prove that they are a spiritual seed? 20. May the 144,000

the children of the flesh, these are not the children of God; but the children of the promise are counted for the seed." And he adds in Gal. 4:28, that, "We, brethren, [Christians] as Isaac was, are the children of promise." And he adds in the next verse, that he was born after the Spirit.

Nothing could be plainer than these testimonies, that there is a spiritual seed, reckoned as the true Israel, perpetuated, not in a literal, but a spiritual, sense.

Because the twelve tribes, therefore, are mentioned in Revelation from whom the 144,000 are sealed, that is no evidence that they are not taken from the gospel dispensation; or even from the closing portion of it. But we have still clearer evidence to present upon this point.

The New Jerusalem, which John saw coming down from God out of Heaven, in which there was the throne of the Lamb, as well as the throne of God, will not certainly be considered a Jewish city; for in the twelve foundations were the names of the twelve apostles. But on the twelve gates of that city, as described in Rev. 21:12, there are names written, which are the names of the twelve tribes of the children of Israel.

Now all the people of God, from Adam to the close of the gospel dispensation, will go into that city through some one of those twelve gates; hence, all will be reckoned, both Jews and Christians, as belonging to some one of the twelve tribes.

No genealogy is kept of those tribes here upon earth, as it is not necessary that men should now

therefore be sealed from Christians even at the close of this dispensation? 21. What city did John see coming down from God out of Heaven? 22. Was this a Jewish or a Christian city? 23. What proves it a Christian city? 24. What does it have upon its twelve gates? 25. What does this prove? 26. Where is the genealogy of the tribes now

understand these distinctions. But Paul speaks of the church of the first born written in Heaven, giving us to understand that the record is kept there. The only object of preserving the tribes distinct in the former dispensation was that the prophecies concerning Christ, who was to spring from a particular tribe, might be fulfilled; and the Jews might thus be able to identify the Messiah. But since Christ has come, that necessity no longer exists; and hence the genealogy of the tribes has been irrecoverably lost.

This company, the 144,000, are again brought to view in Rev. 14:1-5. And here we have indisputable evidence that they are gathered from the last generation of the living. John says, A Lamb stood on Mount Zion, and with him, a hundred forty and four thousand, having his Father's name written in their foreheads. This name is the same as the seal of God brought to view in Rev. 7; hence this company is the same as the 144,000 of chapter 7.

And of these it is said, that they were "redeemed from the earth," and "redeemed from among men." This can mean nothing else but translation from among the living. These first five verses of Rev. 14 belong to chapter 13, and are a continuation of that prophecy. This 144,000 are the ones who pass through the terrible conflict with the two-horned beast power, described in Rev. 13:11-17. But we have shown that this power is a symbol of our

kept? 27. What was the object of preserving the genealogy in the former dispensation? 28. Does that object any longer exist? 29. Where are the 144,000 again brought to view? 30. What conclusion can be drawn from this reference? 31. What does John say of this company? 32. What is the Father's name? 33. What does this show? 34. From what are this company said to be redeemed? 35. What does this expression prove? 36. To what prophecy do the first five verses of Rev. 14 belong? 37. Through what conflict, therefore, do these 144,000 pass? 38. What is the two-horned

own government, is now upon the stage of action, and is the last power which persecutes the church of God. Therefore the 144,000 are the ones who are developed by the third angel's message, and who will be translated from among men at the second coming of Christ.

The sealing work of Rev. 7 results in sealing the number here specified; but as this is identical with the third angel's message, this sealing work has for many years already been going forward; and some whose whole religious experience has been connected with, and is owing to, this work, have fallen asleep since the message commenced. Will they be reckoned with this 144,000? If so, how can it be said that they are redeemed from among men, or translated?

We answer, before Christ comes, there is a partial resurrection to take place, according to Dan. 12:2, and Rev. 1:7. Daniel says, "Many of them that sleep in the dust of the earth shall awake, some to everlasting life, and some to shame and everlasting contempt." This is not the general resurrection of either class; for at the general resurrection of the righteous there are no wicked ones to be raised, and at the general resurrection of the wicked there are no righteous ones included. But here is a mixed resurrection, taking some, a few, of both classes; and this occurs in connection with the standing up of Michael, and the closing time of trouble. We, therefore, infer that at this time, probably when the

---

beast, and when does he do his work? 39. To what conclusion does this lead respecting the 144,000? 40. How long has this sealing work been going forward? 41. What has taken place with some who have been brought out by this message? 42. Will they be numbered with the 144,000, or help compose that company? 43. How can they be said to be redeemed from among men? 44. How is it shown that Daniel's words apply before the general resurrection? 45. At what point are they probably raised? 46. In what condition

voice of God is heard, Joel 3:16, Heb. 12:27, and
Rev. 16:17, some of the pre-eminently wicked will
come forth, and all those who have died in the third
angel's message. Being then raised from the dead,
and taking their place with those who have not died
under this message, they are translated when the
Lord appears; and hence, with the others, may also
be said to be redeemed from among men.

CLASS QUESTIONS ON LESSON XIX., WITH ANSWERS.

1. Are the Seventh-day Baptists included in the
144,000? If so, then what will be done with the
7,000,000 Sabbath-keepers in China as reported
lately in the REVIEW, and many in other portions
of the world, who are keeping the Sabbath?

ANS. The question is not properly put. We cannot tell now who will be included in the 144,000, when
that number is developed. In regard to the 7,000,-
000 Sabbath-keepers in China, there is considerable
doubt hanging over that matter, and we wait for
more definite information before accepting the
report. Should it be asked, (which would be the
proper way of putting the question), will the Seventh-day Baptists be included in the 144,000, we
answer that before the end we understand that the
religious world will be divided into just two classes,
those who keep the Sabbath, and those who oppose
it; and we believe that all the Sabbath-keepers of
whatever name, or perhaps having dropped all distinctive names, will compose that number.

2. Do you understand that all that are saved
from 1844 to the end of time will be included in the
144,000?

---

are they raised? 47. How do they gain immortality? 48.
Can they, like the others, be then said to be redeemed from
among men?

Ans. By no means. For multitudes of honest, sincere, godly people have died since then who knew nothing of this message. And they, living up to the best light they had, will undoubtedly be saved. According to the Scriptures, a person is accountable for the light he receives. And when in all sincerity they serve God according to their best light and knowledge, he accepts them. But when light is brought before them and from selfish or worldly considerations they reject the light, they bring themselves into condemnation, and without repentance and reformation can never be saved. This principle holds in regard to every new truth that has ever been introduced into the world from the days of John the Baptist to the present time.

3. Are the 144,000 the ones which come out of great tribulation mentioned in Rev. 7:14? Are not those that come out of great tribulation the saints mentioned in Dan. 7:21?

Ans. We think the 144,000 are the ones referred to in Rev. 7:14; for John had just seen the great multitude of the redeemed, and says that they came out of all nations, kindreds, peoples and tongues. He understood who these were; but then a company is singled out who were so peculiar that he knew not from whence they came, and when the angel asked him, he simply replied "Thou knowest." The martyrs who are the ones spoken of in Dan. 7:21 are brought to view again in Rev. 20:4, but yet as distinct from those who did not worship the beast, neither his image, nor receive his mark, who are the 144,000. It may be asked then how the 144,000 who were not put to death by persecuting powers can be said to come out of great tribulation in comparison with the martyrs. We reply, they pass through the time of trouble and witness the seven last plagues as they are inflicted upon the wicked, which will present the most fearful scenes ever beheld upon the earth. Those who die in the message escape this fearful trial, and are hence said to be "blessed," Rev. 14:13, are exceptions to this declaration about coming out of great tribulation.

4. Will children of Sabbath-keepers help to constitute the 144,000 of Rev. 14:1?

ANS. This depends upon the standard of computation. If the number is computed according to the rule followed with the children of Israel when they came out of Egypt, it will include only the adult males, the women and children not being reckoned in the number, though still being among the saved. This idea has been suggested, yet we have always supposed that it would take all the Sabbath-keepers, both men, women, and children, to make up the 144,000 when the Lord appears.

5. What is the song sung by the 144,000 which no others could learn?

ANS. The song of their experience. It is called in Rev. 15:3 the song of Moses and the song of the Lamb. The song of Moses was the song which he sang when delivered from his Egyptian oppressors. It recounted their marvelous deliverance and the utter overthrow of their enemies. So the 144,-000, passing through an experience such as no others in all the history of the world have had, are able to sing a song recounting their experience, such as no others are able to sing. It is not only the song of Moses, recounting deliverance from their outward enemies, but the song of the Lamb, recounting their victory over all inward and spiritual foes; for Christ says, "To him that overcometh, will I grant to sit with me in my throne, even as I also overcame and am set down with my Father in his throne."

LESSON TWENTY.

THE SEVEN CHURCHES.

In Rev. 2 and 3 are seven short epistles addressed to seven churches. We regard these, like other lines of prophecy in this book, as prophetic, covering the whole gospel dispensation. A few of the reasons why we regard these as prophetic are as follows:—

There were more churches in Asia than seven. Even if we confine ourselves to that western division of Asia known as Asia Minor, or even that small fraction of Asia Minor where the seven churches were situated which are addressed, there were other important churches in the same territory. Collosse was but a short distance from Laodicea. Miletus was nearer than any of the seven to Patmos, where John had his vision. And Troas, where Paul spent a season with the disciples, was not far from Pergamos.

Why, then, were just seven churches selected out of this number and not all of them addressed, if what is said pertained only to the Christians of those times? The entire book of Revelation was dedicated to the seven churches. But the prophecy of this book was no more applicable to the seven literal churches named, than to other Christians in Asia Minor, those for instance who dwelt in Pontus,

---

REVIEW QUESTIONS ON LESSON TWENTY.

1. How are these churches to be regarded? 2. Among the reasons for considering them prophetic, what is the first one? 3. Where was Collosse situated? 4. What was the situation of Miletus? 5. Where was Troas? 6. How much was dedicated to these seven churches? 7. Did the prophecy concern them particularly and personally? 8. In what other countries were these Christians equally concerned in

Galatia, Cappadocia, and Bithynia. Only a small portion of the book of Revelation could have personally concerned the churches named, or any of the Christians of John's day; for the events it brings to view were mostly so far in the future as to be beyond the life-time of the generation then living.

Again, the seven stars which the Son of man held in his right hand are declared to be the angels of the seven churches. The angels of the churches, doubtless, denote the ministers of the churches. Their being held in the right hand of the Son of man must denote his upholding power, guidance and protection. But are there only seven thus cared for by the Master? Rather, are not all the true ministers of the whole gospel age thus upheld and supported by him?

Still further, John, looking into the Christian dispensation, saw only seven candlesticks representing seven churches, in the midst of which sat the Son of man. His position in their midst must denote his presence with them, his watchcare over them, and his searching scrutiny of all their works. But does he thus regard only seven individual churches in this dispensation? Does not this rather represent his position in reference to all the churches in this age?

Why then were these particular churches chosen that are mentioned? Doubtless for the reason that the names of these churches are significant, indica-

the prophecies of the book of Revelation? 9. When were these events mostly to take place? 10. What do the seven stars denote? 11. Where were these seven stars seen? 12. What did this signify? 13. What does this prove in reference to the seven churches? 14. How many candlesticks did John see? 15. What is signified by Christ's position in the midst of these? 16. What does this prove in reference to the churches? 17. Why then were there seven particular

ting the religious features of those periods of the gospel age which they respectively represent. If for these reasons and others which might be adduced, these epistles are prophetic, we understand them to apply to seven distinct periods of the gospel age, from the days of John to the end of time.

Let us then see if we can find an application of these epistles, which is both Scriptural and consistent, to seven different portions of the gospel dispensation.

First, the church of Ephesus. This word signifies desirable, *chief,* and it may well be taken as expressive of the character and condition of the church in its first state. Christ tells them that they have tried them which say they are apostles and are not. This could appropriately be addressed to a church covering the apostolic age. But even before this period ended, the church had begun to lose her first love and was admonished to repent. The promise to the overcomer, verse 7, reveals the important fact that the tree of life once here upon the earth is now in the paradise of God. We understand this period to cover the age of the apostles and their immediate successors.

The next address is to the church of Smyrna, which signifies *myrrh,* and seems to be a fit appellation for the church of God as it was about to pass through the fiery furnace of persecution and prove itself a "sweet smelling savor" unto God. This church was to have tribulation ten days. If this

churches taken as the ones to whom to address the Revelation? 18. If these epistles are prophetic what do they represent? 19. What is the meaning of Ephesus? 20. How does this apply to the first church? 21. What is said about apostles is this message? 22. What does that prove? 23. What important fact is here revealed in regard to the tree of life? 24. What church is next addressed? 25. What is the meaning of the word Smyrna? 26. What took place to

address to the church is prophetic, those days are prophetic and signify ten years. We have then a notable persecution of ten years duration here brought to view. And it is an undisputable fact that the last and most bloody of the ten persecutions under Diocletian continued just ten years from A. D. 302 to A. D. 312. Buck's Theological Dictionary, pp. 332, 333.

It would be difficult to make an application of this language on the ground that these messages are not prophetic; for in that case only ten literal days could be meant, and we can hardly suppose that a persecution of only ten days on a single church would be a matter of prophecy. But more than this, all the churches suffered in these persecutions; and where, then, would be the propriety of singling out one to the exclusion of the rest, as alone involved in such a calamity?

The direction is to them in verse 10, to be faithful unto death, not *until*, as some understand it. They were to hold fast even at the expense of life itself, and then they had a promise of a crown of life in the future.

The period covered by this church extends from the apostolic age down to the time when the church entered a period appropriately designated by the term Pergamos which signifies *hight, elevation.* The church entered into this period when Christianity had secured the throne of the Roman empire, and Constantine had become a nominal convert to the gospel. The spirit of the world worked mightily in this period; hence the church is addressed as being

make this applicable to the church of this period? 27. What additional reason do we here find for calling these churches prophetic? 28. How far does the period covered by this church extend? 29. What is the signification of the term Pergamos? 30. When did this period commence? 31.

where Satan's seat is. Christ takes cognizance of the unfavorable situation of his people during this period. But disadvantages in situation are no excuse for wrongs in the church, and this church maintained some features for which they were severely censured. They had those in their midst that held the doctrine of Balaam, referring to their falling into spiritual idolatry. They had also those that held to the doctrine of the Nicolaitans. This was a form of heresy said to have originated with one Nicholas, who taught a plurality of wives, etc. The promise to the overcomer in this church is to eat of the hidden manna, and receive a white stone with a new name written thereon. What that is, it would perhaps be unnecessary, as well as useless, to inquire. Wesley says: "Wouldst thou know what that new name will be? The way to this is plain—overcome. Till then, all thy inquiries are vain."

The church of Thyatira. This name signifies, *sweet savor of labor,* or *sacrifice of contrition,* and is an appropriate description of the church during a period of oppression and persecution. If the church of Pergamos reached down to the setting up of the papacy in 538, the period of the church of Thyatira would naturally apply during the whole period of Papal supremacy, 1260 years, from 538 to 1798. This was the period of that tribulation upon the church such as it was never to experience again. Matt. 24:21.

The woman, Jezebel. This name is here used figuratively, denoting, probably, false teachers from

What is meant by the doctrines of Balaam which they held? 32. What by the doctrine of the Nicolaitanes? 33. What is the promise to the overcomer? 34. What is meant by the white stone and new name? 35. What church is next addressed? 36. What is the signification of this word? 37. To what period does this naturally apply? 38. What passage in Matthew applies to this time? 39. What is meant

Rome, some of whom Christians did suffer to preach and teach among them. See History of the Waldenses. "I will put upon you none other burden." Verse 24. This, doubtless, refers to their relief from tribulation, the days of which were shortened by the great Reformation, for the elect's sake. Matt. 24:22.

"Hold fast till I come." This language shows that this period reaches so near the end that some who lived at the close of that time, would live to the coming of Christ.

Church of Sardis. This word signifies *prince* or *song of joy*, or *that which remains*. For the period covered by this church, we come down this side of the Reformation, and of papal supremacy. By the Sardis church is undoubtedly meant, the churches brought out by the great Reformation; and the definition of the name answers well to the condition of the church during this period. What high position has it held ? What favor has it had with the world ? But how has pride and popularity grown apace until spirituality is almost entirely destroyed. This church is to hear the proclamation of the second coming of Christ in all its power; for the true witness says, "If thou shalt not watch I will come upon thee as a thief, and thou shalt not know what hour I will come upon thee." The coming here brought to view is unconditional. By watching they would be prepared for it; and by not watching they would be overtaken as by a thief by this event. This proclamation they have heard in the great Advent movement of the present generation.

by the woman Jezebel? 40. What does Christ mean by saying, I will put upon you none other burden? 41. What is shown by the injunction, "Hold fast till I come"? 42. What is the definition of Sardis? 43. To what period does this apply? 44. What proclamation was this church to hear? 45. Has it heard it, and when? 46. What is re-

In the 5th verse we have some solemn facts stated in regard to the book of life. He that overcometh will not have his name blotted out; and this implies that all those who do not overcome will have their names blotted out from the book of life. This work of blotting out, as we have seen in our investigation of the sanctuary, takes place at the close of Christ's priestly work in Heaven. There will be at the conclusion of that work but two classes: one class having their names retained in the Lamb's book of life, and their sins blotted out of the book of God's remembrance; the other having their names blotted from the book of life and their sins retained to appear against them in the Judgment.

The proclamation of the Advent doctrine to this church results in the introduction of another state of the church, called Philadelphia. This word signifies *brotherly love ;* and this was the great characteristic of that church brought out by the preaching of the Advent doctrine. To this church Christ says, " I have set before thee an open door." The great work of the first message brought us to the cleansing of the sanctuary, when the door into the most holy was opened and there was seen the ark of God's testament. Rev. 11: 19. This church has the promise of being kept from the hour of temptation which shall come upon all the world to try them. This hour of temptation is, doubtless, that brought to view in Rev. 13: 14, and in 2 Thess. 2: 9, 10, which

vealed in the 5th verse of Rev. 3? 47. When is this work to be accomplished? 48. To what did the great proclamation given in this period lead? 49. What is the meaning of the word Philadelphia? 50. What was the great characteristic of the church brought out by the preaching of the soon coming of Christ? 51. What is referred to by the open door set before this church? 52. What promise is given to this church? 53. What will produce this hour of temptation?

will be produced by a still further development of spiritualism, which is already working so mightily in the land. Now, says Christ, "Behold I come quickly." This period brings us down very near to the time of the second coming of Christ.

The last message is to the church of Laodicea. This word signifies, *the judging of the people;* or according to Cruden, *a just people.* And either of these definitions would apply to the time and people between the close of the first message, and the end of time; for in this period of the cleansing of the sanctuary the judgment of the people is going forward, and the result will finally be, "a just people;" a people freed from all their sins.

This applies to the last generation of the church; and there is in this testimony that which should startle and arouse us. This church, with the light respecting the soon coming of Christ shining clearly forth, and that great event even at the door, is found in a lukewarm, half-hearted, indifferent condition; and at the same time, the members deceived with the idea that they are rich and have need of nothing. In this condition they are very offensive to God. Not because in themselves they are worse than other people have been, or are, but because, having greater light, they should occupy a very advanced position. "Therefore," says the True Witness, "I counsel thee to buy of me gold tried in the fire that thou mayest be rich." That is, love and faith working together, hand in hand to make them rich in good works, and rich toward God. They are counseled to buy white raiment; that is, to put on a robe of righteousness, or to have their characters conform wholly to the law of God. They are counseled also, to anoint their eyes with eyesalve that they may see. This eyesalve is the unction from on high, the anointing of the Holy Spirit, which gives us the true discernment in spiritual things. And God's people, during this time, will be rebuked and chastened by him until they become zealous and repent.

Christ stands at the door and knocks; and the promise is to him that will open the door that Christ will come in to him, and sup with him and he with Christ. This denotes a union such as no church has ever before enjoyed; and an outpouring of the Spirit, and an exercising of the heavenly graces beyond anything in the previous experience of the church. This is, without doubt, the arising of the "day star in the hearts" of believers, spoken of in 2 Pet. 1 : 19, and the time of refreshing spoken of by Peter in Acts 3 : 19, which the church is to experience just before the coming of Christ. And they need this work wrought for them to enable them to stand during the fearful scenes with which the world's history shall close.

Here it is, undoubtedly, that the parable of the wedding garment (Matt. 22 : 11–13) applies. The king comes in to see the guests, which is an examination of our characters in the sanctuary above. A man is found there, not having on the wedding garment, or not prepared to stand the test of the Judgment; he is cast out into outer darkness. And right in this critical time, when our cases in the sanctuary are pending, and we are unprepared for that searching test, the True Witness comes to us with an ear-

which they are counseled to procure ? 59. What is embraced in the promise to those who open the door of their hearts ? 60. What parable probably has its application here ? 61. State the points of comparison between the parable and this

nest entreaty to buy of him the white raiment, or to secure while we may the wedding garment to be prepared for the King when he shall come in to see the guests, and to bid those who are ready, to the marriage supper of the Lamb. If we fail to heed this testimony, and so do not provide ourselves with gold, white raiment, and eyesalve, Christ here says, " I will spew thee out of my mouth." The parable says, which is the same thing, that we shall be bound hand and foot, and cast into outer darkness. Both expressions denote an utter and final rejection of the unfaithful.

To the overcomer is here given a promise of sitting with Christ on his throne, as he has overcome and is now sitting with his Father in his throne. This shows that Christ occupies two thrones; first, with his Father, where he is now seated, and has been ever since his ascension to Heaven; and secondly, the throne of his own kingdom, the throne of his father David, when he shall commence his reign immediately after his priestly work is done.

These messages to the churches are both interesting and important, as showing the internal history of the church from the days of the apostles down, and especially important on account of the solemn warning, and the practical duties enjoined upon the last church. In this prophecy we are able to trace the history of the church step by step through this dispensation, finding the most accurate agreement between the testimony of God and the time and condition of the different periods of the church. It can thus be shown unmistakably that we have reached the last period, the Laodicean state of the

prophecy. 62. What is the promise to the overcomer ? 63. What does this prove respecting Christ ? 64. What gives these messages interest and importance ? 65. How is this message calculated to meet our present wants ?

church. And now under the tremendous pressure
of the spirit of the world and of apostasy that pre-
vails in these last days, even that people who have
the truth for this time, and should feel its searching
power and be animated with its life giving spirit,
are lukewarm; neither cold nor hot. But Christ
is at the door; the Judgment is impending; the
King is soon coming in to see the guests; how
important then that some message be given us,
adapted to our condition and our dangers. We
have it in this last message to the church, and if we
faithfully heed it, it will be our salvation; if we
reject it, that rejection will be our eternal ruin.

LESSON TWENTY-ONE.

THE SEVEN SEALS.

THE seals are introduced to our notice in the 4th,
5th, and 6th chapters of Revelation. The scenes
presented under these seals are brought to view in
Rev. 6, and the first verse of Rev. 8. They evidently cover events with which the church is connected from the opening of this dispensation to the
coming of Christ.

While the seven churches present the internal
history of the church, the seven seals bring to view
the great events of its external history.

The first seal presenting a white horse as described
in the second verse of chapter 6, with a rider who
went forth with a bow and a crown conquering and
to conquer, represents the gospel in its first intro-

REVIEW QUESTIONS ON LESSON TWENTY-ONE.

1. Where is the prophecy of the seven seals found ? 2.
What do they embrace ? 3. What is the difference between
the seven churches and the seven seals ? 4. What does the

duction. The whiteness of the horse denoting the purity of the church; and the success of the rider, the marvelous conquests of the gospel.

The second seal introduces a red horse; and under this seal peace is taken from the earth and events of strife and confusion are introduced, represented by a great sword in the hands of him who sat on this horse. This seal is supposed to cover the time from the days of the apostles, at about the close of the first century, to the days of Constantine the Great. In his day the church had so far apostatized that peace was taken from the earth and religious strife became so intense, that, as Mosheim says, there was continual war.

The third seal brings to view a black horse and he that sat upon him had a pair of balances in his hand. Then a voice was heard saying, "A measure of wheat for a penny and three measures of barley for a penny, and see thou hurt not the oil and the wine." The color of this horse, just the opposite of that of the first horse, denotes the terrible apostasy both in doctrine and practice which had taken place in the church. The reference to the balances, the wheat and the barley, sets forth the worldly spirit which had taken full possession of the professed church. The period covered by this seal was from the time of Constantine A. D. 323 to the setting up of the papacy A. D. 538. This was a period of superstition, of darkness and error, during which

first seal represent? 5. What is indicated by the color of the horse? 6. What by the success of him who sat thereon? 7. What takes place under the second seal? 8. What represents this? 9. What time is covered by this seal? 10. To what extent had religious strife increased in the days of Constantine? 11. What is the color of the horse of the third seal? 12. What is indicated by this color? 13. What does the reference to the balances, wheat and barley show? 14. What is the period covered by this seal? 15. What

the principles of the great papal apostasy were rapidly developed.

The fourth seal introduces a scene stranger still. It was a pale horse and the name of his rider was death, and hell (*hades*, the grave) followed with him. "And they had power to kill with sword and with hunger and with death and beasts of the earth." The preceding seal having brought us to the commencement of the papal supremacy, this seal naturally covers that period of its history during which it had in its hands the power of persecution. This was restrained by the great Reformation of the 16th century, as we shall see under the following seal.

The fifth seal brings to view a scene which we will present in the language of the scripture itself: "I saw under the altar the souls of them that were slain for the word of God, and for the testimony which they held: And they cried with a loud voice, saying, How long, O Lord, holy and true, dost thou not judge and avenge our blood on them that dwell on the earth? And white robes were given unto every one of them; and it was said unto them, that they should rest yet for a little season until their fellow servants also and their brethren, that should be killed as they were, should be fulfilled."

This passage is supposed to furnish strong proof in behalf of the conscious existence of disembodied souls. But a little thought will show some insuperable objections to this view. These souls are under the altar; and the altar is the altar of sac-

---

were the characteristics of this period? 16. What scene is presented under the fourth seal? 17. What time does it cover? 18. To what work do the symbols employed appropriately refer? 19. What did John see when the fifth seal was opened? 20. What is this passage supposed to prove? 21. Where are these souls seen? 22. What altar is this?

rifice; for it is where they were slain; but there is no such altar in Heaven. They cried that their blood might be avenged; but the disembodied immortal soul has no blood. If they were in Heaven according to the popular view, they could look over into the vault of hell and behold their persecutors writhing in its inextinguishable flames; for such is their view of the parable of the rich man and Lazarus. Luke 16:19–31. How then could they cry for vengeance upon those who had slain them? Was it not enough to behold them in the flames of hell there to be punished through all eternity?

In view of these difficulties both Adam Clarke and Dr. Barnes give up the idea that this is a literal representation. Clarke says: "The altar was upon the earth," and Barnes says that we are not to suppose that such a scene literally occurred, but that justice cried to God for vengeance upon those who had slain the martyrs as really as if they cried themselves.

But how could they cry if they were not conscious? We answer, By a figure of speech, just as Abel's blood cried, Gen. 4:10, and just as the stone cried out of the wall and the beam out of the timber answered it, Hab. 2:11. The persons here brought to view are those who had fallen under the papal persecutions of the preceding seal. The

---

23. Is there such an altar in Heaven? 24. What do they cry? 25. What is the objection to applying this to disembodied immortal souls? 26. If such souls are in Heaven, what view is constantly before them? 27. What proves that this is the popular view? 28. What then can be said of that view which represents them as crying for vengeance? 29. What does Dr. Clarke say in regard to the altar? 30. What is Barnes' admission? 31. If not conscious, how could they properly be represented as crying to God? References. 32. Who are the persons here brought to view? 33. What can

expression, The souls of them that were slain, being simply a strong expression to denote the persons, with all their capabilities of being, who had been sacrificed by papal fury. Just as Dr. Clarke says that the expressions, "spirits of just men made perfect," Heb. 12:23, and "Father of spirits," Heb. 12:9, and "God of the spirits of all flesh," Num. 16:22; 27:16, "means men not in a disembodied state." Note on 1 Pet. 3:19. And the fact that they had been slain cried like Abel's blood to God for vengeance.

The white robes that were given unto them were robes of character. They had gone down into the grave covered with obloquy and reproach. But the Reformation vindicated them in the eyes of all Christendom. It was seen that they were not the vile heretics that they had been represented to be, but the precious of the earth. They were to rest a little season. A few more were to be slain before the day for the final vindication of the people of God.

This seal covers the period from the beginning of the Reformation in the early part of the sixteenth century to the opening of the sixth seal about one hundred and thirty years later.

Under the sixth seal we have brought to view a great earthquake, the darkening of the sun, the turning of the moon to blood, the falling of the stars, the departing of the heavens as a scroll, and events immediately connected with the second coming of Christ.

The earthquake was the great earthquake of Lis-

be said of the expression, "souls of them?" 34. What was it that cried to God for vengeance? 35. What were the white robes? 36. How were they given? 37. What is meant by their resting a little season? 38. What period is covered by this seal? 39. What is brought to view under the sixth seal? 40. What earthquake fulfilled this proph-

bon which occurred Nov. 1, 1755, which affected at least four million square miles of the earth's surface. The sun was darkened May 19, 1780. The moon refused to give her light the following night; and when it did appear, it bore the appearance of blood as described in this prophecy. The stars of heaven fell Nov. 13, 1833. Other star showers or meteoric displays have been witnessed at different times, but this was the most remarkable and extensive.

Mark speaks of the same signs and locates them at the same time. He says, "In those days, after that tribulation, the sun shall be darkened and the moon shall not give her light and the stars of heaven shall fall." "In those days," before the 1260 years of papal triumph ended, but "after that tribulation," after the persecuting power of the papacy was restrained, between that point and 1798 where the 1260 years ended, these scenes were to appear; and right here history locates the most remarkable of these phenomena that have ever been seen.

It will be noticed that in the fulfillment of this prophecy we stand between the 13th and 14th verses of chapter 6. The next thing here before us is the departing of the heavens as a scroll and the scenes of the great day.

The seventh seal is introduced in Rev. 8:1. The only event mentioned is silence in Heaven about

ecy? 41. When did it occur? 42. How extensive was it? 43. When was the sun darkened? 44. When and how was the testimony relative to the moon fulfilled? 45. When did the stars fall? 46. Is not the character of these phenomena as signs destroyed by the fact that there have been other like exhibitions? And if not, why not? 47. How does Mark speak of those signs? 48. What days does Mark refer to? 49. What tribulation? 50. Between what points of time does this locate these signs? 51. Where do we stand in the fulfillment of the seals? 52. Where is the opening of the seventh seal described? 53. What is the event mentioned

the space of half an hour; and the only time brought to view in the Bible when this could be fulfilled, is that described in Matt. 25 : 31, when Christ appears and "all the holy angels" come with him. Then there can be silence in Heaven; and this event we understand to be the one to which the sixth seal is devoted.

* It will be noticed that the language of the first five seals is symbolical, that of the sixth and seventh literal. We can account for this change in the language only by supposing that the events of these seals being located at the time when the prophecy was to be understood and the doctrine of the second coming of Christ proclaimed is for this reason given in literal and not symbolic language.

* Taken as a whole we may say that these seals represent the great apostasy in the church. The first seal represents the apostolic church in its purity. The succeeding seals, the church in its apostasy. But the true church occasionally appears this side the first seal. It is the oil and the wine of the third seal, the martyrs of the fourth and fifth seals; and those who will be saved at the coming of Christ to which the last seal brings us. While the apostate church will be among those who will call for the rocks and mountains to fall on them and hide them from his presence in the day of His wrath.

---

54. When and by what means can this be fulfilled? 55. Why is there a change between the fifth and sixth seals, from figurative language to literal? 56. How are the true and apostate churches brought to view in these seals?

LESSON TWENTY-TWO.

THE SEVEN TRUMPETS.

THE political events of this dispensation are properly symbolized by trumpets, those heralds of war and revolution. These are brought to view in the 8th, 9th and a part of the 11th chapters of Revelation.

The record of the first trumpet begins with verse 7 of chapter 8. These trumpets are the counterpart of the prophecy of the second chapter of Daniel. That prophecy brings to view the dividing of the Roman kingdom into ten parts as represented by the ten toes of the great image; and the first four of the seven trumpets introduce the events by which this division was effected.

The first trumpet represents hail and fire mingled with blood cast upon the earth. It was fulfilled by the invasion of the Roman Empire by the Goths under Alaric, commencing A. D. 395. This invasion is represented by hail from the fact that the invaders came from the frozen regions of the North. It is further described as fire mingled with blood because the course of the invaders was marked by slaughter and conflagration.

The second trumpet brings us to a new location and another event. A great mountain burning

---

REVIEW QUESTIONS ON LESSON TWENTY-TWO.

1. What do trumpets appropriately symbolize? 2. What period is covered by the seven trumpets of Revelation? 3. Where does the record of the first trumpet begin? 4. Of what are these trumpets the counterpart? 5. What do the first four trumpets introduce? 6. How is the first trumpet described? 7. By what was it fulfilled? 8. When did it commence? 9. Why is it described as hail and fire mingled with blood? 10. What scene does the second trumpet bring

with fire was cast into the sea. The next great invasion of the Roman Empire which shook it to its foundation and conduced to its fall, was that of the Vandals under Genseric. The base of his operations was at Carthage in Africa. The date of his career is marked by the years 428 to 468. His warfare was carried on by sea, well symbolized by a great mountain burning with fire cast into the sea. He ravaged and devastated all those provinces of the Roman Empire which lie upon the Mediterranean.

The frequent reference to the third part, noticed in the trumpets, has allusion to the tripartite division of the Roman Empire. Twice it was divided into three parts before its permanent division into Eastern and Western Rome; and when the third part is spoken of in this prophecy, it refers to that division in which the events of the trumpet under consideration were taking place.

The third trumpet brings to view another invading chieftain, who, like a comet or a blazing star, flamed over the Roman Empire. It was Attila at the head of his warlike Huns. The name of this star is called Wormwood as describing the bitter consequences of this invasion and the terrors and miseries wrought by this war-like chief.

This star fell upon the third part of the rivers and fountains of waters. The scene of Attila's operations was in the northern part of Italy, the

to view? 11. What was the second great invasion of the Roman empire? 12. What was the base of Genseric's operations? 13. What figures mark the date of his career? 14. Why was a burning mountain cast into the sea, a fit symbol of his work? 15. What provinces did he ravage? 16. What is meant by the expression, "the third part?" 17. What conqueror and what people fulfilled the events of the third trumpet? 18. Why is this star called Wormwood? 19. What was the scene of Attila's operations? 20. What did

regions in which so many streams and rivers have
their source. Attila styled himself "The scourge
of God," and made his boast that the grass never
grew where his horse had trod.

ˇ The fourth trumpet is described in the 12th verse
and brings to view the blotting out of the third
part of the sun, moon, and stars. These are
undoubtedly here used as symbols representing the
three highest sources of authority in the Roman
Empire; namely, emperors, consuls and senators;
and we naturally infer from the phraseology of the
text that it denotes their overthrow. We have
now come to the time when the Western Empire
of Rome was extinguished. The date, as given by
Gibbon, is 476 or 479. It was accomplished by
Odoacer who was succeeded by Theodoric the
Ostrogoth; and the events of the trumpet were
finally accomplished by Justinian. The Imperial
office, the sun, was extinguished by Odoacer. Jus-
tantine abolished the Consulship, the moon, and
Narses, the general of Justinion extinguished the
Senate, the stars. Thus in the third part of the
Roman Empire, the sun, moon and stars were smitten, here represented as a third part of these lumi-
naries.

Another angel, not one of this series of seven, is
now introduced declaring that the three remaining
trumpets will be trumpets of woe.

Two of these trumpets, the 5th and 6th, occupy,
in equal portions, the whole of the ninth chapter of
Revelation. The prophet now turns from those

Attila style himself? 21. What was his boast? 22. What
is brought to view under the fourth trumpet? 23. In what
sense are the terms sun, moon and stars, here used? 24.
What do they signify? 25. When was the Western empire
extinguished? 26. Who were the agents in its accomplish-
ment? 27. What may be said of the angel of verse 13? 28.
What chapter, and in what proportion, is occupied with the

agencies which were employed to scourge Rome and break it up into political divisions, to those agencies which were employed to scourge it as an ecclesiastical power after its change from Paganism to the Papacy.

Eleven ? verses are used in describing the fifth trumpet. A star is first seen falling from heaven unto the earth. This star was Chosroes, the king of Persia. He was overthrown by Heraclius, the emperor of the Eastern Empire. His fall was the key by which the bottomless pit was opened For Rome in overthrowing Persia, utterly exhausted herself; and thus the only two powers which were capable of meeting and crushing Mohammedanism, namely, Persia and Eastern Rome, were virtually taken out of the way by this revolution. The bottomless pit symbolizes the wastes of the Arabian desert from which issued a great smoke or the dark and delusive doctrines propagated by Mohammed and his fanatical followers. Chosroes, after his loss of empire was murdered in the year 628; and the year 629 is marked by the conquest of Arabia and the first war of the Mohammedans against the Roman Empire. The locusts that came out of the smoke symbolized the Arabian horsemen as they went forth to fight what they called the battles of the Lord.

Their mission was to torment men five months, but not to kill them. Verses 5 and 10. This period is doubtless prophetic, denoting 150 years.

5th and 6th trumpets ? ˙ 29. From what and to what does the prophet now turn ? 30. Who was the star of verse 1 ? 31. By whom was he overthrown ? 32. What was his fall, and why ? 33. Of what is the bottomless pit here a symbol ? 34. What issued from that pit ? 35. When was Chosroes murdered ? 36. What marks the year 629 ? 37. By what are the Arabian horsemen here symbolized ? 38. How long a period is denoted by the five months ? 39. From what point

The question then arises, From what point are these years to be dated? The 11th verse gives us the key to the solution of the query. They had a king over them whose name is given both in Hebrew and Greek as the destroyer. The conclusion naturally follows that the five months of torment must have taken place under this Ottoman power after its consolidation into a kingly government. Previous to the time of Othman the Mohammedan power was composed of separate and distinct tribes. Under the policy of this man they were consolidated into one government with himself as king. His government was founded near the close of the thirteenth century and has ever since been known, from the name of its founder, as the Ottoman Empire.

The first assault of Othman upon the Eastern Empire took place on the 27th day of July, 1299. Commencing the five months' torment from this event, they would end 150 years later, in 1449, As we inquire for the events which mark the termination of that period, we are brought to the sounding of the next trumpet.

When the sixth angel sounded, a voice was heard, saying, Loose the four angels which are bound in the great river Euphrates. The river Euphrates must here be taken for a symbol of that kingdom of which it was the principal river, which was the Ottoman or Turkish Empire. The four angels are supposed to mean the four chief Sultanies of which that Empire was composed. These were Iconium,

are they to be dated? 40. Why? 41. When did Othman found his government? 42. When was his first assault made upon the Eastern Empire? 43. What was heard when the sixth angel sounded? 44. What does the river Euphrates here symbolize? 45. What are the four angels bound therein supposed to mean? 46. What were these four Sultanies?

Aleppo, Damascus, and Bagdad. They were loosed so that they should hereafter have not simply the power of tormenting, but of destroying. This was accomplished by the following events:—

When the last emperor of the Greeks, John Paleologus, died, leaving no children, Constantine Deacozes succeeded to the empire; but he would not venture to ascend the throne without asking the consent of Amurath, the Turkish Sultan. Thus he virtually surrendered his power into Turkish hands. And this was in the very year when the 150 years of the preceding trumpet ended, namely, in 1449. Amurath, soon after died and was succeeded by Mohammed II. in 1451, who set his heart on possessing Constantinople. The siege commenced April 6, 1453, and the city was taken on the 16th of May following. The eastern seat of the Cæsars thus became the seat of the Ottoman Empire and has so remained to this day.

The principal point for exposition under this trumpet is the prophetic period brought to view in verse 15. The angels were loosed for an hour, a day, a month, and a year. This reduced from prophetic to literal time gives us the following period: A year 360 days, 360 years. A month, 30 days, 30 years, a day, one year, an hour, a twenty-fourth part of a prophetic day, fifteen literal days, making in all 391 years and 15 days. This added to the point in 1449 where the 150 years ended, brings us to August 11, 1840.

---

47. Name the event by which they were loosed so as to have thereafter the power to destroy? 48. By whom was Amurath succeeded, and when? 49. What enterprise did he set his heart on accomplishing? 50. When did the siege of Constantinople commence? 51. When and how did it end? 52. What is the principal point to be explained under this trumpet? 53. How long a period of time is brought to view? 54. Where did this period end? 55. By what means did the

The means by which their conquests were achieved is described in verses 17 and 18 as fire and smoke and brimstone ; and it is a remarkable fact that in this revolution gun-powder was first used for purposes of war. Thus we have a prophecy of the remarkable invention of gun-powder written by John in A. D. 96.

As the prophetic period of this trumpet commenced by the voluntary surrender of power into the hands of the Turks by the Christian emperor of the East, so we might conclude its termination would be marked by the voluntary surrender of that power by the Turkish Sultan back again into the hands of the Christians. In 1838 Turkey became involved in war with Egypt. The Egyptians bid fair to overthrow the Turkish power unless other nations should interfere. To prevent this, the four great powers of Europe, England, Russia, Austria and Prussia interfered to sustain the Turkish government. Turkey accepted their intervention. A conference was held in London at which an ultimatum was drawn up to be presented to Mehemet Ali, the Pacha of Egypt. It is evident that when this ultimatum should be placed in the hands of Mehemet matters would then be committed into the hands of the Christian powers. And on the day when this was submitted to him the Sultan addressed a note to the ambassadors of the four powers inquiring what should be done in case Mehemet refused to comply with the terms which they had proposed. The answer was that he need not alarm himself about any contingency that might arise; for they had made provision for that. And what day was this ? It was the 11th of

Turks achieve their conquest ? 56. What event would be expected to mark the termination of the 391 years and 15 days? 57. What event did take place, on the day when this

August, 1840. Thus the second woe ended, and the sixth trumpet ceased its sounding.

Passing over the 10th and a portion of the 11th chapters of Revelation, the series of trumpets is again taken up in verse 14 of chapter 11. The events of this trumpet are described in the five following verses. They are such as show that this trumpet witnesses the conclusion of all earthly kingdoms and the beginning of the everlasting reign of Christ. Among the events introduced is the opening of the temple of God in Heaven. Verse 19. This was the commencement of the work of cleansing the sanctuary, as explained in the exposition of that subject. This is the same as the finishing of the mystery of God spoken of in Rev. 10:7 which was to mark the beginning of the sounding of that angel. We therefore place the beginning of that trumpet in the autumn of 1844, and the little space termed "quickly" which was to intervene between the second and third woes reached from August 11, 1840, where the sixth trumpet ceased to sound to the autumn of 1844, where the seventh commenced. The 18th verse of Rev. 11 shows that this trumpet covers the concluding troubles of the last days and reaches over to the destruction of the wicked at the end of the thousand years.

---

period ended, and what led to it? 58. Where is the series of trumpets resumed? 59. What is shown by the events brought to view under it? 60. What event is specially noted among others? 61. What was this? 62. How is it spoken of in Rev. 10? 63. What does it there mark? 64. When, therefore, did the 7th trumpet begin to sound? 65. What does this trumpet cover?

LESSON TWENTY-THREE.

THE MINISTRATION OF ANGELS.

JUDE 6: "And the angels which kept not their first estate, but left their own habitation he hath reserved in everlasting chains under darkness unto the Judgment of the great day."

This text brings to view an order of beings called angels, and also shows that there are two classes of them, one which kept not their first estate and another class which have kept it.

Peter speaks of the same. 2 Pet. 2:4. "For if God spared not the angels that sinned but cast them down to hell and delivered them into chains of darkness to be reserved unto Judgment" &c. Here the angels that sinned are those who, as described by Jude, kept not their first estate. The whole host of angels were therefore originally holy, but a part of them have fallen into sin and are reserved unto the Judgment of the great day.

These angels are not the departed spirits of human beings; for Job speaks of the time when the foundation of this earth was laid and says that the morning stars sang together and the sons of God shouted for joy. Job 38:7. These were undoubtedly the angelic hosts, antedating the creation of the world and the history of man.

Moreover Peter in the text already quoted speaks

REVIEW QUESTIONS ON LESSON TWENTY-THREE.

1. What is the testimony of Jude 6? 2. What does this text bring to view? 3. Where does Peter speak of the same? 4. What is his language? 5. How is it shown that Peter refers to the same as Jude? 6. What therefore was the original condition of all the angelic host? 7. Are these angels departed human spirits? 8. What is Job's testimony and where found? 9. What testimony of Peter's proves the same

first of the angels and then of the old world preceding the flood, evidently making a distinction between the angels and the earliest inhabitants of the earth. Again when Adam. and Eve were driven from Paradise before ever a human being had died upon the earth, cherubim were placed at the east garden of Eden to keep the way of the tree of life; and these cherubim are one of the orders of angels. Angels therefore are not the spirits of departed men.

Angels are real beings. They are described in the Bible as possessing face, feet, wings &c. Ezekiel says of the cherubim, "Their whole body and their backs and their hands and their wings," &c. Eze. 10:12. Angels appeared unto Abraham. Gen. 18:1–8. They talked and ate with him. They went on to Sodom and communed with Lot, who, entering into his house baked unleaven bread for them and they did eat. These persons were called angels. David speaks of the manna as the corn of Heaven and angels' food. Ps. 78:23–25.

The case of Balaam, Num. 22:22–31, is an interesting incident. The angel appeared to Balaam with a sword drawn in his hand. The question is sometimes asked how angels can be material beings since we cannot see them. This case illustrates it. The record says the Lord opened the eyes of Balaam and he saw the angel. The angel did not create a body for that occasion. He was just the same as he was before Balaam saw him; but the change

thing? 10. What incident that took place in Eden also shows it? 11. What were these cherubim? 12. What can be said of the reality of angels? 13. How are they described in the Bible? 14. Who appeared unto Abraham? 15. What did they do? 16. What was their course with Lot? 17. How does David speak of them? 18. What may be said of the case of Balaam? 19. What question is sometimes asked? 20. How does this case illustrate it? 21. Into what position

took place in Balaam. His eyes were opened, then he beheld the angel. It was the same with the servant of Elisha when he and his master were brought into a straight place, surrounded by the army of the king of Syria. 2 Kings 6 : 77. Elisha prayed that the eyes of his servant might be opened; and he immediately saw the whole mountain full of horses and chariots round about Elisha.

This may be further illustrated referring to things which we know are material and yet which we cannot see. Air is material, light is material, even thought itself is only the result of material organizations—matter acting upon matter—and yet we can see none of these things. Just so with the angels.

It is further objected to the materiality of the angels that they are called spirits. Heb. 1 : 13, 14. But this is no objection to their being literal beings. They are simply spiritual beings organized differently from these earthly bodies which we possess. Paul says, 1 Cor. 15 : 44, "There is a natural body and there is a spiritual body." The natural body we now have; the spiritual body we shall have in the resurrection. "It is raised a spiritual body." Verse 44. But then we are equal unto the angels, Luke 20:36; then we have bodies like unto Christ's most glorious body. Phil. 3 : 4 and Christ is no less a spirit than the angels. We read that God is a spirit, that is, simply a spiritual being.

They are beings of great exaltation and power.

woro Elisha and his servant at one time brought? 22. What was Elisha's prayer? 23. What did his servant then behold? 24. Who were these beings represented by horses and chariots? 25. Name some other material things which we cannot see? 26. What are angels called in Heb. 1 : 13, 14? 27. What objection is based on this? 28. How is this objection answered? 29. When we have spiritual bodies, to whom are we equal? 30. What may be said of the exalted charac-

At the resurrection of our Lord the presence of one angel struck the Roman guard to the ground like dead men. Matt. 28:3. Even the prophets themselves frequently fell helpless before the majesty of the angels that came to bring them revelations from the Lord. Dan. 10:8, 17; Rev. 19:10; 22:8. An angel destroyed the army of Sennacherib, 2 Kings 19. It was undoubtedly the angels that threw down the walls of Jericho. Josh. 6:20.

These exalted beings are given as ministers of the saints. Heb. 1:14. It appears from Matt. 18:10 that every child of God has an angel to accompany him. The church in Jerusalem understood this; for when the voice of Peter was heard at the gate, they, supposing Peter was in prison, declared that it was his angel. Acts 12:15.

The history of the church is filled with instances of the ministration of these heavenly beings to the people of God. They protected the three worthies in the fiery furnace, Dan. 3:25. They shut the mouth of lions that they should not touch the servant of God. Dan. 6:22. They unloosed the chains and opened the prison doors before Peter. Acts 12:7. David says, "The angel of the Lord encampeth round about them that fear him and delivereth them." Read also other ministrations to Daniel and John as recorded in their writings throughout.

Angels are undoubtedly the ones that make the books of record from which we are all to be judged.

ter of the angels? 31. What incidents prove that they are beings of high power and glory? 32. Who destroyed Sennacherib's army? 33. How many were destroyed and in how long a time? 34. Who threw down the walls of Jericho? 35. What is the office of these exalted beings? 36. What is proved by Matt. 18:10? 37. What incident in Peter's life proves this? 38. Name other instances of their ministration for God's people? 39. What books do the angels pre-

Rev. 20:12. Angels assist in the Judgment. Dan. 7:9, 10; Rev. 5:11. The angels will gather the saints at the coming of Christ. Matt. 24:31; 25: 31; 1 Thes. 4:16, 17.

Such is the work ascribed to the holy angels. Those who have sinned have also their work to do. Their object is to thwart the efforts of the holy angels who are working in our behalf and to lead mankind to sin and finally to ruin. Much speculation has been indulged in regard to the origin of Satan. In the light of the Scriptures this question is involved in no difficulty. God could not consistently constitute creatures other than free moral agents. Being such they had the power of sinning and of falling. The Bible assures us that some angels have so fallen. The leader in this work of rebellion is called Satan. God created him pure and upright. He has by his own action brought himself into this condition of evil. Christ says of him, John 8:44, that he was a murderer from the beginning, that he abode not in the truth, and that he is the father of lies. This shows that all these evils had their origin with him. Isa. 14:12–14; and Eze. 28:13–17 show the exalted position he occupied before his fall, and the cause of his overthrow. His heart was lifted up because of his beauty and he aspired to a higher position than that assigned him by his Creator. Thus pride is shown to be the source of all the evil that has come into the universe.

pare? 40. What do the angels have to do with the judgment? 41. Who will be gathered by them at the coming of Christ? Reference. 42. Are the evil angels active? 43. What is their work? 44. What has resulted from the question of Satan's origin? 45. Explain this question in the light of the Scriptures. 46. What does John 8:44 say of Satan? 47. What scriptures speak of his original condition? 48. What was this condition? 49. What was the cause of

These evil angels are just as real beings as the good. If men can explain away Satan, the devil and demon, by calling them figures of speech, by the same rule we can explain away the good angels, Christ and God himself, leaving the universe without an author or a ruler.

It is asked why God permits these fallen beings to exist. We answer by asking why he permits wicked men to exist. The same principle is involved in each question. The same answer will apply to both. We cannot indeed account for sin. Charles Beecher, in his work entitled "Redeemer and Redeemed," page 82, says: "Sin is, in its own nature, anomalous, and therefore mysterious; it is in its own nature an unaccountable thing; for the moment that it is properly accounted for, *i. e.*, the moment we have assigned a good and sufficient cause for it, that moment it ceases to be sin. A good and sufficient cause, is a good and sufficient excuse; and that which has a good and sufficient excuse is not sin. To account for sin, therefore, is to defend it; and to defend it, is to certify that it does not exist. Therefore the objection that it is inconceivable and unaccountable that sin should enter into such a perfect universe amounts to nothing but saying that sin is exceedingly sinful, inexcusable and destitute of the least defense for justification."

God doubtless permits sin to run its career that its exceeding sinfulness may be seen, and his justice vindicated in finally destroying sin and all its agents forever.

---

his fall? 50. Are the evil angels real beings? 51. What follows from the position of some that the terms Satan, devil, etc., are only figures of speech? 52. Why does God permit these agents of evil to exist? 53. What does Charles Beecher say of the origin and existence of sin? 54. What will doubt-

When Satan sinned he was cast out of Heaven, 2 Pet. 2:4; cast down to Tartarus. This is defined to mean the dark and fathomless void that surrounds the material work of the universe.

Being thus cast out, he, by the temptation and fall of man gained possession of the earth. Gen. 3. By this means he has become the god and prince of this world. The fair inheritance given to Adam has passed over into the possession of Satan, until it shall be redeemed by Christ.

Sinful man is Satan's lawful captive. Rom. 5: 13; Eccl. 3:20. In this condition he is represented as a prisoner. Job 3:17, 18; Isa. 24:22. Of Satan it is said in Isaiah 14:17 that he opened not the house of his prisoners. The grave is called the land of the enemy. Jer. 31:16, 17. Death is called the last enemy of the righteous. 1 Cor. 15:26.

The mission of Jesus is to destroy this work of the enemy. 1 John 3:8; and not only does he destroy the works of the devil, but he is also to destroy the devil himself. Heb. 2:14. This is accomplished by the great plan of salvation. Christ gives himself first to die for man then acts as intercessor in their behalf, pardoning the sins of the penitent. Having finished his work as priest he returns in the cloud of heaven, his second advent, raises the righteous dead and translates the righteous living. Satan is then bound for a thousand years. Rev. 20:1-3. At the end of that period the wicked dead are raised, and, with Satan at their head, they come up around the camp of the saints

---

less be shown by it at last? 55. Where was Satan cast when he sinned? 56. Where is Tartarus? 57. How did he gain a foothold in this world? 58. Who now has dominion of the earth? 59. What is now the condition of sinful man? 60. What is the object of Christ's mission? 61. By what process is this accomplished? 62. Name the order of events?

the beloved city; fire comes down from God out of Heaven and devours them all. This is the fire of the great day spoken of by Mal. 4 : 1 which shall burn as an oven and consume all that do wickedly root and branch, Satan and all his followers, evil angels and evil men. This is the day and this the fire of which Peter speaks, 2 Peter 3 : 7, when he says that the Heavens and the earth are kept in store reserved unto fire against the day of Judgment and perdition of ungodly men. From this fiery ordeal there comes forth new heavens and new earth to be the everlasting abode of the righteous. Verse 13.

LESSON TWENTY-FOUR.

THE SAINTS' INHERITANCE.

" THEN answered Peter and said unto him, Behold, we have forsaken all, and followed thee; what shall we have therefore? And Jesus said unto them, Verily I say unto you, That ye which have followed me, in the regeneration when the Son of man shall sit in the throne of his glory, ye also shall sit upon twelve thrones judging the twelve tribes of Israel." Matt. 19 : 27, 28.

The question here raised by Peter is a very common one. What shall we have? What shall be the reward or inheritance hereafter of the people of God? Christ points them forward as the time of their reward to the regeneration or the re-genesis brought to view in the Scriptures. In harmony with this, we find prophecies of a new heaven and a new earth

63. What scriptures speak of this time when Satan and his followers shall be destroyed? 64. What follows?

to succeed the present. Isa. 65 : 17. " For, behold,
I create new heavens and a new earth; and the
former shall not be remembered, nor come into mind."
Peter in his second epistle, third chapter, describes
the destruction of the present earth by fire in the
great day of the Lord when the elements shall melt
with fervent heat, and the earth also, and the works
that are therein shall be burned up; but he adds:
" Nevertheless we, according to his promise, look for
new heavens and a new earth, wherein dwelleth
righteousness." The promise to which he refers is
the one just quoted from the prophecy of Isaiah.
This certainly is no figure ; and it points plainly to
the future of our earth.

In Isa. 45: 18, we find this purpose expressed by
the Lord in the formation of the earth. " For
thus saith the Lord that created the heavens; God
himself that formed the earth and made it; he hath
established it, he created it not in vain, he formed it
to be inhabited. I am the Lord; and there is none
else."

He certainly did not form it to be inhabited by a
wicked race of beings that now dwell upon it. It
must be inhabited by those who are in harmony with
his own will, and this purpose will be carried out.
Accordingly we find promises made to the righteous
that they shall inherit the land. Ps. 37 : 11. " The
meek shall inherit the earth." Prov. 2 : 21, 22.

REVIEW QUESTIONS ON LESSON TWENTY-FOUR.

1. What question is a very natural one to be raised by
Christians ? 2. What disciple put this question to our Lord?
3. To what time did Christ point him? 4. What is the
regeneration? 5. What prophecies harmonize with this
view? 6. To what promise does Peter refer to support the
idea of a new heaven and new earth? 7. What does this
language certainly bring to view? 8. What purpose does the
Lord express in Isa. 45 : 18? 9. Has this purpose ever
been accomplished? 10. Will it be accomplished? 11. What

"For the upright shall dwell in the land, and the perfect shall remain in it. But the wicked shall be cut off from the earth, and the transgressors shall be rooted out of it." So says our Lord himself in his first recorded sermon : "Blessed are the meek, for they shall inherit the earth," Matt. 5:5. This is not fulfilled in this world, nor can it be till a new dispensation shall be ushered in.

The promises made to the ancient worthies, bring to view the same thing. Heb. 11:13. "These all died in faith, not having received the promises." Heb. 6:12. "That ye be not slothful, but followers of them who through faith and patience inherit the promises." Then Paul refers to the promise made to Abraham ; and he shows our connection with it; for he says that it was given that we might have strong consolation who have fled for refuge to lay hold of the hope set before us."

The promise to Abraham is recorded in Gen. 12: 1–3. "In thee shall all the families of the earth be blest." Gen. 22:18. "And in thy seed shall all the nations of the earth be blest." This promise must be universal, and it must reach through all time; otherwise, all the nations of the earth would not be blessed in him. Rom. 4:13, shows that this is the view to be taken of the promise to Abraham. "For the promise that he should be the *heir of the world*, was not to Abraham, or to his seed, through the law, but through the righteousness of faith."

promises are made to the righteous respecting the earth, and where recorded? 12. Why cannot these promises be fulfilled in this present state? 13. When will they be fulfilled? 14. What is brought to view in the "promises?" 15. To what does Paul refer in Heb. 6:13? 16. How is our connection with this promise shown? 17. Where are the original promises to Abraham found? 18. Quote them. 19. How extensive is this promise, and why? 20. What view does Paul take of this promise, in Rom. 4:13? 21.

By the promise Abraham is therefore made heir of the world; and yet we are told that he died, not having received the promise. How then can the promise be fulfilled? Answer: Only by a resurrection of the dead. Paul says in Acts 26 : 6, 7: " And now I stand and am judged for the hope of the promise made of God unto our fathers; unto which promise our twelve tribes, instantly serving God day and night, hope to come. For which hope's sake, king Agrippa, I am accused of the Jews. Why should it be thought a thing incredible with you that God should raise the dead?" Here the whole promise rests upon the future resurrection of the dead.

Paul in Gal. 3 : 8 calls this promise to Abraham the Gospel. "And the scripture, foreseeing that God would justify the heathen through faith, preached before the gospel unto Abraham, saying, In thee shall all nations be blessed." He says further in verse 16, that the promise to the seed is to Christ; and in verse 29, that we become Abraham's seed, and heirs to the promise by becoming connected with Christ. "And if ye be Christ's, then are ye Abraham's seed, and heirs according to the promise." Heirs of what? We have just seen that Abraham is heir of the world, and if we become heirs with him, then our heirship embraces the world.

This is in harmony with the scriptures already quoted affirming that the meek shall inherit the earth. The promises then embrace all that Christ

When was this promise fulfilled to Abraham? 22. How then can it be fulfilled? 23. What does Paul show in Acts 26 : 6, 7? 24. What does Paul in Gal. 3 : 8, call this promise to Abraham? 25. Who is meant by Abraham's seed to whom the promise was made? 26. How do we become related to the prophecies by a connection with Christ? 27. Of what are we thus made heirs? 28. With what does this view

has undertaken in our behalf. They include the whole plan of salvation. By coming to Christ and accepting of him we become Abraham's seed, and heirs according to the promise. And this plan of salvation can be carried out only by a resurrection of the dead, when eternal life shall be given to all God's people, and by the regeneration of this earth, when a new heavens and a new earth shall be created and given to the saints as their everlasting possession. Then the meek shall inherit the earth, then the promise of Peter as quoted can be fulfilled. Then the saints shall take the kingdom under the whole heaven to possess it forever and ever as described by Daniel in his interpretation of the great Image of Nebuchadnezzar in Daniel 2, and in his vision of the four beasts in chapter 7: "And the kingdom and dominion and the greatness of the kingdom under the whole heaven, shall be given to the people of the saints of the Most High." The stone cut out of the mountain representing the kingdom of Christ, became a great mountain and filled the whole earth.

This new heaven and new earth, the everlasting abode of the saints is described by John in Revelation 21. The New Jerusalem which comes down from Heaven, the city of beauty and glory, is its grand metropolis. All tears are wiped away. There is no more death, sorrow or care. Pain never enters, and the former things are passed away. All things are made new. The son of God and the Lamb

---

harmonize? 29. How much then do the promises embrace? 30. How can these promises be fulfilled, or the plan of salvation be carried out? 31. What will the meek then inherit? 32. What promise mentioned by Peter will then be fulfilled? 33. What prophecies of Daniel will then be fulfilled? 34. Can they be fulfilled in any other way? 35. What does John describe in Rev. 21? 36. What is to be the metropolis of this new earth? 37. What is to be the condition of the

is the light of it and the nations of the saved bring their honor and glory into it. There will be no night there! Nothing ever enters in to defile or to destroy, and they only possess it who are written in the Lamb's book of life.

Isaiah describes it as the place where the eyes of the blind shall be opened, and the ears of the deaf unstopped, and the lame man shall leap as an hart, and the tongue of the dumb shall sing; in the wilderness waters break forth and streams in the desert. The parched ground becomes a pool, the thirsty ground springs of water; and the ransomed of the Lord come to Zion with songs of everlasting joy upon their heads.

There is the river of life; that stream which makes glad the city of God, and the tree of life which is for the service of the nations. Then God's original purpose concerning the earth will be carried out. His glory will fill the earth as the waves fill the sea. And then the wicked, having all been destroyed, the universal song of jubilee heard by John in vision on Patmos will rise to God, when every creature which is in heaven, and on the earth and under the earth and such as are in the sea and all that are in them will be heard saying: "Blessing and honor, and glory, and power be unto him that sitteth upon the throne, and unto the Lamb forever and ever." Rev. 5 : 13.

----

people of God there? 38. What description does Isaiah give of it? 39. What purpose will then be carried out? 40. Where do we find prophecies that the glory of the Lord shall fill the earth? 41. When will these prophecies be fulfilled? 42. What has then become of the wicked? 43. What song will then be heard?

LESSON TWENTY-FIVE.

GIFTS OF THE SPIRIT.

PAUL in 2 Cor. 3, calls this dispensation, in comparison with the former, the "ministration of the Spirit." From this it appears that this dispensation was to be characterized by the outpouring and influence of the Spirit of God. In the prophecy which brings it to view, Joel, 2:28, quoted by Peter on the day of Pentecost, Acts 2:17, the Lord says: "And it shall come to pass in the last days, I will pour out of my Spirit upon all flesh." The last days here signify the whole gospel dispensation; and they are the last when taken in connection with the whole history of the world from the time of its creation, six thousand years ago.

The effect of this outpouring of the Spirit on all flesh was to be seen in the following results: "Your sons and your daughters shall prophesy, and your young men shall see visions, and your old men shall dream dreams."

When we speak of the doctrine of the gifts of the Spirit, we simply mean the operation of the Spirit in the ways here indicated; and that the Spirit was designed to operate in this manner through this dispensation, much proof can be found in the New Testament. In his last commission to his disciples, Jesus said: "Lo, I am with you alway, even unto the

1. What is this dispensation called by the apostle? 2. By what is it to be characterized? 3. What prophecy brings it to view? 4. What does the prophecy declare? 5. What do the last days here signify? 6. How can this whole dispensation be called the last days? 7. How was the effect of this outpouring of the Spirit to be seen? 8. What is meant by the doctrine of the gifts of the Spirit? 9. What did Christ

end of the world." Mark, in recording this, shows
the manner in which he would be with them: "And
these signs shall follow them that believe." Verse
17. And again, verse 20: "And they went forth
and preached everywhere, the Lord working with
them, and confirming the word with signs following."

This was the way in which our Lord continued
with his disciples, by the influence and operations of
the Holy Spirit; and that this was to continue to
the end, is certain from his own promise: "Lo, I am
with you alway, even to the end of the world."

Peter, on the day of Pentecost, said to those who
were convicted: "Repent, and be baptized every
one of you in the name of Jesus Christ for the remission of sins, and ye shall receive the gift of the Holy
Ghost. For the promise is unto you, and to your
children, and to all that are afar off, even as many
as the Lord our God shall call." This shows again
that the promise of the Holy Ghost covers the whole
dispensation and was to continue to the end.

Paul, in 1 Cor. 12, dwells upon this subject in full.
He says: "Now concerning spiritual gifts, brethren,
I would not have you ignorant." Verse 1. In verse
4, he continues: "Now there are diversities of gifts,
but the same Spirit." Verse 6: "And there are
diversities of operations, but it is the same God
which worketh all in all. But the manifestation of
the Spirit is given to every man to profit withal.
For to one is given by the Spirit the word of wisdom; to another the word of knowledge by the same
Spirit; to another faith by the same Spirit; to

in his last commission say to his disciples? 10. What does
Mark's record show? 11. How was Christ with his disciples?
12. How long was he to continue to be with them in this
manner? 13. What did Peter say to those convicted on the
day of Pentecost? 14. What do Peter's words show? 15.
Where does Paul take up the subject at length? 16. What
source do all the diversities of gifts have in common? 17.

GIFTS OF THE SPIRIT.

another the gifts of healing by the same Spirit; to another the working of miracles; to another prophecy; to another discerning of spirits; to another divers kinds of tongues; to another the interpretation of tongues. But all these worketh that one and the self-same Spirit, dividing to every man severally as he will."

Here it is very clearly stated that all the operations are the work of the same Spirit; they are simply the different channels through which it manifests its presence. Paul proceeds to illustrate this by reference to the human body, speaking of its different members, and the particular offices which these members are to perform; and in making this application at the conclusion of the chapter, he says: "Now ye are the body of Christ, and members in particular. And God hath set some in the church, first apostles, secondarily prophets, thirdly teachers, after that miracles, then gifts of healings, helps, governments, diversities of tongues."

That these gifts were once in the church, all admit, for we are assured that God formally and officially set them in the church. And who has taken them out of the church? If God has done this should it not be recorded in as explicit a manner as that he once established them therein?

In his letter to the Ephesians, Paul again takes up the subject. He says, Eph. 4:11: "And he gave some, apostles; and some, prophets; and some, evangelists; and some, pastors and teachers." These gifts are called in verse 8, gifts which he gave unto men, "when he ascended up on high."

What different operations are here mentioned? 18. By what does Paul now illustrate his subject? 19. What application does he make? 20. What conclusion follows from the statement that God has set these gifts in the church? 21. What does Paul say in Eph. 4:11? 22. What are these things

Now he states that the object of these gifts was for the perfecting of the saints, for the work of the ministry, for the edifying of the body of Christ.

He states how long they are to continue. "'Till we all come into the unity of the faith, and of the knowledge of the Son of God unto a perfect man, unto the measure of the stature of the fullness of Christ."

From the end and object of these gifts, as here stated, it will be seen at once that they are just as much needed at one point in this dispensation as another; just as necessary in the closing up as in the beginning. Some say these gifts were needed when the gospel was first introduced, but the necessity having passed away, they are no longer demanded; but is not the unity of faith, the knowledge of the Son of God, and the attainment unto the measure of the stature and the fullness of Christ, still desirable in the Christian dispensation?

But if we may judge from the practices of the whole Christian world, they believe in only a partial abolition of these gifts of the Spirit. Do they not have evangelists? Do they not ordain pastors? Do they not believe in teachers? On what ground? Because Christ commanded his disciples to go forth and teach all nations and to continue this work even to the end of the world. But the commission did not limit the work to these branches, but promised the gift of the Spirit as we have already shown in its diversities of operations to the end of the world. If we take this ground, that the gifts have been

called? 23. What does he state as the object of these gifts? 24. To what time does he say they were to continue? 25. What follows from this? 26. What objection is raised by some? 27. How is it answered? 28. What does the practice of the Christian world show? 29. What gifts do they still employ? 30. What is their authority for this? 31. What else was promised? 32. If the gifts have ceased, what

taken from the church, that the operation of the Spirit in these special methods was designed to cease, and has ceased, then we must no longer plead for evangelists, pastors, teachers, nor sustain by any special means, the work of the ministry.

If these gifts were to continue through the Christian dispensation, it is asked, why we have not examples of their manifestations. We answer that there have been instances in every age of the operation of the Spirit in some of these marked and special ways. The reason of their being no more frequent is found in the occurrence of the great apostasy so plainly predicted in the Christian church. Men have departed from God. All Christendom has been sunk in the darkness of error and superstition with which the world has been flooded by the Romish church. The true children of God have been few and obscure.

For examples of the manifestations of these gifts in the Gospel age the reader is referred to books entitled "Miraculous Powers," and the "Spirit of God," published at the *Review and Herald* Office, Battle Creek, Mich.

It might be expected that so important an agency in the Christian church would be counterfeited by the powers of darkness; hence we have the injunction, "Try the spirits," and the warning that many false prophets have gone out into the world. We are called upon to discriminate carefully between the true and false. We are not to reject all gifts because some of them are counterfeited. We do not throw away money, or refuse its use, because there

position must we take in reference to pastors, evangelists, and teachers? 33. Have there been examples of the gifts in every age? 34. Why have they not been more frequent? 35. In what works is found abundant testimony showing instances of their manifestation? 36. What kind of opposition might be expected? 37. What instructions are therefore

are counterfeits in the land. Everything valuable we must expect to be counterfeited. We guard ourselves by learning how to test the false by the true.

On the subject of the gifts our Lord gives us an infallible rule : " By their fruits ye shall know them." See Deut. 13 : 1; 18 : 21. If that which is predicted by the prophet comes not to pass, it is proof that he is not sent of God ; but even if it does come to pass, if its tendency is to lead away from God, it is to be rejected as false. The spiritualists of these modern times, and the Mormons, furnish remarkable instances under both these heads.

We have referred to a prophecy which speaks of this dispensation in general, and proves the existence of the gifts throughout the Gospel age. We have seen why they have been so little manifested ; it is because of the great apostasy. Now as the Church comes out from the wilderness and the errors of the dark ages. by true and genuine reformation, we naturally conclude that the gifts will be restored and that this dispensation will close, as it commenced, with remarkable manifestations of the work of the Spirit of God.

In accordance with this we have prophecies which plainly point to the revival of the gifts in the closing days of this dispensation. See Rev. 12 : 17 : "And the dragon was wroth with the woman, and

---

given us. 38. How are we to guard ourselves against deception in this matter ? 39. What rule does our Lord give us by which to test those manifestations which claim to be gifts of the Spirit ? 40. If an event predicted does not come to pass, what is the conclusion ? 41. If what the prophet says does come to pass, but he leads away from the true God, what is the conclusion then ? 42. What two great religious movements of these days furnish examples under both these heads ? 43. What should we naturally conclude would take place in the last days ? 44. What do we have to sustain this idea ? 45. What is the testimony of Rev. 12 : 17. 46. What

went to make war with the remnant of her seed, which keep the commandments of God, and have the testimony of Jesus Christ." By the woman we are to understand the church; by her seed, the members of the church throughout this dispensation. Therefore the remnant of her seed can refer to only one body of people, the last generation of Christians upon the earth. These are characterized by keeping the commandments of God, and having the testimony of Jesus Christ. In Rev. 19: 10, we have the definition of what is here called the "testimony of Jesus Christ." Said the angel to John, "The testimony of Jesus is the spirit of prophecy." This the reader will at once recognize as one of the gifts set in the church.

1 Cor. 1: 6, 7, shows that the church that are waiting for the coming of Christ are to come behind in no gift. The 5th chapter of 1 Thess. is evidently addressed to the church when the day of the Lord is about to come. In that chapter we have this instruction from the apostle: "Despise not prophesyings;" showing that these will then appear in the church. And we may reasonably infer that the prophecy of Joel 2: 1, 28, 31, quoted by Peter in Acts 2, being given in reference to the coming of the great day of the Lord would be fulfilled in as remarkable a manner as we draw near to that day, as it had been in any part of the Gospel dispensation. That the gift of prophecy is manifested according to the Scriptures in connection with the

is meant by the woman? 47. What by her seed? 48. Where, then, do we look for the remnant of the woman's seed? 49. By what is this remnant characterized? 50. What is the testimony of Jesus defined to mean, and where? 51. What is shown by 1 Cor. 1: 6, 7? 52. To whom is the 5th chapter of 1 Thessalonians addressed? 53. What instruction do we there find? 54. What is shown by this? 55. What may we reasonably expect as we draw near to the great

third angel's message we refer the reader to works published at the *Review and Herald* Office, entitled the " Spirit of Prophecy," and the " Testimony to the Church."

LESSON TWENTY-SIX.

BAPTISM—ITS RELATION TO THE DIVINE LAW IN THE WORK OF TRUE CONVERSION.

" IF ye then be risen with Christ, seek those things which are above, where Christ sitteth on the right hand of God." 2 Col. 3:1.

This scripture has been applied to three things: 1. To a resurrection from dead works in being reclaimed from a backslidden state. 2. To the literal resurrection of the just at the second coming of Christ. 3. To being raised up out of the water in baptism.

We inquire, To which of the three do the words " risen with Christ" apply ? Not to the first. Christ never had a resurrection from dead works. He was without sin. He did not have such a resurrection. Mark this : Whatever this resurrection may be Christ had one like it; for it is a resurrection with him.

The text cannot refer to the resurrection of the just, for that event is when the seeking time is in the past, and the saints themselves are above. The seeking of the heavenly treasure is before it is given, at the resurrection. We are then shut up to the position that

3. The text does refer to water baptism. Here

day of the Lord ? 56. What works show that the spirit of prophecy is manifested in connection with the third angel's message ?

the follower of Christ has a resurrection with his Master. In death Christ was laid in the grave, from which he arose by the power of God. So his followers are laid in the water in baptism, and are raised up out of the water.

But positive proof is found in Chap. 2:12, that the disciple is raised with Christ in baptism : "Buried with him by baptism wherein also ye are risen with him through the faith of the operation of God, who hath raised him from the dead." We here notice :—

1. The text plainly states that in baptism we are buried and risen with Christ.

2. This is done in the faith that the Father raised his Son from the dead. In the morning of the first day of the week God operated in the resurrection of Jesus, and baptism is received in faith of it.

Again the apostle speaks to the point to the church at Rome : " Therefore we are buried with him by baptism into death, that like as Christ was raised up from the dead by the glory of the Father, even so we also should walk in newness of life." Rom. 6:4.

The following points are worthy of notice :—

1. The disciple is buried in the water, and raised up out of the water in faith of the burial and resurrection of Christ, and in faith of the resurrection of the just at the coming of Christ.

2. And as Christ entered upon a new life at his resurrection, so the new life of the Christian properly commences at baptism. We do not say that

---

REVIEW QUESTIONS ON LESSON TWENTY-SIX.

1. Quote the text at the head of this lesson. 2. What is the first thing to which it has been applied ? 3. The second ? 4. The third ? 5. Why can it not refer to the first or second ? 6. To what does it refer ? 7. Where is positive proof of this found, and why ? 8. What is Paul's testimony to the Romans on this subject ? 9. What points are worthy

none will be saved only those who have been immersed. We believe that thousands who have never been baptized will be in the kingdom of God. All will be judged according to the light they have had. As with the Papal baptism so with the Papal Sabbath. Those who had not the clear light on these subjects, but in honesty of soul followed their teachers who had Papal errors clinging to them will be judged according to the light they had, and the obedience they manifested. Those who have the clear light upon these subjects will also be judged according to that light, and the manner in which they walk in that light. The Bible standard of truth and duty is the only safe one. Those who take up with an anti-scriptural baptism and Sabbath because the founders of their churches when just emerging from the darkness of Papal error brought them into different branches of the Protestant churches run fearful risks.

The apostle expresses the form of baptism in the strongest terms. He not only uses the word " buried," but in Rom. 6 : 5 he uses even stronger language if possible : " For if we have been planted together in the likeness of his death we shall be also in the likeness of his resurrection." What should we think of the farmer who would ·sprinkle a few grains of sand on his seeds and say that he had buried them ? But planting seems a strange figure.

But let it be particularly noticed that the very manner or likeness of burial in baptism is distinctly stated. It is to be done in the likeness of Christ's death. The reader will please go with us to Joseph's

---

of notice here ? 10. What is the Bible standard of judgment on this matter ? 11. In what language does the apostle set forth the form of baptism ? 12. How is this illustrated in the work of the husbandman ? 13. What is the force of the words, " likness of Christ's death "? 14. Why cannot the can-

new sepulcher and see the dear Saviour lying there upon his back as we lay out the dead. The very position in the water is to be in imitation of Christ's in death. Can this be done by sprinkling a few drops of water into a babe's face? Answer: "Planted in the likeness of his death." Can it be accomplished by pouring a gill of water on the head of the candidate to run down the clothing? Is there the least resemblance in this dabbling in water to the position of Christ in the tomb? We know of no more complete refutation of this error than the words used by the apostle—*buried*—*planted*.

Will it not do quite as well to plunge the candidate into the water face formost as the Dunkers do? We inquire, Did the friends of Jesus place their dear Lord in the sepulcher upon his face? The thought is revolting. Again we reply in the words of Paul: "Planted in the likeness of his death."

Three events in the history of the first advent of Christ represent three steps in leaving a life of sin, and reaching that of obedience. These are his crucifixion, burial and resurrection. The sinner is first crucified with Christ. "Knowing this, that our old man is crucified with him, that the body of sin might be destroyed." Rom. 6:6. This crucifixion represents true conviction of sin. It is spoken of in the same epistle under the figure of death. "What shall we say then? Is the law sin? God forbid. Nay, I had not known sin, but by the law. For I had not known lust, except the law had said, Thou shalt not covet. But sin, taking occasion by the commandment wrought in me all manner of concupiscence. For without the law sin was dead. For I was alive without the law once; but when the

didate be plunged into the water face foremost? 15. What three events in the history of the first advent represent three steps in the sinner's conversion? 16. What is the instrument

commandment came, sin revived, and I died." Chap.
7 :-7–9. Please notice :—

1. The instrument by which the sinner is crucified, is slain, truly convicted, is the moral code.

2. That Paul means the ten commandments in the
use of the word *law* is evident from the fact that he
refers to the tenth precept of that code as especially
instrumental in his case.

3. The word *alive* does not refer to natural life,
but to a careless state of the mind, when without a
true sense of the holiness of God's law. Neither does
death refer to the cessation of natural life, but to true
conviction of sins by the light of the sacred law.

The second step in conversion is burial with
Christ by baptism. "Therefore, we are buried with
him by baptism into death." Rom. 6 : 4. Here the
burial of Christ, or his position in the sepulcher represents the true mode of baptism.

The third step in conversion is a resurrection with
Christ from a watery grave. " If ye then be risen
with Christ." Col. 3 : 1.

We now see the relation which baptism sustains
to the law of God in Scriptural conversion. With
correct views of the mode of baptism, and what is
meant by law, all is plain. The apostle is giving in
this connection his own experience, hence those who
seek apostolic religion should mark well the means
employed in his case. The moral code is God's great
looking-glass into which he looked and saw the im-
perfections of his moral character. This prepared
the way for him to come to Christ for pardon and

---

by which the sinner is slain ? 17. What does Paul mean by
the word "law ?" 18. What does he mean by the words,
"alive," and " death ?" 19. What is the second step in
conversion ? Reference. 20. What is the third step ? Reference. 21. What is shown by these scriptures ? 22. What
does the apostle give in this connection ? 23. By what does

justification through his precious blood. This epistle to the Romans was written in the year 60, about
thirty years after the handwriting of ordinances
were nailed to the cross. Paul's conversion occurred several years after the abolition of the Jewish
system of worship.

The apostle James illustrates the use of the royal
law by a looking-glass : "But be ye doers of the word,
and not hearers only, deceiving your own selves.
For if any be a hearer of the word, and not a doer,
he is like unto a man beholding his natural face in
a glass ; for he beholdeth himself, and goeth his way,
and straightway fogetteth what manner of man he
was. But whoso looketh into the perfect law of
liberty and continueth therein, he being not a for-
getful hearer, but a doer of the work, this man shall
be blessed in his deed." Chap. 1: 22–25.

The first great work, then, of the gospel minister
as he labors for the conversion of sinners, is to hold
before them God's great mirror, that they may see
what sin is and know its exceeding sinfulness. The
reason why many who profess religion were never
converted is because they were not convicted, and
the reason why they did not have genuine conviction is because they have never seen the corruptions
of the heart in God's mirror, the ten commandments.
A popular gospel keeps that from the people, and
moves upon the sinner's sympathies and fears, producing a conviction more nervous than intelligent.
Such conviction does not result in a change of life
as required by the sacred Scriptures. Intelligent
convictions produced by the claims of the law of
God changes the mind, the heart, and the life. This

James illustrate the use of the law ? 24. What is the first
work of the gospel minister in laboring for the conversion of
sinners ? 25. Why is it that so many who profess religion
are not converted ? 26. What results from intelligent con-

change is illustrated in the text by the change from
life to death. A man walks to-day in the strength
of manhood, to-morrow he is a corpse. What a
change! Yet inspiration has chosen it to illustrate
the first great work in true conversion. Thus far
we have followed the apostle in his experience, and
have learned from him the character and use of the
law of God in the present dispensation. He saw its
excellence, its holiness, its justice and goodness, and
felt its searching, slaying power, and says, " I died."
But he does not leave us here. Burial follows death.

But what is the pre-requisite, or scriptural preparation for the ordinance of baptism? When viewed
in the light of a burial, or funeral, the answer is at
hand. Before burying our dead we must feel
assured that they are really dead. So before burial
with Christ by baptism we should know that the
candidate has experienced that conviction that may
be represented by death, that he has been crucified
with Christ. Burial alive is a horrid thought. And
it is no less horrid to the thorough Christian to be
buried in baptism while using tobacco, or wearing
jewelry and other outward ornaments forbidden in
the word of God. But to lay these aside for the
occasion effects no real change in the candidate.
When the sinner really dies to sin these drop off,
never to return.

But would you not have the candidate wait until
he has experienced the love of God, and comes out
shouting happy before receiving baptism? Not
unless there is some precept or example of the kind
in the New Testament. There is nothing joyful in
the burial of our dead friends. We do not regard

viction produced by the law? 27. By what is this change
illustrated? 28. What is the pre-requisite of baptism? 29.
What will give evidence of this scriptural death? 30. Should
the candidate wait for joyful emotions before baptism? 31.

joyful feelings as the Scriptural evidence of preparation for baptism. Brokenness of spirit, with tears, confessions and mourning on account of sins and feelings of unworthiness are the best evidences of preparation of mind and heart for baptism. The New Testament furnishes evidence that the truly convicted person should not wait a single hour. In fact every instance of baptism furnishes evidence that the truly convicted soul should not wait.

We first cite the case of Saul. No one questions his conversion. The work was accomplished in him by the word and Spirit of God. We have seen what the moral code did for him. And if it be thought necessary that the Holy Spirit act a part in conviction and conversion, then we cite Saul's experience as he was on his way to Damascus to persecute the saints. Most certainly the Spirit of God will work in harmony with the law of God. The Lord who appeared to Saul in the way sent him to Ananias to be instructed more fully. Jesus might have shown Saul his whole duty and thus set aside all human instrumentality, but he chose to honor the instrumentalities he had placed in the church. This great man must sit at the feet of Ananias, and there learn his first duty. By the hand of Ananias Saul first received his sight. Next came baptism. "And now," says Ananias, " why tarriest thou? Arise and be baptized." Acts 22:16. There was no occasion for waiting. In this remarkable conversion of a great man baptism followed immediately after conviction of sin.

The case of the jailor is another where baptism closely followed conviction. He was convicted that

---

What would rather be suggested by the illustration of burial? 32. What evidence does the New Testament furnish? 33. What were the great features of Saul's conversion? 34. How long did he wait before baptism? 35. What is shown

he was a sinner in the night of the imprisonment of
Paul and Silas, and anxiously inquired of them:
"Sirs, what must I do to be saved?" He was told
to believe on the Lord Jesus Christ. They then
preached the word of the Lord to his family, and
that very night baptized them. These ministers,
who fully understood their business, did not wait
until this family should experience religion, as it is
termed, and come out shouting happy before they
baptized them; but the same hour of the night that
the jailor was convicted of sin he and his family
were baptized, after which came the rejoicing.

The case of the eunuch is also to the point. He
was a man in great authority. His experience
should have a decided bearing on the subject. He
was riding in his chariot reading from the prophet
Isaiah: "He was led as a sheep to the slaughter, and
like a lamb dumb before his shearer so opened he
not his mouth." "Of whom speaketh the prophet
this?" inquired the eunuch, "of himself, or of some
other man?" This question reveals the astonishing
ignorance of the eunuch. Right there, as teacher
and pupil were riding in the chariot, the evangelist
Philip commenced a course of instruction. The
record says that he preached Jesus to the eunuch.
Just then they came upon a body of water of sufficient depth for immersion. It might have been at
a sudden turn in the road. They seem to have come
upon it unexpectedly. "See, here is water," cries
the eunuch, "what doth hinder me to be baptized?"

But why is this novice speaking of baptism? The
record does not state that Philip had as much as
mentioned the ordinance. It is evident, however,

by the case of the jailor? 36. What is the next case in point?
37. What reveals the ignorance of the eunuch? 38. What
did Philip preach to him? 39. To what did they suddenly
come? 40. What did the ennuch then say? 41. Why does

that in preaching Jesus, Philip had introduced baptism, or the eunuch would not have thought of it. Philip preached Jesus. His text was in Isaiah, which speaks of his humiliation and death. Yes, he fully instructed him respecting the death, burial and resurrection of Christ. He must believe on the Lord Jesus Christ before receiving baptism. He must have faith that he died for our sins, that he was buried, and that he arose for our justification. And as faith without works is dead, he must show that faith by the very act which the gospel provided to show that faith. These facts must have entered into Philips discourse in order for his hearer to make the intelligent inquiry in reference to his receiving baptism. He who preaches Jesus aright will preach baptism.

But the point especially under consideration is that baptism immediately follows true conviction of sin. Did Philip tell the eunuch that he had better wait three or six months, and that at some more convenient season they could have a large gathering at which time the ordinance could be administered before the crowds ? The record does not mention any such delays. No, the coachman is commanded to halt right there, and then and there " they went down into the water, both Philip and the eunuch, and he baptized him. And when they were come up out of the water, the Spirit of the Lord caught away Philip, and the eunuch went on his way rejoicing." Acts 8 : 26–40. Here, again, rejoicing does not go before, but follows baptism.

The reader will bear in mind that we do not say that the comforts of the Holy Spirit are not in many instances experienced before being baptized. We do say, however, when the subject is presented in

he so abruptly speak of baptism ? 42. What is the point to be especially noticed here ? 43. What bearing has the bap-

the true light, and the several steps in leaving a life of sin for one of obedience and holiness are taken in rapid succession, according to the examples given in the New Testament, the rejoicing in hope will be after baptism. The descent of the Holy Spirit in the form of a dove upon Christ after his baptism greatly strengthens this position. It would have been a great relief to John and his friends if the dove had appeared while Christ stood upon the banks of Jordan asking baptism, designating him as the Son of God. For it seems that the administrator's mind was not clear. After John was cast into prison he sent word to Jesus inquiring : " Art thou he that should come, or do we look for another ? " Neither did the dove appear while administrator and candidate stood in the waters of Jordan. But when he who was our substitute and pattern had been plunged into the water, had been raised up out of the water, the Holy Spirit came upon him, marking the very period when we may expect the blessing of God to witness the act of obedience in the baptismal vow. The manifestation of this is not always the same. With some it is like the descent of the gentle rain, producing a heavenly smile, indicating the peace that reigns within, while in the cases of others shouts of the high praises of God are heard.

We see that baptism is closely related to conversion. In fact, it seems to be a part of conversion. It is the outward act by which believers show their faith in Christ. But while some have removed baptism from this close relation to conversion, and regard the ordinance of little importance, others regard it the act by which sins are remitted. Those who regard baptism of little importance sometimes cite 1

tism of Christ upon this part of the subject ?   44. What relation, then, has baptism to conversion ?   45. What use is

Peter 3 : 21, as sustaining their lax position : " The like figure whereunto even baptism doth also now save us, not the putting away the filth of the flesh, but the answer of a good conscience toward God by the resurrection of Jesus Christ." " I was sprinkled," says one, " and that answered my conscience." " And my conscience was answered by being poured," says another. This may all be true ; but are our friends, who differ with us on baptism, sure that they have a good conscience on this subject ? Peter says : " But the answer of a *good* conscience." Pagans and Papists may be very conscientious, and their blinded consciences not be good. Protestants may be in a like condition on some points. But it is a fact of much interest that the apostle in the last clause of the passage raises a standard to which we may bring our consciences, and know that they are right " by the resurrection of Jesus Christ from the dead." On the other hand, some evidently overlook the necessary work to be wrought upon the mind and heart before baptism. They do not see the use of the divine law, that it must slay the sinner, that he be dead before he is buried, hence it is to be feared that some, at least, are buried alive ! Some teach that Christ is put on in the simple act of baptism, which teaching has a strong tendency to set aside not only the work of the law of God in conversion, but that also of the Holy Spirit.

But Gal. 3 : 27, may be urged : " For as many of you as have been baptized into Christ have put on Christ." It should here be noticed that the text does not say that the Galatian brethren had put on

sometimes made of 1 Pet. 1 : 23 ? 46. What may be said about the conscience in these cases ? 47. What is the standard given to which we are to bring our consciences ? 48. What is taught by some classes ? 49. What is shown by Gal.

Christ in the sole act of baptism. They had put on Christ by faith, baptism being the corresponding work, an act by which they manifested their faith in Christ.

It is also asserted that baptism is for the remission of sins. Very true; but there are also other means for the remission of sins. Christ's blood was shed for the remission of sins. Matt. 26 : 28. Christ was to give knowledge of salvation unto the people for the remission of their sins. Luke 1 : 77. It became Christ to suffer, and to rise from the dead the third day, that repentance and remission of sins might be preached in his name. Chap. 24 : 46, 47. Repentance and baptism are for the remission of sins. Acts 2 : 38. Faith is for the remission of sins. " Whosoever believeth in him shall receive remission of sins." Chap. 10 : 43; also Rom. 3 : 25. In the arrangement for the remission of sins, baptism holds its place in the divine whole.

In the investigation of the subject of scriptural conversion thus far, we see that it is by the divine law that the sinner obtains a knowledge of his sins. He cannot understandingly repent of his sins until he sees them; therefore, the gospel minister, who labors to convert the sinner, is under the most solemn obligation to hold before him God's great mirror. His first work is to show the character, perpetuity and claims of the moral code. And in so doing he follows the example of his divine Master. In Christ's first recorded sermon he said, " Think not that I am come to destroy the law, or the prophets; I am not come to destroy, but to fulfill; for verily I say unto you, Till heaven and earth

3 : 27 ? 50. What may be said on the declaration that baptism is for the remission of sin ? 51. How does the sinner obtain a knowledge of his sins ? 52. What view does this

pass, one jot or one tittle shall in no wise pass from the law, till all be fulfilled." Matt. 5 : 17, 18.

The sinner sees the holiness and justness of the divine law, that he is exposed to the wrath of God, and feels its slaying power. He yields to the requirements of all its precepts, and is dead. The gospel then points him to Jesus. He hears the story of the cross, the burial in Joseph's sepulcher, the glory of the resurrection, and the ascension of Jesus to the Father's right hand, where he ever lives to intercede for poor sinners. He raises his head and ventures to believe that Jesus will pity and save him. And as he believes, let him immediately show his faith in the burial and resurrection of Christ by being baptized.

He has now put off the "old man," and has put on the "new man." The Christian warfare and race is begun. He has now the faith of the gospel, and the exhortation of Peter is especially applicable: "Giving all diligence, add to your faith, virtue; and to virtue, knowledge; and to knowledge, temperance; and to temperance, patience; and to patience, godliness; and to godliness, brotherly kindness; and to brotherly kindness, charity. For if these things be in you and abound, they make you that ye shall neither be barren nor unfruitful in the knowledge of our Lord Jesus Christ." 2 Pet. 1 : 5–8.

In Rom. 7, the apostle first makes an important declaration; second, gives an illustration; and third, states his conclusion. These we will notice in their order :—

1. His declaration. "Know ye not, brethren, for

give him of the law ? 53. To what does the gospel then point him ? 54. What does the sinner then do ? 55. Into what condition does he thus bring himself ? 56. What does Paul give us in Rom. 7 ? 57. What is his declaration ? 58.

I speak to them that know the law, how that the law hath dominion over a man as long as he liveth?" Verse 1. The words, *he liveth*, do not refer to natural life. This is not the subject upon which the apostle is treating. In harmony with his discourse in these chapters, the phrase must have reference to what he calls *the old man*, or the *carnal mind*. Then we understand Paul to declare that the law has dominion over a man as long as he lives in transgression of it. We will give an illustration.

Passing a bridge in the State of New York, we met three men, each carrying a large leaden ball. Each man was chained to the ball he carried, and an officer followed them. These men had been breaking the law, and it had dominion over them, because they had not kept it. We walked with freedom where our business led us, for we had kept the law. Our feelings were in perfect harmony with every good law in the State. To say that those who keep the law of God are in bondage, under the dominion of the law, is a stupid blunder. They are not the men.

2. His illustration. "For the woman which hath an husband is bound by the law to her husband so long as he liveth; but if the husband be dead, she is loosed from the law of her husband. So then, if, while her husband liveth, she be married to another man, she shall be called an adulteress; but if her husband be dead, she is free from that law, so that she is no adulteress, though she be married to another man." Verses 2, 3. In this illustration there are mentioned the woman, the law of marriage, the first husband, and her second husband. We now look for an application, consistent with the subject upon which the apostle is here treating.

What is his illustration? 59. What is his conclusion? 60.

The woman represents candidates for everlasting life, to whom the gospel call is given. The law of marriage represents the law of God. The first husband represents the old man, and the second husband represents the *new man,* which is the Lord Jesus Christ. We will here give a few direct texts which speak of the old and new man. "That ye put off concerning the former conversation the old man, which is corrupt according to the deceitful lusts; and be renewed in the spirit of your mind; and that ye put on the new man, which after God is created in righteousness and true holiness." Eph. 4:22-24. "Lie not one to another, seeing that ye have put off the old man with his deeds, and have put on the new man, which is renewed in knowledge after the image of him that created him." Col. 3:9, 10. See, also, Gal. 2:20; Rom. 6:6.

Now mark, Before the woman could be legally married to the second husband, her first husband must die. Did his death affect the law of marriage? Certainly not. The same law that bound her to her first husband, bound her to the second. And before the sinner can be united to Christ, the new man, the old man must die. Does this death affect the divine law? Not in the least. The same moral code that held the sinner in condemnation, is now his rule of obedience, and binds him to Christ. The apostle's conclusion shows that we have correctly applied his illustration.

3. His conclusion. "Wherefore, my brethren, ye also are become dead to the law by the body of Christ; that ye should be married to another, even to him who is raised from the dead, that we should bring forth fruit unto God." Verse 4.

This conclusion of the apostle shows that the

What is meant by the expression, "That being dead wherein

first husband represents that which is said to become dead. Some say it is the law; but Paul says, " Wherefore, my brethren, *ye* also are become dead."

Verse 6 : " But now we are delivered from the law, that being dead wherein we were held, that we should serve in newness of spirit, and not in the oldness of the letter."

Being delivered from the law must be understood in harmony with Paul's statement of its use and perpetuity. It is not by the death of the law, but, by that being dead wherein we were held by the law, which is the carnal mind, or " the old man ; " or with the marginal reading, " being dead to that wherein we were held."

Says Paul, " The carnal mind is enmity against God, for it is not subject to the law of God, neither, indeed, can be." Rom. 8:7. This carnal mind, which is represented by the first husband, must be slain before the person can be united to Christ; then the enmity against God and his holy law is gone, and he is subject to the divine law, and keeps all its precepts with delight. But to set the ten commandments aside, and teach that sinners may be married to Christ without being first slain by the moral law, is to teach spiritual adultery.

Turn to Acts 20:20, 21, dear reader, and you will there learn that the gospel preached by Paul is in harmony with his own experience and his teachings in his epistle to the Romans. He says, " I kept back nothing that was profitable unto you, but have shown you, and have taught you publicly, and from house to house, testifying both to the Jews, and also to the Greeks, repentance toward God, and

we were held ?"   61. What does Rom. 8 : 7 say of the carnal mind ? 62. By what is the carnal mind represented? 63. That being slain what takes place ? 64. What is shown by acts 20 : 20, 21 ? 65. Why did he teach first repentance

faith toward our Lord Jesus Christ." Here are the two great foundation timbers of the gospel, as preached by Paul; first, repentance toward God; and, second, faith toward our Lord Jesus Christ. He taught that sinners must first manifest repentance toward God for the transgression of his holy law, before believing in Jesus Christ. He kept back nothing that was profitable. He did not keep back the law; for by it is the knowledge of sin. He first presented the claims of the divine law, and showed the sinner that his first work was to exercise repentance toward its Author; then he taught the sinner that faith in Christ was the only remedy for sin.

Therefore, in the present dispensation, God the Father is our lawgiver, and Christ is our advocate. And before sinners can be benefited by the mediation of Christ, they must manifest repentance toward the lawgiver for the transgression of his holy law. With this the words of the beloved disciple agree: "Sin is the transgression of the law." 1 John 3:4. "And if any man sin, we have an advocate with the Father, Jesus Christ the righteous." Chap. 2:1.

But if Christ is our lawgiver, as some teach, who is our advocate? We have none. But as Jesus Christ is the sinner's advocate with the Father in this dispensation, it follows that the Father's law of ten commandments is in full force.

"Do we then make void the law through faith? God forbid; yea, we establish the law." Rom. 3:31. Faith in Jesus Christ as a sacrifice for sin, and now an advocate with the Father, for our sins—"trans-

toward God? 66. Why faith in Jesus Christ? 67. Who then is our lawgiver? 68. What office does Jesus Christ perform? 69. If Christ is our lawgiver, who is our advocate? 70. What do these facts show respecting the perpe-

gression of the law "—is the strongest proof of the perpetuity of the law of ten commandments.

Hence, the closing testimony of the third angel: "Here is the patience of the saints; here are they that keep the commandments of God and the faith of Jesus." Rev. 14:12. Also, the dragon is to make war with the *remnant*, the Christians in the closing generations of time, "which keep the commandments of God, and have the testimony of Jesus Christ." Chap. 12:17.

These are Christian commandment-keepers. Their observance of the Sabbath of the fourth commandment stirs the ire of the dragon host.

But those who endure his wrath, and stand faithful in the closing conflict, will soon receive the great reward promised by Him who says, Rev. 22, "Behold I come quickly, and my reward is with me." "Blessed are they that do his commandments, that they may have right to the tree of life, and may enter in through the gates into the city."

LESSON TWENTY-SEVEN.

CHRIST IN THE OLD TESTAMENT.

WHEN all was lost in Adam, the plan of redemption through Jesus Christ was immediately instituted; hence he is represented as the "Lamb slain from the foundation of the world." Rev. 13:8. In the patriarchal and Jewish ages Christ was slain in

tuity of the law? 71. What is the closing testimony of the third message? 72. What are the characteristics of the remnant, of Rev. 12:17? 73. What is the promise of Christ in Rev. 22:14?

REVIEW QUESTIONS ON LESSON TWENTY-SEVEN.

1. When was the plan of redemption instituted? 2. In what sense was Christ slain in the patriarchal and Jewish dis-

figure. In the Christian age he is slain in fact. The Scriptures reveal but one plan by which fallen men may be saved. It is true that in the development of the plan of grace through Christ there has been in each dispensation an increase of light. But there is no intimation in all the Bible of three plans, one for the patriarchal age, one for the Jewish, and one for the Christian age.

Jesus Christ is the Redeemer of sinners in all the ages of human probation. "Neither is there salvation in any other; for there is none other name under heaven given among men, whereby we must be saved." Acts 4 : 12. We protest, in the name of reason and revelation, against the vague heresy that the law of the Father and the gospel of the Son are opposed to each other, the one designed to take the place of the other; as if the men of former dispensations were saved by the law without the gospel, and those of the present dispensation are saved by the gospel while disregarding the moral law. It was not possible for sinful man in the ages past to secure a fitness for the inheritance of the saints in light by the divine law alone. There is no ability in law to redeem the transgressor. It is not the province of law, human or divine, to pardon the transgressor of law. The moral law is a rule of right action, condemning the transgressor, and holding him as such until he shall suffer the penalty. The divine law can do no more for the sinner. It is the gospel alone that offers pardon and salvation. And without the gospel of the Son of God none of the men of the patriarchal and Jewish ages could be saved.

pensations? 3. In what sense in the Christian age? 4. How many plans of salvation are there? 5. How many ages does the work of Christ as Redeemer embrace? 6. Are the law and the gospel opposed to each other? 7. Was it possible for man in past ages to be saved by the law? 8. What would be the hope of the patriarchs without the gospel? 9.

The gospel is the *joyful message* of redemption
through Jesus Christ. We inquire, How early in
the sad history of the fallen race was the gospel proclaimed ?   Was it first given in the days of Christ?
of Moses ? of Abraham ? or of Adam ?   We distinctly trace the faith and hope of the gospel of the
Son of God in that early denunciation of wrath upon
Satan, that the seed of the woman should bruise the
serpent's head. Gen. 3 : 15. In this decree against
the author of sin and death, we hear the gospel of
the Redeemer as verily as in the song of the angels
over the plains of Bethlehem, to the shepherds as
they watched their flocks by night.   Luke 2: 8–14.

And when the first sons of Adam brought their
offerings to the Lord, Cain in unbelief brought of the
first-fruits of the ground.   But Abel, in faith of the
great Sacrifice for sin to be manifested in the distant future, brought of the firstlings of his flock.
Through that lamb Abel saw the Lamb of God, the
Redeemer of the world, and set his hope upon him.
In the blood of that firstling, Abel saw the blood of
Jesus Christ as truly as we see the dying Saviour in
the broken bread and the fruit of the vine at the
Lord's supper. In these emblems we see Christ
shedding his blood for our sins on the cross.   Abel
saw the same in the bleeding, dying firstling which
he offered.

" And the Lord had respect unto Abel and to his
offering ; but unto Cain and to his offering he had
not respect." Gen. 4: 4, 5. The sacred narrative
states that while Abel's act of faith in the Redeemer
to come sealed his righteous character, cost him his
life, and placed him at the head of the holy martyrs
of Jesus, Cain's infidelity was regarded as sinful, and
was the stepping-stone to the high crime of the mur-

What is the gospel?   10. How early was it proclaimed ?   11.
What was the difference between the offering of Abel, and

der of his brother, which sealed his character as a vagabond in the earth. See Heb. 11:4; 1 John 3:12.

We pass down the sacred record of the fallen race to Abraham, and there we find the joyful news of redemption through Jesus Christ, to be extended to the nations of the earth, proclaimed to the trusting, obedient patriarch. Paul speaks of it thus: "And the scripture, foreseeing that God would justify the heathen through faith, preached before the gospel unto Abraham, saying, In thee shall all nations be blessed." Gal. 3 : 8. The apostle here quotes from Gen. 12 : 3. See verse 7 ; Chap. 13:14, 15 ; 17:7, 8; 26 : 3; 28 : 13, where this promise is extended to Abraham's seed.

The gospel of the Son of God was proclaimed to Abraham in this promise, in that it is really a promise of Christ, as argued by the apostle in Gal. 3 : 16.

The gospel was preached to the children of Israel in the days of Moses. In his epistle to the Hebrews, Paul states : " Unto us was the gospel preached, as well as unto them; but the word preached did not profit them, not being mixed with faith in them that heard it." Heb. 4 : 2. That the gospel was preached to their fathers in a former dispensation, the apostle treats as a well known fact, and states that it was preached in his day as well as then, making it appear that the gospel of the Son of God was alike common in both the Jewish and Christian ages. He also testifies of the Hebrews in the wilderness, that they " were all baptized unto Moses in the cloud and in the sea, and did all eat the same spiritual meat, and did all drink the same spiritual drink ; for they drank of that spiritual Rock that followed them, and that Rock was Christ." 1 Cor. 10 : 2–4.

Moses and the believing Jews had the faith and

that of Cain? 12. How was the gospel preached to Abraham? References. 13. How was the gospel preached to the

hope of the gospel. Through the blood of the sacrificial offerings, they saw Christ, and by faith embraced him. Their hopes of the future life were not in the law, but in Christ. The typical system was but the shadow of good things to come, of which Christ, as a sacrifice and mediator, is the center.

Christ was with Moses and the children of Israel in the wilderness. The angel that went before them, Ex. 23 : 20, 21, 23 ; 14 : 19 ; 32 : 34 ; 33 : 2, 14 ; Num. 20 : 16 ; Josh. 5 : 13, 14 ; Acts 7 : 37, 38, was the Lord Jesus Christ. The record states that Joshua was by Jericho, and that " he lifted up his eyes and looked, and, behold, there stood a man over against him with his sword drawn in his hand. And Joshua went unto him, and said unto him, Art thou for us, or for our adversaries ? And he said, Nay ; but as captain of the host of the Lord am I now come." Josh 5 : 13, 14.

We must not understand by this declaration of the angel that he had come to supersede Joshua in the command of the armies of Israel. Joshua was still commander, as is seen by Chap. 6 : 2 : " And the Lord said unto Joshua, See, I have given into thine hand Jericho, and the king thereof, and the mighty men of valor." But the angel had come to Joshua's aid, as captain of the heavenly host of loyal angels.

The captain of the host of the Lord is the head over angels, or the Archangel of Jude 9, and the Lord himself of 1 Thess. 4 : 16. And while it was appointed to Joshua to lead the armies of Israel around Jericho, a portion of the priests bearing the ark of God containing the ten commandments, and seven priests bearing seven trumpets of ram's horns

children of Israel? 14. What texts show that Christ was with Moses and the children of Israel? 15. To what does Josh. 5:13, 14, refer ? 16. Who did the work of overthrow-

before the ark of God, the Son of God was to lead on the invisible armies.

Joshua had no battering rams with which to break down the walls of Jericho. At his command the armed men passed on before the priests that blew the trumpets, and those that carried the ark of God. And the rearward came after the ark. In this simple display there was no manifestation of physical force. The work of casting down the massive walls of Jericho was left to the invisible hands of the heavenly host led on by the Son of God.

The day was gained. "So the people shouted when the priests blew with the trumpets. And it came to pass when the people heard the sound of the trumpet, and the people shouted with a great shout, that the wall fell down flat so that the people went up into the city every man straight before him, and they took the city." Josh. 6 : 20. And it is an exceedingly interesting fact to those who keep "the commandments of God and the faith of Jesus " under the third message, Rev. 14 : 12, that prominent among the united agencies employed to achieve that grand victory, away back in the days of Joshua, were the ten commandments in the ark, and the leadership of the Son of God.

And it is not a common angel that is spoken of in Ex. 23 : 20, 21 : " Behold, I send an angel before thee, to keep thee in the way, and to bring thee into the place which I have prepared. Beware of him, and obey his voice, provoke him not ; for he will not pardon your transgressions ; for my name is in him." Such language can be applied to no other than the Son of God.

Christ is the angel that was with Moses in the

ing Jericho ? 17. What interesting fact appears in this narrative ? 18. To whom does Ex. 23:20, 21, refer ? 19. Who is meant by the angel who was with Moses in the mount ? 20.

Mount Sinai.   In that last address of the holy martyr, Stephen, he bears this important testimony. The words in brackets express our convictions relative to the persons meant in Acts 7 : 38 : " This [Moses] is he that was in the church in the wilderness with the angel [Christ] which spake to him [Moses] in the Mount Sinai, and with our fathers, who received the lively oracles to give unto us." The conclusion seems irresistible that the Son of God spoke the ten commandments from Sinai.

The eternal Father is never called an angel in the Scriptures, while what angels have done is frequently ascribed to the Lord, as they are his messengers and agents to accomplish his work.   It is said of Him who went before the Hebrews to deliver them, "My name is in him."   In all the stupendous events of that deliverance the mind of Jehovah was represented in Jesus.

The typical system was given to Moses by the Son of God in the Mount Sinai.   Jesus Christ, the minister of the " true tabernacle," showed Moses patterns of it, and of the vessels of the heavenly sanctuary, that he might know how to form the typical.   And as Moses is instructed relative to the tabernacle, even the several parts of the golden candlestick, Ex. 25 : 31–40, the boards and bars, Chap. 26 : 15–30, and the altar with its staves, pans, shovels, and other particulars, Chap. 27 : 1–8, he is charged, as quoted by Paul, Heb. 8 : 5, " See that thou make all things according to the pattern showed to thee in the mount."

The church of all the ages is the church of Jesus Christ.   He is the world's only Redeemer.   Those

---

By whom, probably, were the ten commandments spoken from Sinai?   21. What is the Father never called?   22. To whom is the work of angels frequently ascribed, and why? 23. By whom was the typical system given?   24. What is the church of all the ages?   25. What is the foundation of

who shut themselves up to the New Testament, and have the foundation of the church laid at the resurrection, or at pentecost, are building too narrow a structure. The apostle states the foundation of the true church in these words : " Now, therefore, ye are no more strangers and foreigners, but fellow-citizens with the saints, and of the household of God, and are built upon the foundation of the apostles and prophets, Jesus Christ himself being the chief corner-stone." Eph. 2 : 19, 20.

When the angel said to John in Patmos, " The testimony of Jesus is the spirit of prophecy," he meant more than expositors generally suppose. His words reach far back to the days of fallen Adam, when the plan of redemption was instituted, and embrace the entire prophetic word of both Testaments.

The manifestation of the spirit of prophecy was designed for all dispensations. The Sacred Record nowhere restricts it to any particular period of time, from the fall to the final restitution. The Bible recognizes its manifestation alike in the patriarchal age, in the Jewish age, and in the Christian age. Through this medium God communed with holy men of old.

Christ and his angels are the connecting link between God and fallen man. Here is the order by which prophetic truth is communicated from the throne of heaven to the children of men. God gives it to Christ. Christ gives it to his angel. The angel shows it to the chosen prophet of God. And the prophet reveals it to the people.

The plan of salvation by which man is reconciled to God and God to man was devised by both the

this church ? 26. For what dispensations was the spirit of prophecy designed ? 27. What is the connecting link between God and fallen man ? 28. By whom was the plan of salva-

Father and the Son. And in carrying it out, the counsel of peace is between them both. Zech. 6:13. But it was given to the Son to reveal this plan in the several stages of its development to the fallen race in the several ages.

All things pertaining to the grand scheme of redemption, whether in the figures of the former dispensation, or in the facts of the present, were revealed to the fallen race by our adorable Redeemer. He is therefore no more the author of the Christian than of the Jewish system. And those who contrast Moses with Christ, and the Jewish with the Christian system, are virtually arraying Christ against Christ.

The Spirit of Christ inspired the prophets of the former dispensations. It testified through them of his sufferings at his first advent, and of the glory that should follow at his second coming The apostle, speaking of the great salvation which had come to the church through Jesus Christ, says that the prophets "inquired and searched diligently, who prophesied of the grace that should come unto you ; searching what, or what manner of time the Spirit of Christ which was in them did signify, when it testified beforehand the sufferings of Christ, and the glory that should follow." 1 Pet. 1:10,11.

In this is seen the harmony of both Testaments, that the Spirit of Jesus inspired the writers of both. And while the blind Jew shuts himself up to the Old, and the equally blind Christian virtually shuts himself up to the New Testament, we thank God for a whole Bible. In the writings of both Testaments we see the entire plan of salvation in all stages of its development, in the several

tion devised ? 29. By whom was it revealed ? 30. What spirit inspired the writers of both the Old and New Testa-

dispensations, and the Spirit of Christ inspiring the divine whole.

The Spirit of Christ was in Enoch the seventh from Adam, testifying through him: "Behold, the Lord cometh with ten thousands of his saints, to execute judgment upon all, and to convince all that are ungodly among them of all their ungodly deeds which they have ungodly committed, and of all their hard speeches which ungodly sinners have spoken against him." Jude 14, 15. And so extended was the range of his prophetic vision, and so minute, that he could look down over long ages, and describe the coming of the Lord, and the execution of the last judgment upon the ungodly.

The Spirit of Christ was in Abel, testifying of the sufferings of Christ through the blood of the firstling of his flock. And the Spirit of Christ was in Moses, testifying of the sufferings of Christ through the blood of those beasts which was typical of the blood of the Son of God.

The Spirit of Christ was in Daniel, testifying in his prophecy of the sufferings of Christ in the midst of the seventieth prophetic week: "And after threescore and two weeks shall Messiah be cut off." "And in the midst of the week he shall cause the sacrifice and the oblation to cease." Chap, 9 : 26, 27. The Spirit of Christ in the prophet also testified of the glory that should follow, in these words: "I saw in the night visions, and behold one like the Son of man came with the clouds of heaven, and came to the Ancient of Days, and they brought him near before him. And there was given him dominion, and glory, and a kingdom." Chap 7 : 13, 14.

---

ments ? 31. By what spirit was Enoch moved ? 32. Abel 33. Noah ? 1. Pet. 3:17–20. 34. Moses ? 35. Daniel ?

The blessed Christ of the New Testament had the supervision of giving this important prophecy to Daniel. In proof of this proposition we first cite the statement of the angel that appeared to Daniel in his vision of the tenth chapter : " There is none that holdeth with me in these things but Michael your prince." Verse 21. There were only three persons connected with the giving of the prophecy; Daniel, Michael, and another, which Chap. 8 : 16, shows to be Gabriel. " And I heard a man's voice between the banks of Ulai which called and said, Gabriel, make this man to understand the vision." This command to Gabriel to further instruct the prophet Daniel came from Michael, as no other held with him in the things of the prophecy. Hence Michael, or the Son of God, having received the great things of the prophecy from the Father, shows them to the angel Gabriel, with the order for him to reveal them to the prophet Daniel.

There is a striking similarity in the manner in which the prophecy of this book was given in the Jewish dispensation, and the manner in which the last book of the New Testament was given in the Christian dispensation. Both came from the Father to the Son, and both were shown to angels by the Son, to be revealed by them to Daniel and to John, for the benefit of the servants of God. The object of one was to show " what shall be in the latter days," Dan. 2 : 28, and the object of the other is to show the " things which must shortly come to pass." Rev. 1 : 1.

---

36. Who had the supervision of giving the prophecy of Daniel? 37. Who is Michael in Dan. 10:21? 38. To what three persons was the giving of this prophecy confined? 39. In what particulars was the giving of the Old Testament similar to that of the New? 40. What spirit testified through

The Spirit of Christ was in Isaiah, testifying of the sufferings of Christ in these words: "He is despised and rejected of men; a man of sorrows and acquainted with grief." "He was wounded for our transgressions, he was bruised for our iniquities. The chastisement of our peace was upon him; and with his stripes we are healed." Chap. 53:3, 5. The Spirit of Christ in Isaiah also testifies of his glory: "Of the increase of his government and peace there shall be no end, upon the throne of David, and upon his kingdom, to order it, and to establish it with judgment and with justice from henceforth, even forever." Chap. 9:7.

We might continue these quotations to almost any length. The whole ground, however, is briefly covered by these remarkable words of the Saviour: "All things must be fulfilled which were written in the law of Moses, and in the prophets, and in the Psalms, concerning me." Luke 24:44.

Moses was a prophet. The Spirit of Christ was in this leader of the tribes of Israel, and testified, as quoted by Peter: "A prophet shall the Lord your God raise up unto you of your brethren like unto me." Acts 3:22; Deut. 18:18. The phrase *like unto me,* in the above passage, has reference to Christ and Moses as prophets or teachers. In many respects Moses and Christ were unlike; but as prophets they were alike. The principles which they declared to the people came from Him who had said, "I change not." God spoke through them both. Neither Moses nor Christ were law makers. Christ disclaims having anything to do with legislation. "My doctrine is not mine, but his that sent me." John 7:16. "I do nothing of myself but as

Isaiah? 41. What remarkable words of Christ cover the whole ground? 42. In what respect was Moses like Christ? 43. Were Moses and Christ law makers? 44. What is

318 THE BIBLICAL INSTITUTE.

my Father hath taught me, I speak these things."
Chap. 8 : 28. " The word which ye hear is not mine,
but the Father's which sent me." Chap. 14 : 24.
And speaking of the Son, the Father says, " He
shall speak unto them all that I shall command
him." Deut. 18 : 18.

In their efforts to hold before the people the
Jewish and Christian dispensations in as wide contrast as possible, certain religious teachers would
make it appear that the doctrines and principles
taught by Christ were unlike those taught by
Moses. But any amount of reasoning from false
premises, or unwarrantable assertions on their part
cannot change the word *like* in the above passages
to unlike. There the word stands, challenging the
efforts of those who would hold in wide contrast
God's two grand ministrations of truth and love,
covering the periods of the Jewish and Christian
ages.

In the development of the plan of redemption
through Jesus Christ in all the ages, from the time
that hope first dawned upon fallen Adam to the
crucifixion, resurrection, and ascension of Christ,
and the glory of Pentecost, there have been degrees
of light and glory. Hence the comparison of the
dispensations. The great plan is one, unfolding
with degrees of increased light and glory in the
successive ages. Paul's comparison of the two ministrations in 2 Cor. 3, is worthy of special study.
Mark well the clearness and strength of his expressions, which we here give side by side not for contrast, but for

Christ's testimony respecting himself? References. 45.
Why may the two dispensations past and present be compared? 46. Where does Paul set forth a remarkable comparison of the two dispensations? 47. With whom did the

COMPARISON.

JEWISH MINISTRATION.	CHRISTIAN MINISTRATION.
But if the ministration of death, written and engraven in stones was glorious,	how shall not the ministration of the Spirit be rather glorious. Verses 7, 8.
For if the ministration of condemnation be glory,	much more doth the ministration of righteousness exceed in glory. Verse 9.
For even that which was made glorious had no glory in this respect,	by reason of the glory that excelleth. Verse 10.
For if that which is done away was glorious,	much more that which remaineth is glorious. Verse 11.

The typical system did not originate with Moses. It came from Heaven. It originated with the God of love, and the merciful Christ of the New Testament. The first covenant, of itself, in its time, was glorious with blessings to the obedient. It is an impeachment of the character of God as a changeless being of love and wisdom to say that any part of his plan to redeem fallen man is defective and bad, whether it be in figure in the first covenant, or in fact in the second.

The unqualified strength of scripture expression in a few instances in both the Old and New Testaments seems at first reading hardly to agree with the position here taken. But these texts must be viewed in a comparative sense in harmony with the general scope of scripture testimony, the character of God and the special comparison of the apostle in declaring the ministration of the Jewish age glorious, while that of the Christian age is simply more glorious than the one that preceded it.

typical system originate?   48. To whom do all the redeemed

And why should the two ministrations be held in contrast? They both came from the same Divine Source, in behalf of the same race of sinners, to perfect that holiness of character in all the saved from all the ages, necessary for the same holy heaven. Hence John in prophetic vision, looking forward, saw them all gathered to the immortal shores, from the time of the holy martyr Abel down to the last ransomed sinner near the close of the Christian age, "a great multitude which no man could number, of all nations, and kindreds, and people, and tongues." He heard them all unite in the same acclamation, "Salvation to our God which sitteth upon the throne, and unto the Lamb." Rev. 7:9, 10.

Why should there be a wide contrast between ministrations under which the unit family of the immortal world find eternal redemption? Why? God is the one Father of all the adopted sons and daughters of grace from all the ages, and Christ is their only Saviour and Redeemer. Angels that excel in strength are the holy guardians of the obedient and faithful of every age, and the Holy Spirit is their sanctifier. The pious dead of all the ages sleep in the one Jesus; 1 Cor. 15:17, 18; and his voice will awaken them all at his coming. John 5:28, 29. They will all be caught up together to meet the Lord in the air, and upon the sea of glass all will receive the crown of glory and the palm of victory from the hand of Jesus. Then why should there be a wide contrast between God's moral government of fallen men in the Jewish and Christian ages?

---

at last ascribe their salvation? 49. Who is the Father of all? 50. Who is the Saviour of all? 51. Who are the guardians of all? 52. In whom do all the pious dead sleep? 53. By whom will they all be crowned at last?

LESSON TWENTY-EIGHT.

THE FIRST DAY OF THE WEEK.

WE affirm that the only weekly Sabbath of the Old and New Testaments is the seventh day. The terms, Jewish Sabbath, and Christian Sabbath, are not Bible terms. The term used by the Author of the moral code is, "The Sabbath of the Lord thy God." Ex. 20:10. The Jews had annual sabbaths which are termed "your sabbath," and "her sabbaths;" but the weekly Sabbath of the Bible is called by way of eminence, The Sabbath, in both the Old and New Testaments.

The Bible does not recognize two weekly Sabbaths, one in the Old Testament, to be observed on the seventh day of the week, and one in the New Testament, to be observed on the first day of the next week. There is but one weekly Sabbath taught in all the Bible. The Sabbath of the Old Testament is the Sabbath of the New Testament. On the seventh day of the first week of time God rested from the work of creation. This he did not do on any other day of that week. He sanctified the very day of his rest. That is, he set it apart to a holy use. This he did not do with regard to any other day of the week. He put his blessing upon the seventh day, the day of his rest. This he has not done to any other day of the week. God has

---

REVIEW QUESTIONS ON LESSON TWENTY-EIGHT.

1. What is the only weekly Sabbath in the Bible? 2. What may be said of the terms Jewish and Christian Sabbath? 3. What term does the author of the Sabbath use? 4. What were the annual sabbaths called? 5. How many weekly Sabbaths does the Bible recognize? 6. What were the steps by which the Sabbath was instituted? 7. Do these apply to any other day of the week but the seventh?

commanded the sacred observance of the day of his rest. He has not commanded the sacred observance of the first, or any other of the six secular days of the week.

While it is freely admitted that the seventh-day Sabbath is taught in the Old Testament, the general impression is abroad in the Christian world that the observance of another day is taught in the New Testament. It is in hope of removing this false impression from the minds of candid readers that we come directly to the New Testament, and risk the discussion of this subject at this time on the testimony of inspired Christian writers.

And, first, we inquire, When was the New Testament written? Answer: In the Christian age. Matthew, it is said, wrote his gospel six years after the resurrection of Christ. The other books of the New Testament were written later, and at different dates during a period of sixty-five years, after the establishment of the Christian church. Again we inquire, Who wrote the New Testament? Answer: Christian men, who had been converted from Judaism. And for whose benefit was the New Testament written? Answer: The men of the Christian age. How was the New Testament written? Answer: By inspiration of God. Then, if the New Testament was written in the Christian, and not in the Jewish, age; by Christian, and not by Jewish, men; for the benefit of the men of the Christian, and not the men of the Jewish, age; and by inspiration of God; it follows that the terms used in the New Testament are the inspired terms for the Chris-

---

8. What day has God commanded to be kept? 9. Has he commanded the observance of any other? 10. What is the particular subject of this lesson? 11. When was the New Testament written? 12. By whom and for whom was it written? 13. How was it written? 14. What follows from

tian church. Now there are two days named in the
New Testament, standing side by side, each claimed
by different bodies of Christians as the Sabbath of
the Christian church. These are the last and the
first days of the week. The Seventh-day Baptists,
and the Seventh-day Adventists, observe the seventh day of the week as the Lord's Sabbath, while
the Christian world generally hold that the first
day of the week is the Sabbath for Christians.
But how does this matter of these two days stand
in the New Testament?

The first day of the week is mentioned in the
New Testament only eight times, and is not in a
single instance spoken of as a Sabbath, a day of
rest, or a sacred day. It is simply called the first
day of the week. On the other hand, inspiration
gives the seventh day of the week in the New Testament the sacred title of the Sabbath fifty-nine
times. We will here give the eight texts which
mention the first day of the week, and see if they
prove what they are said to prove.

FIRST TEXT.—Matt. 28:1. "In the end of the
Sabbath as it began to dawn toward the first day
of the week, came Mary Magdalene, and the other
Mary to see the sepulcher." Here two days are
mentioned. One is called the Sabbath, and the
other, the day following it, is called the first day of
the week. Which of the two days is the Sabbath
for Christians? Is it the one that is simply called
the first day of the week, and is never called the
Sabbath, or spoken of as a day of rest in the New
Testament? Or, is it the day which inspired
Christian writers, in the Christian age, writing for
the benefit of the men of the Christian age, call the
Sabbath?

these facts? 15. How many times is the first day of the
week mentioned in the New Testament? 16. Give the first

SECOND TEXT.—Mark 16 : 2. "And very early in the morning, the first day of the week, they came unto the sepulcher at the rising of the sun." We give this passage, and the following three, because we are giving every text in the New Testament that mentions the first day of the week. They only show that the first day of the week is called simply the first day of the week.

THIRD TEXT.—Verse 9. " Now when Jesus was risen early the first day of the week, he appeared first to Mary Magdalene, out of whom he had cast seven devils."

FOURTH TEXT.—Luke 24 : 1. "Now upon the first day of the week, very early in the morning, they came unto the sepulcher, bringing the spices which they had prepared, and certain others with them."

FIFTH TEXT.—John 20 : 1. "The first day of the week cometh Mary Magdalene early, when it was yet dark, unto the sepulcher, and seeth the stone taken away from the sepulcher."

SIXTH TEXT.—Verse 19. " Then the same day at evening, being the first day of the week, when the doors were shut where the disciples were assembled for fear of the Jews, came Jesus and stood in the midst and said unto them, Peace be unto you." From this text it is asserted that the disciples met on the day of our Lord's resurrection to commemorate that event, and that Jesus sanctioned this meeting by uniting with them. To this assertion we reply :—

The disciples at that time did not believe that their Lord had been raised from the dead. Mark 16 : 9–14 proves this. It is there stated that he first appeared to Mary, who "went and told them that had been with him, as they mourned and wept. And they, when they had heard that he was alive, and had been seen of her, believed not." Verse 11. They did not believe Mary.

"After that he appeared in another form unto two of them as they walked, and went into the country. And they went and told it unto the residue; neither believed they them." Verses 12, 13. They would not believe the two disciples to whom Jesus had that day made himself known at Emmaus. Read Luke 24:13–36.

"Afterward he appeared unto the eleven as they sat at meat, and upbraided them with their unbelief and hardness of heart, because they believed not them which had seen him after he was risen." Verse 14. Jesus reproved the disciples for their unbelief in regard to his resurrection. And it is not remarkable that he should find his disciples together that evening, inasmuch as they had one common abode. Acts 1:13. "And when they were come in, they went up into an upper room, where abode both Peter, and James, and John, and Andrew, Philip and Thomas, Bartholomew and Matthew, James the son of Alphæus, and Simon Zelotes, and Judas the brother of James." See also Mark 3:19. And our Lord appeared to them "as they sat at meat."

The simple facts in the case, then, are that Jesus appeared to his disciples at their home, as they were enjoying a common meal, and that they did not, two excepted, believe that he had arisen from the dead. But ministers gravely assert that they were assembled for religious worship, commemorating the resurrection of their Lord! Whether asser-

---

the occasion of Christ's meeting with them ? 24. What text

tions of this kind be made in ignorance of the facts in the case, or to deceive the people, it is time that those who make them be rebuked, and the people read the facts in the case for themselves out of the New Testament.

It is also asserted that Christ often appeared to his disciples on the first day of the week. But only one text (John 20:26) is cited to prove this assertion, and this proves nothing to the point. "And after eight days again his disciples were within and Thomas with them; then came Jesus, the doors being shut, and stood in their midst, and said, Peace be unto you." The text says, the disciples *were within,* which does not mean they had *gone out* to meeting. They were at home. Again, after eight days does not mean seven, but carries us past the next Sunday to Monday night, at least. But here we are met with the assertion that the phrase, *after eight days* is indefinite, therefore does not prove that Christ appeared to his disciples on Monday evening. But if it be indefinite, who knows that it means just one week? In the name of common sense we protest against making the phrase indefinite in order to remove the circumstances from Monday, and then making it definite to establish it on Sunday. The phrase is either definite, or it is not. If it is not definite, then no one can tell the day on which Jesus met with his disciples the second time. If it be definite, then the second time that Jesus appeared to his disciples was as late as Monday night.

SEVENTH TEXT.—Acts 20:7. "And upon the first day of the week, when the disciples came

is quoted to prove frequent meetings of Christ with his disciples? 25. Where were the disciples then? 26. To what day would "after eight days" carry us? 27. What is the seventh text? 28. What is claimed as the purpose for

together to break bread, Paul preached unto them, ready to depart on the morrow, and continued his speech until midnight."

It is asserted that the disciples after the ascension of their Lord, assembled on the first day of the week to commemorate his resurrection by the breaking of bread. We reply that the communion does not commemorate the resurrection, but the crucifixion of our Lord. 1 Cor. 11 : 26. And as it was celebrated at Troas on a different day from that on which it was first instituted by our Lord, we conclude that it was not designed to be celebrated on any one particular day of each week. The meeting at Troas seems to have been an occasional meeting to break bread as Paul was to depart on the morrow.

From the circumstance of there being "many lights in the upper chamber" where the disciples were assembled to break bread, we conclude that it was an evening meeting. Paul preached all night, and at day-break started off on foot to Assos, and there joined his brethren in a ship, and came to Mitylene.

Now comes the inquiry, On what day of the week did that meeting hold all night? Answer : "Upon the first day of the week." As each day commences at sunset, according to God's division of time [Gen. 1], that meeting at Troas was held on what is called Saturday night, and Paul and his brethren started off on their long journey to Jerusalem in the morning of the first day of the week. Here is apostolic example for labor on the first day of the week.

which the disciples assembled on the first day of the week ? 29. What does the communion commemorate ? 30. Is it confined in the Scriptures to any particular day ? 31. What is proved by the "many lights," used on that occasion ? 32. What part of the day must this night meeting have been held ? 33. On the following light part of the day, what did Paul do ?

If it be said that the meeting at Troas was held on Sunday night, and that the disciples started on their journey Monday morning, we reply that in that case the meeting was held on the second day of the week; and those who with this position plead apostolic example from Acts 20:7, should keep Monday as the Christian Sabbath.

But leaving the question in regard to what night this meeting was held, there is an important fact which places the subject beyond all controversy. The first part of each of the seven days of the week is night, the last part is the day. The disciples held a meeting in the first part of the day at Troas, and journeyed on the last part of the same day. If, then, this day received the stamp of sacredness by this meeting of the apostles in the first part of it, their journeying in the last part of it removed the stamp of sacredness from it.

EIGHTH TEXT.—1 Cor. 16:2. "Upon the first day of the week, let every one of you lay by him in store, as God hath prospered him, that there be no gatherings when I come." It is inferred from this text that Paul enjoins a public collection; therefore the Corinthian church met for worship each first day of the week; therefore it is the Christian Sabbath. But it is an important fact that the apostle enjoins exactly the reverse of a public collection. He says, "Let every one of you lay by him in store." This is an individual work for each to attend to at home.

Justin Edwards, in his notes on the New Testament, comments on this text thus: "Lay by him in store; at home. That there be no gatherings;

that their gifts might be ready when the apostle should come."

Prof. J. W. Morton, late missionary to Hayti, in his Vindication of the True Sabbath, says: "The whole question turns upon the meaning of the expression, 'by him'; and I marvel greatly how you can imagine that it means ' in the collection-box of the congregation.' Greenfield, in his Lexicon, translates the Greek term, 'by one's self, i. e. at home.' Two Latin versions, the Vulgate and that of Castellio, render it, 'apud se,' with one's self, at home. Three French translations, those of Martin, Osterwald, and De Sacy, 'chez soi,' at his own house, at home. The German of Luther, 'bei sich selbst,' by himself, at home. The Dutch, 'by hemselven,' same as the German. The Italian of Diodati, 'appresso di se,' in his own presence, at home. The Spanish of Felipe Scio 'en su casa,' in his own house. The Portuguese of Ferreira, para isso,' with himself. The Swedish, 'naer sig sielf,' near himself. I know not how much this list of authorities might be swelled, for I have not examined one translation that differs from those quoted above."

There is another text which is so commonly urged in favor of the first day of the week as the Sabbath, that it may properly be noticed here. Rev. 1:10: "I was in the Spirit on the Lord's day."

It is claimed that this was the well-known title of the first day of the week when John wrote. How then does it happen that the same writer in his gospel, which was written two years later (see Bible Dictionary, Barnes' Notes, etc., Hist. Sab. p. 189), calls the first day simply "first day of the week," without any title whatever? John 20:1, 19. So far from its being true that Sunday was then called the Lord's day, history conclusively shows that no authoritative instance of the application of that term to the first day can be found till the time of Tertullian, A. D. 200.

What day, then, does John mean by the term Lord's day? That he means some day of the week is evident; for it would be absurd to refer the expression to the gospel dispensation, and untrue to refer it to the future day of judgment. And inasmuch as the day of the week is not specified in the text, we must look to other scriptures to determine which day is meant.

We lay it down as a self-evident proposition that that day must be the Lord's day which he has claimed as his. He has never so claimed the first day in any manner either by word or act. He never rested upon that day, never blessed it, never set it apart, never attached any title of sacredness to it, and never gave any command for its observance. But all these things he has done in reference to the seventh day. He rested upon it and sanctified it, or set it apart to a holy use, at creation. Gen. 2:2. In the fourth commandment he styles it, "the Sabbath of the Lord thy God." Ex. 20:8-11. In Isaiah he emphatically calls it "my holy day." Isa. 58:13. And finally Christ himself declares, "The Son of man is Lord also of the Sabbath." Mark 2:27. Whether therefore it is the title of the Father or the Son that is involved it pertains equally to the seventh day and to no other.

If anywhere in the New Testament a record could be found stating that the Son of man is Lord of the first day of the week, that fact would be held as conclusive in favor of that day; and any man who should question it would be reviled for his obstinacy. Why then not give the same weight to the fact that such a record is found for the seventh day of the week, the Sabbath of the Lord ?

We have noticed in the foregoing pages the eight texts which mention the first day of the week in the New Testament, and find no commandment to keep the day, no intimation of a change of the day of the Sabbath, and no grounds for inference that the day possesses any more sacredness than the five days that follow it.

In contrast, we find that the Sabbath is mentioned fifty-nine times in the New Testament, and in every instance reference is made to the last day of the week, on which the Creator rested from his work, the day he set apart as his, the day on which he put his blessing. We here give reference to the texts in the New Testament which call the seventh day of the week the Sabbath. Matt. 12 : 1, 2, 5 (twice), 8, 10, 11, 12 ; 24: 20 ; 28 : 1 ; Mark 1 : 21 ; 2 : 23, 24, 27 (twice), 28 ; 3 : 2, 4 ; 6 : 2 ; 15 : 42 ; 16 : 1 ; Luke 4 : 16, 31 ; 6 : 1, 2, 5, 6, 7, 9 ; 13 : 10, 14 (twice), 15, 16 ; 14 : 1, 3, 5 ; 23 : 54, 56 ; John 5 : 9, 10, 16, 18 ; 7 : 22, 23 (twice); 9 : 14, 16 ; 19 : 31 (twice); Acts 1 : 12 ; 13 : 14, 27, 42, 44 ; 15 : 21 ; 16 : 13 ; 17 : 2 ; 18 : 4.

We do not propose to notice all these texts at this time, as many of them contain no other proof to the point than that the Sabbath is the inspired name of the seventh day of the week in the Christian dispensation. And we might here add, that if the phrase, " Christian Sabbath," be admissible, the

learn from the eight texts ? 47. How many times is the Sabbath mentioned in the New Testament? 48. To what day

seventh day of the week is the Christian Sabbath. We will notice a few of the above texts.

Matt. 24:20. "And pray ye that your flight be not in the winter, neither on the Sabbath day." It is generally believed that this text has reference to the flight of Christians from the city of Jerusalem at the time of its destruction. Then our Lord recognized the existence of the Sabbath, A. D. 70, as verily as the seasons of the year. The text also shows that our Lord regarded the Sabbath as a definite day in the week. Some teach that the Sabbath is not a definite day of the week, but only "a seventh part of time," or "one day in seven and no day in particular." If this be a proper definition of the Sabbath, we may use the definition for the word in the text defined. This would make our Lord say, "But pray ye that your flight be not in the winter, neither on a seventh part of time!" If such a prayer had been answered so that the poor Christians might not leave on one day in seven, we would like to know when they could have made their flight.

Mark 2:27, 28. "And he said unto them, The Sabbath was made for man, and not man for the Sabbath; therefore the Son of man is Lord also of the Sabbath." The Jews supposed that the Sabbath was Jewish—made for them alone. They had the institution buried up with their traditions so that in their bigotry they even dared to charge the Lord of the Sabbath and his followers with desecrating it. Jesus rebuked them. "The Sabbath," said he, "was made for man"—for the entire race. Many hold the limited view of the Sabbath which the Jews held, and cry, "It's Jewish;" but Christian Sab-

do these texts refer? 49. What is proved by Matt. 24:20? 50. Explain Mark 2:27, 28. 51. What important point is established by Luke 23:56?

bath-keepers are happy to know that Jesus is Lord of the Sabbath of the fourth commandment which they observe and teach.

Luke 23 : 56. "And they returned, and prepared spices and ointments, and rested the Sabbath day according to the commandment." This is spoken of Christ's intimate friends who had followed their Lord to the sepulcher. It was probably near the close of the sixth-day when Jesus died upon the cross. He was taken down and borne to the sepulcher. The Marys returned and prepared the spices. The Sabbath came as the sun went down. They rested. How? "According to the commandment." The Sabbath, and the commandment guarding it, lived after Christ's death, and Luke, writing as is supposed twenty-eight years after the crucifixion, records the observance of the Sabbath according to the commandment by Christians after the death of Christ, as an important fact for the Christian church.

LESSON TWENTY-NINE.

THE BIBLE SABBATH.

WE now come to the book of Acts. Those who would follow apostolic example will come with us to this book with peculiar interest. But first we would remark that apostolic example when in harmony with divine precept is clothed with authority. Without precept, it has no real force. Paul and Barnabas had a sharp contention (Acts 15:29), yet no one feels bound to follow their example in this respect. Now if it could be shown that the disciples often assembled in the day-time of the first-day of the week, this would fall far short of proving a change of the Sabbath. But only one text (Acts 20 : 7) is claimed from the book of Acts for first-day observance, and we have shown from the facts stated in that chapter that the disciples were in meeting the first part of that day—Saturday night—and journeyed the last part—Sunday. We will now show that apostolic example is on the side of the Sabbath.

Acts 13 : 42 : " And when the Jews were gone out of the synagogue, the Gentiles besought that these words might be preached to them the next Sabbath." The Gentiles had no respect for the Sabbath, but, rather, were opposed to the institution honored by the Jews ; yet they invite this Christian minister to preach the same discourse to them the next Sabbath. " And the next Sabbath day came almost the whole city together to hear the word of God." Verse 44.

Chap. 16 : 13 : " And on the Sabbath we went out of the city by a river side, where prayer was wont to be made, and we sat down and spake to the women which resorted thither." This Sabbath meeting was not held in a Jewish synagogue. Lydia believed, and was baptized, and her household. But was the Sabbath Paul's regular preaching day ? Was this his manner ? Let chap. 17 : 2, answer. " And Paul, as *his manner was*, went in unto them, and three Sabbath days reasoned with them out of the Scriptures."

Chap. 18 : 1–11, contains important testimony on this subject. Paul at Corinth abode with Aquila and Priscilla, and worked with them at tent-making. " And he reasoned in the synagogue every Sabbath,

many texts are quoted to show apostolic example for keeping Sunday ? 3. What does Acts 13 : 42 show in regard to apostolic example ? 4. What bearing have Acts 16 : 13, and 17 : 2, on this question ? 5. How many Sabbaths did Paul

and persuaded the Jews and the Greeks." Verse 4. How long did he remain at Corinth? "And he continued there a year and six months, teaching the word of God among them." Verse 11. Here is apostolic example for seventy-eight successive Sab= baths. And it will be seen by verses 5–8, that the apostle occupied the synagogue a part of these Sab- baths, until the Jews opposed and blasphemed, then he went into the house of Justus, where he preached the remaining portion to the Gentiles.

That Paul never had, at any time during his min- istry, regarded the seventh day of the week as a secular day, and never had regarded the first day of the week as the Sabbath in its stead, is evident from his testimony in the last chapter of the book of Acts, before an assembly of the chief of the Jews at Rome. He addresses them with great boldness thus : "Men and brethren, though I have committed nothing against the people or customs of our fa- thers, yet was I delivered prisoner from Jerusalem into the hands of the Romans." Acts 28: 17.

It was the custom of their "fathers" to observe the seventh day of the week as the Sabbath, con- cerning which the Jews were very strict in Paul's day. If the apostle had left the observance of the seventh day, and had given the influence of his teachings and his example in favor of the first day of the week as the Sabbath for Christians, his mouth would have been closed at once after testifying that he had done "nothing against the customs of the fathers." But the closing verses of the book of Acts show that the apostle remained at Rome preaching the gospel with great confidence, unmolested by any one, which could not have been the case had he

observe at Corinth? 6. What is shown by Acts 28 : 17? 7. What was the custom of the fathers? 8. Then what did Paul's statement show him to be? 9. What assertion is

ceased to be a Sabbatarian. "And Paul dwelt two whole years in his own hired house, and received all that came in unto him, preaching the kingdom of God, and teaching those things which concern the Lord Jesus Christ, with all confidence, no man forbidding him." Verses 30, 31.

Here, dear reader, is apostolic example in harmony with that divine precept which was spoken under circumstances of awful grandeur from Sinai, and written with the finger of God, hence it has tremendous force.

Christians who take the Bible as the rule of truth and duty freely admit that before Christ, the seventh day of the week was observed in commemoration of the rest of the Creator on the seventh day of the first week, after he had completed the six days of creation. This position is fully sustained by the record of the first seventh day, Gen. 2 : 1–3, and by the Sabbath precept of Ex. 20 : 8–11.

But it is asserted that the work of redemption is greater than the work of creation, and that Christians should no longer observe the seventh day in commemoration of the completion of the work of creation ; but they should now observe the first day in commemoration of the completion of the work of redemption at the resurrection of Christ on the first day of the week. These assertions sound out well from Sunday pulpits, and read smoothly in print to those who wish them true ; and if they were sustained by the Bible, the Christian world could safely receive them. But what spoils this pleasing fable is the fact that there is not a single text in all the word of God to sustain it.

Redemption greater than creation? Our first-day friends themselves are compelled to admit that

made respecting creation and redemption ? 10. Where are

God has never said this. What right, then, has any man to make such an assertion, and then base the change of the Sabbath upon it. But suppose that redemption is greater than creation, who knows that we should observe a day of the week to commemorate it? God has not required men to keep any day as a memorial of redemption.

But if it were a duty to observe one day of the week for this reason, most certainly the crucifixion day presents the strongest claims. It is not said that we have redemption through Christ's resurrection; but it is said that we have redemption through the shedding of his blood. "And they sung a new song, saying, Thou art worthy to take the book, and to open the seals thereof; for thou wast slain, and hast redeemed us to God by thy blood, out of every kindred, and tongue, and people, and nation." Rev. 5:9. "In whom we have redemption through his blood, the forgiveness of sins, according to the riches of his grace." Eph. 1:7; Col. 1:14; Heb. 9:12, 15. Then redemption is through the death of the Lord Jesus; consequently the day on which he shed his precious blood to redeem us, and said, "It is finished," John 19:30, is the day that should be kept as a memorial of redemption, if any day should be observed for that purpose.

Nor can it be pleaded that the resurrection day is the most remarkable day in the history of the first advent of our Lord. It needs but a word to prove that in this respect, it is far exceeded by the day of the crucifixion. Which is the more remarkable, the act of the Father in giving his beloved and only Son to die for a race of rebels, or the act of that Father

the texts of scripture to sustain this? 11. What right then has any one to assert this? 12. But if redemption is greater than creation, then what? 13. If we should keep a day to commemorate redemption, what day should it be? 14.

in raising that beloved Son from the dead? There is only one answer that can be given: It was not remarkable that God should raise his Son from the dead; but the act of the Father in giving his Son to die for sinners was a spectacle of redeeming love on which the universe might gaze, and adore the wondrous love of God to all eternity. Who can wonder that the sun was vailed in darkness, and that all nature trembled at the sight! The crucifixion day, therefore, has far greater claims than the day of the resurrection. But God has not enjoined the observance of either. And is it not a fearful act to make void the commandments of God by that wisdom which is folly in his sight? 1 Cor. 1: 19, 20.

The learned and godly Paul lived, and preached, and wrote after the resurrection of Christ. And he is so far from teaching that the first day of the week should be observed to commemorate redemption, that he exhorts the church in view of a future day of redemption. "And grieve not the Holy Spirit of God whereby ye are sealed unto the day of redemption." Eph. 4: 30. And Christ speaks of his second coming, and the signs of that event, in these words: "And then shall they see the Son of man coming in the clouds with power and great glory. And when these things begin to come to pass, then look up, and lift up your heads, for your redemption draweth nigh." Luke 21: 27, 28. The day of redemption is still future. But when the Lord shall appear the second time to finish the plan of redemption, to give immortality to all his saints, to remove the curse from the earth, and "make all things new," then if it please God that the redeemed family shall observe the first, or any other day of the week, to

What was the most remarkable day in the history of the first advent of our Lord? 15. Is redemption yet finished? 16. What text from Paul proves this? 17. What other texts show the same thing? 18. When will redemption be

commemorate the completion of redemption, those who observe the Bible Sabbath here will be very happy to take part in that grand celebration. But meanwhile we will be content, while waiting for the day of redemption, to celebrate the Rest of the Lord on the day in which the Creator rested from his work of creation. Our Sunday friends are just one dispensation ahead of time.

But if Christians would commemorate our Lord's death and resurrection, the great events which lie at the very foundation of the plan of human redemption, there is no need of robbing the Lord's rest-day of its holiness in order to do it. God has provided us with memorials, bearing his own signature; and these we may observe with the blessing of Heaven. Would you commemorate the death of our Lord? You have the Lord's supper. 1 Cor. 11 : 23–26.

Would you commemorate the burial and resurrection of the Saviour? You need not keep the first day of the week. The Lord ordained a very different and far more appropriate memorial, in the ordinance of baptism. Rom. 6 : 3–5 ; Col. 2 : 12.

The Catholic and Protestant churches have changed this ordinance to sprinkling, so that this divine memorial of the Lord's resurrection is destroyed. And that they may add sin to sin, they lay hold of the Lord's Sabbath and change it to the first day of the week, thus destroying the sacred memorial of the Creator's rest, that they may have a memorial of Christ's resurrection.

But here we are met by a certain class of opponents of the primeval Sabbath with the assertion

finished? 19. How much ahead of time, then, are Sunday-keepers? 20. What true memorials has God given us of the death and resurrection of Christ? 21. What have both Catholic and Protestant churches done? 22. What assertion do we sometimes meet in reference to the command-

that only nine of the ten commandments are given in the New Testament, and that the Sabbath is purposely left out. This view is expressed in different terms. It is sometimes stated that "every other precept of the decalogue is re-affirmed in the New Testament excepting the Sabbath." And it is not unfrequently the case that ministers will so far presume upon the ignorance and credulity of the people as to affirm that nine of the ten commandments are given *verbatim* in the New Testament, and that the Sabbath of the Old Testament is carefully kept out of the New.

We freely admit that the fourth commandment is not given *verbatim*, that is, word for word, in the New Testament. And it is just as true that only the three short commandments are thus repeated. The sixth, seventh and eighth only are repeated in the New Testament. Does this fact release men from keeping the first, second, third, fourth, fifth, ninth and tenth? No, indeed. "Thou shalt not kill; thou shalt not commit adultery; thou shalt not steal," are the only precepts of the decalogue which are repeated word for word in all the New Testament. Let the most critical eye search this matter fully. We state the facts in the case.

What, then, can be said of those ministers who will state to audiences hasting to the bar of God to be judged by the moral law, and in the very face of Heaven, that nine of the ten commandments are given *verbatim* in the New Testament? Their egregious assertions must be attributed either to inexcusable ignorance of the subject, or to the custom of handling the word of God deceitfully. If they are so grossly ignorant of the subject as to shield them from the charge of clerical trickery, and uttering deliberate falsehood in the house of God, they have no business meddling with the subject, until they have studied it.

The ten precepts of the moral code did exist from the days of fallen Adam, and were binding on the people before they were spoken from Sinai, and written upon tables of stone. This is evident from the fact that the Bible contains a record of the very sins which are the violation of each one of the ten commandments, as existing before the law was declared in the hearing of the people at Sinai. Where there is transgression there must be law. Remove law, and sin ceases to exist. "For where no law is, there is no transgression." Rom. 4: 15. The sin of Sabbath-breaking was rebuked as early as thirty days before the ten commandments were spoken from Sinai. This fact is fully established by comparing Ex. 16 : 1, 23–30 ; 19 : 1.

And there is no intimation in all the Old Testament that God would at any time change any of the precepts of his moral code. That law being in its nature changeless as the very throne of heaven, once written in the Old Testament, accompanied with the record of the circumstances of awful grandeur that attended its rehearsal at Sinai, the Lord has not seen fit to have it written a second time in the New Testament. The Holy Ghost never undertook to give the divine law over again on a new account in the New Testament.

---

assertion ? 27. How far back were the precepts of the moral code binding ? 28. What shows this ? 29. What is the statement of Rom. 4 : 15 ? 30. How long before Sinai was Sabbath breaking rebuked ? 31. What change of the moral code is intimated in the Old Testament ? 32. Was it necessary that it should be written again in the New Testament ?

The apostles in their writings long years after the death and resurrection of Christ appeal to the moral code as given in the Old Testament as the highest living authority in heaven, or on the earth. They state moral duties and obligations, and refer to the precepts of the moral code to sustain their propositions. If it had been left to Paul, Peter, James, John and Jude, to give the moral code, or nine-tenths of it over again in the New Testament, those faithful men would have done it, and we should be able to read those precepts word for word in their writings.

Our opponents see as clearly as we do that it is necessary to their position that nine of the ten commandments should appear in the New Testament, word for word. Hence the temptation before the minds of those ministers who feel that they must preserve the unity of their flocks to give a false impression to quiet the minds of the people upon the Sabbath question.

This fact crops out in the statement of those opponents who manifest more regard for party than a clear conscience in the statement that nine of the ten commandments are given *verbatim* in the New Testament. They see the need that it should be so; and, feeling it important that the people should view the matter thus, in order that they be shielded from the claims of the fourth commandment, they seem to adopt the policy of the Roman church, that " the end justifies the means," and give themselves up, even in the house of God, to the utterance of a deliberate untruth.

<hr>

33. To what did the apostles appeal long after the death of Christ ?   34. If the re-enactment of the law had been left to the apostles, what should we find ?   35. What is necessary to the position of our opponents ?   36. What temptation does this put them under ?   37. What acts does it lead them

We stand upon the grand old moral code, the only document in the universe that has the honor to have been spoken by the voice of God in the hearing of the assembled people, and to have been engraven with his finger on the tables of stone. Do our opponents declare that moral code revised, so that only nine of its precepts should be observed by Christians? Then we inquire: What prophet has foretold that this should be done? What apostle has recorded the fact that this has been done? The Bible is silent upon the subject. No such revision of the moral code has taken place.

Do any still urge that the apostles have revised the moral code so as to release men from the claims of the fourth commandment? Then we again inquire: Where is the revised code? What scribe ever copied it? What printer ever printed it? What book-seller ever sold it? What colporteur ever carried it about the country to throw into laps of the dear children to impress them with the fact that there are nine commandments, and only nine, for Christians to observe?

We are at this time dealing with plain facts in a pointed manner. And, may be, we shall be pardoned by the candid public for inquiring: Do these men who have the moral code revised, or changed in some way, so as to release Christians from the observance of the Sabbath of the fourth commandment, really believe that any such revision has taken place? If they do, why not produce a copy of the revised code? Please pass it in, gentlemen. When you will produce the new code, brought into existence by as good authority as that which originated the old, we will be happy to accept it as the moral

to? 38. Upon what do we stand? 39. What must our opponents show to move us? 40. Do those who claim a revision of the moral code, believe in any such revision? 41.

law for Christians, and cease to agitate the public mind with the Sabbath question. But until you do this, we shall cling to the original document, and plead for the observance of all its precepts by Christian men.

Again we inquire: Do these men believe what they say, when they tell the people that the fourth precept of the moral code has been revised, or so changed that Christians are released from the observance of the last day of the week? We make this pointed appeal with the fact in full view, known everywhere, that in the several branches of the mammoth Sunday-school institution the old moral code of ten commandments has been thrown into the laps of a million of the dear youth of our land, printed word for word as God spoke it from Sinai, and as he wrote it on the tables of stone. If the divine law has been revised, why do not the managers of the American Tract Society, which has the support of nearly a score of the leading denominations of our land, publish the new code for all the Sunday-schools? Why not print the revised code, make a correct impression on the minds of the youth, and free the subject from present embarrassment, if they believe what they teach?

It will appear evident to every candid mind that these religious bodies who are printing and circulating the original moral code do not really believe that it has been revised. To say the least, want of faith in the revision doctrine has kept them from getting the several precepts of the revised code together in due form, and publishing it to the Christian world. And so they continue to print the ten commandments just as they read in Ex. 20. We give the two codes side by side:—

If the ten commandments have been revised and changed, why are they still printed in their old form? 42. In the

ORIGINAL CODE.

1. Thou shalt have no other gods before me.

2. Thou shalt not make unto the any graven image, or any likeness of any thing that is in heaven above, or that is in the earth beneath, or that is in the water under the earth. Thou shalt not bow down thyself to them, nor serve them ; for I the Lord thy God am a jealous God, visiting the iniquity of the fathers upon the children unto the third and fourth generation of them that hate me, and showing mercy unto thousands| of them that love me, and keep my commandments.
3. Thou shalt not take the name of the Lord thy God in vain ; for the Lord will not hold him guiltless that taketh his name in vain.

5. Honor thy father and thy mother, that thy days may be long upon the land which the Lord thy God giveth thee.

6. Thou shalt not kill.
7. Thou shalt not commit adultery.

8. Thou shalt not steal.
9. Thou shalt not bear false witness against thy neighbor.
10. Thou shalt not covet thy neighbor's house ; thou shalt not covet thy neighbor's wife, nor his man-servant, nor his maid-servant, hor his ox, nor his ass, nor anything that is thy neighbor's.

REVISED CODE.

1. Get thee behind me, Satan ; for it is written, Thou shalt worship the Lord thy God, and him only shalt thou serve. Luke 4 :8.
2. Then Paul stood in the midst of Mar's hill, and said, Ye men of Athens, I perceive that in all things ye are too superstitious. For as I passed by, and beheld your devotions, I found an altar with this inscription, TO THE UNKNOWN GOD. Whom therefore ye ignorantly worship, him declare I unto you. God that made the world and all things therein, seeing that he is Lord of Heaven and earth, dwelleth not in temples made with hands. Acts 17 : 22–24.
3. But above all things, my brethren, swear not, neither by Heaven, neither by the earth, neither by any other oath ; but let your yea be yea, and your nay, nay, lest ye fall into condemnation. James 5 :12.
5. Children, obey your parents in the Lord, for this is right. Honor thy father and thy mother, which is the first commandment with promise, that it may be well with thee, and thou mayest live long on the earth. Eph. 6: 1–3.
6. Thou shalt not kill. Rom. 13 :9.
7. Thou shalt not commit adultery. Rom. 13 :9.
8. Thou shalt not steal. Rom. 13 :9.
9. Thou shalt not bear false witness. Rom. 13: 9.
10. Thou shalt not covet. Rom. 13 : 9.

Before calling special attention to the quotations which are said to constitute the new moral code for Christians, we wish to make some general remarks :

1. There is general agreement among our opponents as to the passages in the New Testament which constitute the new code of nine precepts as we have given them. If, however, any feel dissatisfied with

revised code what is the first commandment? 43. What scripture is appealed to for the second ? 44. What for the third ? 45. The fifth ? 46. The sixth, seventh, eighth, ninth and tenth ? 47. If the decalogue was ever abrogated,

these, they are urgently invited to make improvements as shall please them. We are anxious to meet the real positions of opponents.

2. All talk about the " re-affirming of the nine commandments," and the " revised moral code," is on the supposition that the ten commandments, were abrogated at the death of Christ. Mark this : The position is that all ten of the commandments were in full force up to the time of the death of Christ, and that, with the death of the world's Redeemer, the moral code also died.

3. As the decalogue was the living moral code throughout the entire ministry of the Son of God until the hour of his death upon the cross, it would be more than childish to quote any of Christ's words spoken during his public ministry, as re-affirming any of its precepts. Whatever, therefore, may be claimed from the New Testament as re-affirming nine of the precepts of the decalogue, must be found in the Acts and Epistles of the apostles.

4. But, bad for their theory, this gives a period between the death of the moral code at the cross and the re-affirming of the nine precepts by the apostles, in which there is no law. And "where no law is, there is no transgression." Rom. 4 : 15. This view gives a sinless period to the world of more than twenty long years. Not sinless however because of any change in men ; but because of the supposed decease of God's Moral Detecter, " For by the law is the knowledge of sin." Rom. 3 : 20.

Beginning with the first, we now briefly notice the passages which these gentlemen who have the divine law abolished, and a part of it re-enacted,

when was it done ? 48. Where then must we look for a re-affirming of that law ? 49. According to this how long a period intervened between the abolishing and re-enactment ?

would have the Christian world believe are the new code for the Christian age. For their first commandment they cite Luke 4:8. The reader will please notice the passage as we have placed it in juxtaposition with the original first commandment of the decalogue. But right here these gentlemen face fearful absurdities.

1. According to their position, the first commandment for the Christian church was addressed to the devil. We naturally inquire whether this Christian precept was given for the especial benefit of his Satanic majesty? Or did the great Head of the church give the second edition of the first commandment to the Christian church through the devil?!

2. The original first commandment was announced from Sinai by the voice of the Lord, as the trembling people stood before the burning, quaking, mountain. The scene was awfully grand. But in this case the first commandment was re-affirmed in the wilderness of temptation when but two beings were present; one the Son of God in his humility; the other the devil! "Be ye astonished, O ye heavens, at this!" Right here, in the desolate wilderness, we are told, the first commandment of the divine law was re-affirmed to the Christian church through the devil!!

3. But as the very climax of all absurdities, the position of these gentlemen has the first commandment re-affirmed at the commencement of Christ's ministry, at least three years and a half before the supposed decease of the ten at the close of his ministry. This gives eleven commandments for the period of three and a half years! And if, according

to our law-abolishing friends, all the precepts of the divine law were swept by the board at the cross, clean work was made, not only of the ten, but of the one prematurely re-affirmed to Satan, leaving the Christian church but eight precepts in the new moral code, instead of nine, and the devil not one!

So much for the first precept of the new code. And of the second re-affirmed precept we will here state that it is simply a record of facts in Paul's visit and labors in Athens that is given in Acts 17: 22–24, having no form of a precept whatever. Neither can the second precept of the decalogue be found in any of the books of the New Testament. Reference is made to the sin of violating the second commandment, and Christians are warned against it; but we search in vain for the second precept of the decalogue in the New Testament.

When the second commandment has been urged against the images of the Romish church, Papists have proudly trampled it under their feet as a Jewish precept, declaring that it was not in the New Testament. Hence the second commandment is left out of their numerous catechisms. And now a host of Protestants use the same old papal argument to excuse their practice relative to the fourth commandment. When we urge the claims of the Sabbath law upon Protestants, they in their turn reply, "The Sabbath precept is not given in the New Testament."

But if it be still urged that Paul did re-affirm the second precept of the decalogue from Mars' Hill for the Christian church, then we reply that there is

mandments then were there during that period? 54. And then what took place at the cross? 55. What is the so-called second precept in the revised code? 56. What is the position of the Romish church on the second commandment? 57. How does the position of some Protestants on the fourth commandment compare with this? 58. How many follow-

no evidence that there was a single follower of
Christ in the city of Athens to hear it. Read Acts
chapter seventeen. It was when Paul's attendants
had returned to Berea, leaving the apostle alone,
that he addressed the people. And did the great
apostle then and there re-affirm the second precept
of the decalogue for the Christian church through
the curious, Christless crowd of that city wholly
given to idolatry, and not one Christian present?

And further it may be worthy of note that Paul's
speech at Mars' Hill was full twenty years after the
death of Christ. If, therefore, the decalogue was
abrogated at the cross, and the second precept was
really re-affirmed in the apostle's memorable address
at Athens, all men were released from the second
commandment for the space of twenty years!

We pass to the third commandment, and again
call the reader's attention to the old moral code,
and to those passages supposed to constitute the
new Christian code, as we have placed them side
by side on page 345. Please read the two, and then
answer the inquiries. Has the apostle James
re-affirmed the third commandment in the text
quoted? If he has, why change the language
employed. Has the apostle improved upon the
style of the High and Holy One? The Friends, and
thousands besides, hold that the apostle here
opposes the judicial oath. He probably refers to
that which is forbidden by the third commandment, but it is preposterous to say that the apostle
is here resurrecting the third commandment, and
giving it over a second time for the Christian
church.

The apostle claimed no such thing; but in the

ers of Christ were there in Athens to hear Paul's revision of
the second commandment? 59. What may be said of the
revised third commandment from the book of James? 60.

same epistle he says: "There is one Lawgiver, who is able to save and to destroy." If the work of revising, or re-affirming the moral code, was left to the apostles, then there were twelve lawgivers instead of one, as affirmed by the apostle. James 4:12. He wrote A. D. 60. Was there no third commandment for more than a quarter of a century?

We pass to the fifth precept. Paul states a moral duty, and cites the fifth commandment as his authority. He is not re-affirming the fifth precept of the decalogue in his letter to the church at Ephesus, therefore does not repeat it *verbatim* and entire. See page 345. This epistle was written A. D. 64. Did the fifth commandment lie dead, from the blow it received at the death of Christ, for more than thirty years?

The sixth, seventh and eighth precepts are repeated in Paul's epistle to the church at Rome *verbatim*. And why? Is it because the apostle is re-affirming them, or giving them over again on a new account? No! He is doing no such thing! If this work of re-affirming nine of the precepts of the decalogue had been left to the trusty men who wrote the New Testament, we should find all nine precepts in the New Testament word for word.

These three short precepts only of all the ten are quoted *verbatim*, because of their brevity. The writers of the New Testament state moral duties, and appeal to the moral code, which was to them in the first century, and is to us in the nineteenth century, the highest authority in all heaven and earth. Paul's letter to the Romans was written

How many lawgivers does James set forth? 61. Why does not Paul to the Ephesians give the fifth commandment verbatim? 62. Where are the sixth, seventh and eighth precepts found verbatim? 63. Why are they thus given? 64.

A. D. 60. Were the precepts against murder, adultery and theft lying dead more than twenty-five years?

We now come to the last, the tenth. What difference between the two! See page 345. There is in the old edition the sum of thirty-three good words. But in what is supposed to be the new, re-affirmed precept, there are only the first four words of the old. Was the Lord too lengthy in the first edition, making it necessary for the learned apostle to improve upon his work? Or, was "the law of the Lord perfect" as it came from its Author, and was Paul unfaithful to duty? These inquiries are made on the supposition that it was left to Paul to re-affirm the tenth commandment for the benefit of the Christian church. But no; the apostle assumed no such position as belonging to a fraternity of lawgivers. He simply cites the tenth precept of the decalogue, quotes enough of it to be understood, and honors it, a quarter of a century after the death of Christ, as resting on its original, immutable basis, the highest living authority in the universe.

Driven from the position that all the precepts of the divine law, excepting the fourth, are re-affirmed in the New Testament, this class of opponents are compelled to admit that in the case of the second commandment reference is made only to the principle or facts upon which the precept is based This is all they can possibly maintain. When fairly and squarely on this ground, then we are prepared to say to them that the term "Sabbath," in the singular number, which expresses the very institution sustained by the fourth precept of the moral code, is mentioned fifty-nine times in the New Testament.

In the tenth commandment, old edition, how many words are there? 65. How many in the new? 66. What conclu-

So that when it comes to this, that in some of the nine precepts reference is made by the apostles to only the principle or fact which gave rise to the precept, then it will be seen that Sabbatarians are ahead, having fifty-nine references to the Sabbath of the fourth commandment in the New Testament. Can as many references be shown from the New Testament to any other one of the ten precepts of the decalogue? Search and see.

But why labor to dodge the point? The Sabbath is either abrogated, or it is not. The Sabbath is not partly right and partly wrong. It has either been changed from the seventh to the first day of the week, or it has not been changed. We should observe the first day of the week as the Christian Sabbath, or we should not. We should observe the seventh day, or we should not.

Where is the plain proof from the New Testament that the Sabbath has been abrogated or changed? What prophet of God has declared that the moral code of the Infinite One should be abolished, or changed? And what apostle has stated in plain terms that anything of this kind has taken place? But Christ, in his memorable sermon on the mount seems to anticipate the discussion of the law question in the Christian church, and as a rebuke of wrong positions upon the subject, and as a guide to correct thoughts, says: "Think not that I am come to destroy the law or the prophets; I am not come to destroy but to fulfill. For verily I say unto you, Till heaven and earth pass, one jot or one tittle shall in no wise pass from the law, till all be fulfilled." "And let all the people say, Amen."

sion does this lead to? 67. What advantage do Sabbath-keepers still have in reference to the Sabbath? 68. What language of Christ should guide us on this subject?

INDEX

We'd love to have you download our catalog of
titles we publish at:

www.TEACHServices.com

or write or email us your thoughts,
reactions, or criticism about this
or any other book we publish at:

TEACH Services, Inc.
254 Donovan Road
Brushton, NY 12916

info@TEACHServices.com

or you may call us at:

518/358-3494